EMBRACING

the

FUTURE

EMBRACING

the

FUTURE

Preparing for Life After Retirement

GENERAL EDITOR

Roy A. Prete

ASSOCIATE EDITORS

LeRoy E. Whitehead, Douglas E. Brinley,
and Elder Dennis B. Neuenschwander

DESERET
BOOK

SALT LAKE CITY, UTAH

Visit us at DeseretBook.com

ISBN 978-1-60908-906-1

Printed in the United States of America
Malloy Lithographing Incorporated, Ann Arbor, MI

10   9   8   7   6   5   4   3   2   1

The future is as bright as your faith.

PRESIDENT THOMAS S. MONSON
APRIL 2009 GENERAL CONFERENCE

CONTENTS

PREFACE

There are many books on preparing for later life, but none directed uniquely to Latter-day Saints. This book was written to fulfill that need. As they approach later life, Latter-day Saints share many concerns with people of all faiths, such as financial planning, maintaining good health, and future association with family and friends. But some things are unique. Latter-day Saints live longer and have a different set of values than people of other faiths, which impels them toward a more active life of service and personal development. The high value they place on family life also makes a significant difference. Finding fulfillment in later life will depend on a number of factors, several of which are within our own volition. As we "embrace the future," with all its opportunities and challenges, we should remember with Longfellow that "age is opportunity no less Than youth itself, though in another dress."[1]

Retirement, aging and related issues are very hot topics these days, with items in the news nearly every day. Why is that so? The fact is that people are living longer—much longer. Those who are now 65 will live on average an additional 21 years![2] Questions therefore arise as to the growing practice of delayed retirement, the viability of the Social Security system, and coverage of seniors' health and welfare needs. These questions are particularly acute, as they impinge heavily on public policy. As those 60 and over now occupy nearly 20 percent of the population in the United States, Canada and other places, they have become a political force that needs to be reckoned with at every level of government.[3]

Many issues associated with retirement and aging are even more poignant for Latter-day Saints, who, on average, will live six years longer than the population at large.[4] This gives Church members an extended period of potentially productive life and service. At the same time, in the gospel plan, there is no retirement from service in the Lord's Church. In fact, the Church encourages an active and engaged lifestyle, with emphasis on "enduring to the end."

This book is intended to address some of the issues related to preparing for later life within a Latter-day Saint context. Some basic questions addressed are the purpose of aging in the divine plan, when to retire from employment, how to prepare financially for later life, how to maintain better health, how to prepare for missionary and other service, and how to remain vibrant and productive. The joys of service and grandparenting are underscored, and the importance of family communications and preserving family histories and heritage are emphasized.

This is an honest book. The challenges of later life are also treated in chapters on adapting to new spousal relationships after retirement, declining sexual function, and how to cope with problems of aging such as potential illness, disability, bereavement, and even dying and the role of medical technology. One chapter addresses the special issues faced by singles in later life. Planning for the division of inheritance and finding fulfillment in later life are also discussed. The final chapter delineates our post-mortal existence on the pathway leading to exaltation and eternal life.

As Church members, by following correct principles, we can make those lengthy years following retirement more meaningful, productive and fulfilling. Particularly applicable are principles of preparation, communication, service, positive attitude, staying active and engaged, developing talents and capacities, and focus on the family. Service may take many forms, including serving missions, temple work and family history, volunteering, and service within the family. Rock-solid gospel principles, such as faith in Christ, keeping covenants and commandments, and following the counsel of the living prophets, are sure guides to happiness and success in later life.

Spiritual progress is the key. The closer we draw to our Heavenly Father and Jesus Christ, the greater will be our spiritual growth and enjoyment, and the greater will be our joy as we prepare for the next phase of our eternal journey. Our greatest joy will undoubtedly derive from family associations with children and grandchildren and the peace that comes with a life well-lived. Later life may indeed be very fulfilling and meaningful despite declining physical powers.

A word of caution. You will find in the pages of this book many tantalizing suggestions for self-improvement, improved family relations, spiritual development, and service. But you won't be able to do them all—at least, not all at once. Whatever your family circumstance, as a couple or single, the suggestion is to make a prayerful selection of items you wish to work on, and then to work on them on a priority basis. The Lord will guide your footsteps. As King Benjamin averred: "It is not requisite that a man should run faster than he has strength. . . . [but] that he should be diligent, that thereby he might win the prize."[5]

Many vicissitudes and trials may befall elderly people—illness, disabilities, loss of skills and functions, loss of a spouse, and various other afflictions. While these may be difficult for them and their families, the basic concept is that "if ye are prepared ye shall not fear."[6] Certainly, all things that befall us in our human journey have purpose in the Lord's plan. The purpose of this last stage of life, with all its blessings, opportunities and challenges, must ultimately be to provide a unique window to help us in our quest to acquire godly attributes[7] and to "be perfected" in Christ.[8]

It is intended that this book be a helpful guide with practical helps that are user-friendly. In order to draw together in a single place many of the ideas and information found here and there in fragments, the editors have brought together a team of faithful scholars. Some have drawn from professional training as doctors, lawyers, and marriage and family consultants; others have drawn from their own-lived experience and research. Many of the contributors have been selected from the Emeritus Seventy and general Church officers who are retired from active service but who are rich in Church experience and specialized expertise. Contributors have each spoken in their own language and in their own way. The reader will derive the greatest enjoyment from each chapter in imagining that he or she has just had a chat with the author for a period of 30–45 minutes on a subject of particular interest.

The volume is directed particularly to those aged 50 and older, for whom the preparation for life after retirement has become an immediate issue. But persons of any age can profit from reading it to better understand the needs of seniors and how to better prepare themselves and their families for a future time, not many years hence, when they will be in a similar situation. This is largely a self-help book for those approaching later life and only deals in passing with family, professional and institutional support and care for seniors. Several good books, applicable to both Latter-day Saints and other social groups, may be consulted on that subject.[9]

Many people contributed to the preparation of this volume. LeRoy E. Whitehead encouraged the project at the outset and was a close collaborator throughout. Elder Alexander B. Morrison and Dr. Donald B. Doty were early promoters of the endeavor and contributed chapters. Elder Morrison, in addition, suggested several distinguished contributors from among the former seventy and general Church officers. Others deserve special mention: Ardeth G. Kapp and Douglas E. Brinley, who wrote chapters and suggested additional contributors; the many authors who took time from their busy schedules to distill their particular measure of wisdom; the editorial team who labored so assiduously to refine the text; Heather Moore and Annette Lyon, for their conscientious copy edit; and in particular, Jana Erickson, Product Director at Deseret Book, for her enthusiasm and support for the project.

I would especially like to thank my wife, Carma, for her unfailing support and assistance, and our many early-morning conversations, which were particularly meaningful in helping shape ideas. Other family members also assisted: daughters Becky Doig and Sarah Kohrman, who reviewed some chapters and made helpful comments; son Joseph Prete, who suggested from his acquaintances no less than two contributors; and son-in-law Christian Bryner, who reviewed chapters and provided pro-bono legal advice.

The opinions expressed in this book are those of their authors alone, and are not the official views of either the publisher or of The Church of Jesus Christ of Latter-day Saints.

Roy A. Prete
Editor
September 11, 2011

Notes

1. "Brainy Quote, Henry Wadsworth Longfellow quotes" at
   http://www.brainyquote.com/quotes/authors/h/henry_wadsworth_
   longfellow.htmlgmsteacy@gmail.com. gmsteacy@gmail.com (consulted Oct.
   25, 2010).
2. "In the 20-year period between 1970 and 1990, the average life expectancy
   of a 65-year-old increased modestly, about 15 percent. In the *12-year period*
   that followed, *average life expectancy increased 50 percent*. Today, the average
   65-year-old will live 21 years, to age 86!" (Scott Keffer, "Avoiding the Great
   Retirement Dilemma," *Physician's News Digest*, Mar. 2006, 3, at
   http://www.physiciansnews.com/finance/306.html (consulted Oct. 20,
   2009).
3. "Senior Citizen Longevity & Statistics: Senior Citizen Population on Brink
   of Explosion in World and in United States: Census Bureau," *Senior Journal:
   Today's News and Information for Senior Citizens & Baby Boomers*, June 24, 2009, at
   http://seniorjournal.com/NEWS/SeniorStats/2009/
   20090624-SenCitPopulation.htm (consulted Oct. 20, 2009). According to

census numbers cited in the table, "US Population by Age and Sex: 2008," in the United States, 18.9 percent of the population was 60 or over in 2008.

4. See "Life Expectancy Among LDS and Non-LDS in Utah," in *Demographic Research*, vol. 10, 61–82, Mar. 12, 2004, at http://www.demographic-research.org/volumes/vol10/3 (consulted Oct. 20, 2009). BYU demographer Ray M. Merrill, in a 2004 study, concludes from an analysis of data for white males and females in Utah from 1994 to 1998 that, "life expectancy was 77.3 for LDS males, 70.0 for non-LDS males, 82.2 for LDS females, and 76.4 for non-LDS females."

5. Mosiah 4:27.

6. D&C 38:30.

7. 2 Peter 1:3–8.

8. Moroni 10:32.

9. See Holly Whittelsey Whiteside, *The Caregiver's Compass: How to Navigate with Balance & Effectiveness Using Mindful Caregiving* (Fremont, NH: Possibility Guild, 2010); Hugh Delehanty and Elinor Ginzler, foreword by Mary Pipher, *Caring for Your Parents: The Complete Family Guide—Practical Advice You Can Trust from the Experts at AARP* (New York: Stirling, 2008); Paul Hogan and Lori Hogan, *Stages of Senior Care: Your Step-by-Step Guide to Making the Best Decisions* (New York: Kindle [paperback] 2009); Joseph L. Matthews, *Long-term Care: How to Plan and Pay for It*, 8th ed. (Berkeley: Nolo, 2010).

1

AGING IN THE DIVINE PLAN

Elder Alexander B. Morrison

The genius of William Shakespeare reminds us that "all the world's a stage and all the men and women merely players." In *As You Like It,* Act II, Scene 7, the "immortal bard" writes of the seven ages of mankind, which each of us plays out in his or her own unique time and way. The first on the scene is the infant, "mewling and puking in the nurse's arms." Then, in sequence, we play out the roles of the whining schoolboy, "creeping like snail unwillingly to school;" the lover, "sighing like furnace;" the soldier, "sudden and quick in quarrel;" the justice, "in fair round belly;" and "lean and slipper'd pantaloon, with spectacles on nose, and pouch on side, his youthful hose well sav'd a world too wide for his shrunk shank; and his big manly voice, turning again towards childish treble." Finally, says Shakespeare, we end "this strange eventful history, in second childishness and mere oblivion, sans teeth, sans eyes, sans taste, sans everything."

But is that all there is to our mortal journey? Is mortality bound on the one hand by the cradle, and, on the other, by the grave? Does life not have *real* meaning? To be sure, mortal life is short. In his time

Elder Alexander B. Morrison, First Quorum of the Seventy (emeritus), is a noted pharmacologist, former senior civil servant, internationally recognized health expert, the recipient of several humanitarian awards, and the author of eight books, including *Valley of Sorrow: A Layman's Guide to Understanding Mental Illness.*

of trouble, Job averred that man "cometh forth like a flower, and is cut down: he fleeth also as a shadow, and continueth not."[1] The Psalmist agreed that man's days "*are* as grass: as a flower of the field . . . for the wind passeth over it, and it is gone; and the place thereof shall know it no more."[2] But the wise Solomon retorted: "To every *thing there* is a season, and a time to every purpose under the heaven: A time to be born, and a time to die."[3] Isaiah summarized, "The grass withereth, the flower fadeth: but the word of our God shall stand forever."[4] I conclude, therefore, that there is much more to our eternal existence than Shakespeare's incomplete tale of mortality's seven stages.

MORTALITY AND ETERNITY

This is neither the time nor the place to even attempt to outline the totality of so-called "Mormon doctrine" on the meaning of mortality and eternity. But Latter-day Saints recognize that our mortal birth did not herald our beginning. We have always lived; mortality is but a part—a way-stop, if you will—of a great and grand cosmic drama. We lived with God our Father in our pre-mortal existence, our "first estate." There we were distinct, unique, conscious spirit beings, with volition, gender and moral agency. Our "first estate" was in preparation for our "second estate," mortality. Latter-day Saints are in accord with the expressions of the poet William Wordsworth, who penned these lines:

> Our birth is but a sleep and a forgetting:
> The Soul that rises with us, our life's Star,
> Hath had elsewhere its setting,
> and cometh from afar:
> Not in entire forgetfulness,
> And not in utter nakedness,
> But trailing clouds of glory do we come
> From God, who is our home.[5]

Understanding that God is our Father, and our true home is with Him, allows our thoughts to transcend the dark despair of the grave and counter the nearly instinctive fear of death and extinction. Much of the divinely revealed information about mankind's relationship with God was lost, we aver, soon after Christ established His church in the meridian of time.

A GLORIOUS RESTORATION

Latter-day Saints believe that following Jesus Christ's establishment of His Church upon the earth, there occurred a great apostasy which resulted in a loss of divine authority, unacceptable changes in church governance, distortion of essential doctrines, covenants and practices, and a long period of spiritual darkness. Not that there were not good people on the earth at all times, but the approval of God was missing and had to be restored. So, too, did His authority for all that is done in His name.

That restoration began on a spring day in 1820, when Joseph Smith, a farm boy from upstate New York, saw and talked with the Father and the Son in a glorious epiphany which Latter-day Saints call "The First Vision." The Prophet Joseph Smith records part of that conversation in these words: "I was [told] that I must join none of [the churches of the day], for they were all wrong; and the Personage who addressed me [Jesus Christ] said that all their creeds were an abomination in his sight."[6]

The dawning of a brighter day had burst refulgent on the world. It would sweep away the errors and misunderstandings of nearly two millennia and replace them with the simple restorative and rejuvenating truths of Christ's gospel. Establishment of The Church of Jesus Christ of Latter-day Saints thus represents a revelatory restoration.[7]

Our Father in Heaven, knowing beforehand of our trials and tribulations, our sins and shortcomings, provided for us the means by which we may return to His presence. His Great Plan of Happiness for His children is described in various ways in the scriptures, including the plan of salvation,[8] the plan of redemption,[9] and the merciful plan of the Great Creator.[10]

THE PLAN OF SALVATION

What is the plan of salvation? It is many things. It is all-encompassing, as would, perhaps, be expected, considering the fact its author is the Father Himself. It includes the Latter-day Saint belief that the knowledge of a Savior and the plan of salvation has been revealed to mankind several times.

As the noted LDS scholar Robert Millet states, "Christian doctrines have been taught and Christian sacraments administered by Christian prophets since the beginning of time. Adam and Eve were Christians . . . Abraham and Moses and Isaiah and Jeremiah and Ezekiel were Christian prophets."[11] In short, God has revealed Himself and His plan of salvation during the various dispensations of time, the first of which was the Adamic dispensation.

All of the prophets testify of Christ. Each bears solemn and sacred witness of Him. He is "the Shepherd and Bishop of your souls,"[12] the "lamb without blemish and without spot."[13] His was the only perfect life. He and He alone remains sinless, though he was tempted as we all are. In short, He is much more than a prophet: omniscient, omnipotent, all-knowing, all-powerful, the Redeemer and Savior of all mankind. His Atonement makes it possible for all men and women everywhere and in every period of history to be forgiven, redeemed, and born again, as His sons and daughters.[14]

Mortal life, then, has as one of its main purposes the gaining of earthly experience "to progress toward perfection and ultimately [for each to] realize [his or her] divine destiny as [an heir] of eternal life. The divine plan of happiness enables family relationships to be perpetuated beyond the grave. Sacred ordinances and covenants available in holy temples make it possible for individuals to return to the presence of God and for families to be united eternally."[15]

THE INFINITE ATONEMENT

The Atonement of Jesus Christ is the centerpiece of the plan of salvation. I acknowledge that the pull of living in a sinful world, and of the Fall of Adam, will ever be with us in mortality—that all of us are subject to the effects of sin and death—and hence, in our unredeemed state are separated and alienated from the full presence and influence of God our Father. However, our Father, who loves us and wishes the very best for us, whose very purpose is to bring to pass the immortality and eternal life of man,[16] has provided the means, through His Son's sacrifice, by which we may be given relief from the pain and penalties of our sins and shortcomings. That can occur because of the Atonement of Jesus (literally *at-one-ment*), which brings us back to unity with God. The victory of the grave and the sting of death are forever swallowed up in Christ's great sacrifice. This is the sublime message which all true Christians throw in the face of a disbelieving world.

There are, Latter-day Saints believe, two components to the Atonement. The first is a free gift to all of mankind. Resurrection is provided to all of God's children. It is universal. We need do nothing to achieve it. It is provided freely to all, both the good and the bad, the evil and the righteous. Its first fruit was Jesus Himself. He became the first fruits of them that slept, the first to be resurrected, as the prophets remind us over and over again. One day, all of us will rise from death to life, and our bodies will be reunited with our spirits, never again to be divided. "For as in Adam all die, even so in Christ shall all be made alive."[17] Thus, all of us, regardless of what we've done in mortality, are saved from the dark extinction of the grave through Christ's great gift to all. He opened the door for all to rise from death to life. We are all assured of immortality.

But there is another component to Christ's Atonement. It can never

be earned, but it must at least be struggled for. It applies at the level of
the individual. It is not universal, but is given only to those who follow
Christ. There are certain things which must be done if God's divine
grace and mercy are to be activated in human hearts. In short, we must
come to Christ, accepting Him as our Lord and Savior. We must repent
of our sins, have faith in His divine name, receive baptism and the gift
of the Holy Ghost and strive to keep His commandments until, in His
good time, we have completed our mortal journey. Thus, Jesus is "the
author of eternal salvation unto *all them that obey him*."[18] Exaltation is
more than immortality, if that be possible. It is eternal life, endless life
with God. It is the highest form of salvation.

As Amulek, the great Book of Mormon prophet, explained:
"He [Christ] shall come into the world to redeem his people; and he
shall take upon him the transgressions of those who believe on his
name; and these are they that shall have eternal life, and salvation cometh to none else."[19]

The means by which Christ carried out His atoning sacrifice is
mainly a mystery, and probably always will be to mortal man. The
Atonement, quite simply, is incomprehensible to our finite mortal
minds. It began in the Garden of Gethsemane and reached its full
fruition on the cross of Calvary. Jesus, in His agony for the sins of the
world, sweat great gouts of blood,[20] and in a way we mortals simply
cannot understand, took responsibility for our individual and collective
sins. That includes *my* sins and *your* sins, and those of all who have lived
or ever will live on earth. It is so glorious, "I scarce can take it in!"[21]

AGING IN THE DIVINE PLAN

What has all of this got to do with aging? For one thing, each of us
will die. Death, with its inevitable separation of body and spirit, comes
to all, yet none is beyond the reach of Christ's power to save; no soul
is beyond the strength of His mercy and grace. Thus, though Latter-
day Saints do not subscribe to the erroneous (and damnable) doctrine

of predestination, we believe it is never too late in mortality to come to Christ, repent of our sins, exercise faith in Him, accept holy ordinances, and then remain faithful to His commandments until the end of mortal life.

That includes the making and keeping of sacred covenants. "He that hath my commandments, and keepeth them," said Jesus, "he it is that loveth me."[22] Jesus will soon return again to earth, with healing in His wings, to set His people free and to reign as King of Kings and Lord of Lords. The gospel of Christ is open to all, both young and old, whether youth or greybeard. Better late than never, is our dictum. Our responsibility is simple: We are to "call upon the nations to repent, both old and young, both bond and free, saying: Prepare yourselves for the great day of the Lord."[23]

Thus, we proclaim to all the world that all people, everywhere, literally are the sons and daughters of God, of His lineage, possessed in embryo of His perfection and power, and with the potential to become more like He is. As Professor Robert Millet has noted, "birth and death are inextricably intertwined. We are born to die and die to live. We . . . pass beyond this vale of tears [if we are faithful] to inherit a far greater and grander existence; it is in dying that we are born into immortality. In mortal death we leave the realm of time and return to eternity."[24]

PATHWAYS TO FINDING FULFILLMENT

What other counsel can be given under the general rubric of concern for the aging?

I hesitate to give counsel to others. Too much of the snippets of understanding I've been able to glean and gather have come from the hard knocks encountered in every life. However, as I move deeper into the twilight of mortality, my thoughts turn increasingly to consideration of what is involved in a life well-lived, and to the components of what the Greek philosophers called the "well-ordered soul." I confess that earlier in life, I loved to associate with the best and the brightest.

I enjoyed (probably too much) the cut and thrust of high-level intellectual debate, the rough and tumble of differing views. Now, much
of that seems irrelevant or pretentious. Whereas, as a young man I
enjoyed being with the *brightest*, I now wish to be with the *best*.

Time and space permit mention of only a few items of counsel. I
am encouraged that other authors throughout this book have ampli-
fied these and others. Every member should read and ponder President
Ezra Taft Benson's classic 1989 general conference address, "To the
Elderly in the Church."[25] To those who are at or approaching that
"certain age," may I suggest the following:

1.   Put Emphasis on the Family.

It is important to note that traditionally, family units contained
much more than the nuclear family. Elder J. Richard Clarke said:
"In earliest biblical culture, the family was more than a parent and
child unit. It included all who were related by blood and marriage.
This kindred family, as I prefer to call it, was strongly linked by natural affection and the patriarchal priesthood. The elderly were ven-
erated for their experience and wisdom. There were [*sic*] strength
and safety in numbers, and, through love and support, members
established solidarity and continuity."[26]

In such an extended kindred family, relatives travel—sometimes
for great distances—to support family activities, weddings, funerals, missionary farewells. Cousins, uncles, aunts, grandparents
strengthen each other in making and keeping gospel covenants.
Grandparents have special roles to play in the family. They often
act as family historians, informing current generations about their
progenitors and earlier members of the family.

They serve as vital links between generations of the family,
and in the process, teach much about the importance of continuity
and intergenerational experiences. Preparing life histories for each
child is something only a parent can do. Copies make wonderful
birthday or Christmas presents. In today's world, with its dizzying

array of technology, we can bestow the gift of an audio and/or video letter to each child, even to infants and the yet unborn. This gift can appropriately include encouragement, testimony and "the things of your soul."

Grandparents traditionally have served as mentors and teachers of younger family members. That role remains extant today. As grandparents assume their patriarchal and matriarchal roles within the extended kindred family unit, they demonstrate both leadership skills and moral principles of lasting importance. In doing so, they build family togetherness. President Ezra Taft Benson, speaking to the elderly in the Church, called upon them to organize their families into cohesive units. Family reunions, where fellowship and family heritage can be felt and learned, can do much to further this essential sense of togetherness.

"Some of the sweetest memories I have," President Benson said, "are of our own family reunions and gatherings."[27]

All in all, grandparents can, said President Benson, "have a profound influence on their grandchildren."[28] As time permits (and usually time is not generally so encumbered for retirees), they [grandparents] can teach from the "best" books and the "best" stories.[29] In this way, honor, love and respect for *all* generations, and *all* circumstances, are taught in never-to-be-forgotten ways.

2. *Take the Time to Learn Your Genealogy; Honor and Succor Your Roots.*

Alex Haley, the famous author of *Roots*, is quoted as saying: "In all of us there is a hunger, marrow-deep, to know our heritage—to know who we are and where we come from. Without this enriching knowledge, there is a hollow yearning. No matter what our attainments in life, there is still . . . an emptiness, and the most disquieting loneliness."[30]

I have a dear friend with whom I carpooled for many years, a faithful Christian man, though not of my faith, who exemplifies Haley's belief. Late in life, after my friend's retirement, he has found joy in learning about his ancestors who first arrived in Canada from Ireland in the early 1850s. He plans to visit Ireland and meet long-lost cousins as soon as he can. He has found that— as with all families—his "roots" extend back through history and forward through eternity. His ancestors became more than names on dim and dusty pages of the family Bible. They become real to him, people who felt much like he feels, who loved and laughed, and wept in joy and sorrow. His heart has turned to his fathers in fulfillment of the Spirit of Elijah, and the sacred relationships of mortality are extended forever. When blessed by priesthood power, families on earth can become families in heaven.

"The greatest responsibility in this world that God has laid upon us," said the Prophet Joseph Smith, "is to seek after our dead. . . . It is necessary that those who are going before and those who came after us should have salvation in common with us; and thus hath God made it obligatory upon man."[31]

3. *Plan for Your Financial Future.*

As we move through life towards retirement, it is wise to begin as soon as possible to prepare for the years which follow fulltime employment. That planning, *and acting,* should not wait until retirement is upon us. Start now, and follow your plan! Unnecessary debt must be avoided as the plague. So too should get-rich schemes and uncertain ventures. Most emphatically, *do not live beyond your means.* In almost all instances, if you don't have the money, do without. Our pioneer forefathers lived by the adage: "Fix it up, wear it out, make it do, or do without." That is still good advice today! All of us know, perhaps personally, of the many terrible tragedies which have come to those who unwisely borrow for things they don't need. Curb your wants, live frugally, and be prudent in your spending.

4. *Never Stop Learning*.

Make a commitment to learning; let it become and remain the hallmark of your life. Read, read, read! Reading, as President Thomas S. Monson has noted, is one of the true pleasures of life. It is, he says, both "mind-easing and mind-inspiring to sit down privately with a congenial book."[32]

"Seek ye out of the best books words of wisdom; seek learning, even by study and also by faith,"[33] the Lord instructed Joseph Smith. Every president of the Church since Joseph Smith has echoed these words, reminding us that all of us, if we are but willing, are able to walk with the great minds of history. The "mindless drivel" of the countless hours of television many watch must be replaced by efforts to really learn from the great men and women of the past.

"Get all of the education you can," said President Gordon B. Hinckley. "The Lord will have you learn things both secular and spiritual. He has placed upon you . . . a compelling mandate." [34]

The Lord has said, "And I give unto you a commandment that you shall teach one another the doctrine of the kingdom . . . [and] of things both in heaven and in the earth, and under the earth; things which have been, things which are, things which must shortly come to pass; things which are at home, things which are abroad; the wars and the perplexities of the nations, and the judgments which are on the land; and a knowledge also of countries and of kingdoms."[35]

President Hinckley continues: "I know of no other people or any other system of theology which includes a God-given mandate to acquire secular knowledge as well as spiritual knowledge." Speaking to students, he said: "I hope you will do the very best you can to prepare yourselves to make a significant contribution to the society of which you will become a part."[36]

It matters little what course of study you follow, in the sense that whether one is a plumber, a physician, nurse, accountant, farmer, carpenter or garbage collector probably matters little to God as long as we are honest and diligent. The important thing is to continue to learn, "whether you are thirty or whether you are seventy. Your industry in so doing will cause the years to pass faster than you might wish, but they will be filled with a sweet and wonderful zest that will add flavor to your life and power to your teaching."[37]

In all of your learning, which must demand your full heart and be a constant preoccupation, remember that not all knowledge is equal. As Elder Neal A. Maxwell, my beloved friend and mentor, explained: "All knowledge is not of equal significance. There is no democracy of facts! They are not of equal importance. Something might be factual but unimportant . . . Some truths are salvationally significant, and others are not."[38]

President Boyd K. Packer explains further, talking about events in his own family: "They [family members] will not be judged on how many degrees they hold or how extensive their schooling may be, but on how well educated they are in those things which are of eternal value."[39]

So put first in your list of educational priorities that body of knowledge which will lead you to God and His ways. Jacob, the Nephite prophet, warned us of those who, "when they are learned they think they are wise, and they hearken not unto the counsel of God, for they set it aside, supposing they know of themselves, wherefore, their wisdom is foolishness and it profiteth them not. And they shall perish. But to be learned is good if they hearken unto the counsels of God."[40]

"Our purpose" [i.e., that of the Church], President Packer explains, "is to produce students who have that rare and precious combination of a superb secular education, complemented by faith in the Lord, a knowledge of the doctrines He has revealed, and a testimony that they are true."[41]

Learn always: Let that counsel be the light which beckons you onward, the lamp which lights your path.

5.   *Continue to Serve Others.*

You will never grow too old to serve others. You'll never be too old to help the unfortunate. Doing so is the measure of your Christian discipleship. It will sanctify you and make you more holy. It will bring you closer to God and His Son.

What is there about service that purifies hearts and brings souls to Christ? There is no single answer but rather several. Service drives out selfishness, the great enemy of spirituality. The "natural man," carnal, sensual, and devilish, is deeply selfish, caring not for the unfortunate, uninterested in helping to meet the needs of others. He sees them only as creatures to be used to gratify *his* wants and then to be thrown away. His ears are stopped up against the pleas of the oppressed, the poor, those in pain. Their cries of suffering are of no consequence or interest to him.

Service helps us develop compassion, that most Christ-like of virtues. Compassion is more than sympathy. It involves empathy— an ability to feel deeply the pain of others as though we were one with them. "For behold, are we not all beggars?" asked compassionate King Benjamin. "Do we not all depend upon the same Being, even God, for all the substance which we have, for both food and raiment, and for gold, and for silver, and for all the riches which we have of every kind?"[42]

Compassion goes beyond empathy to action, impelling us to bind up the wounds, "succor the weak, lift up the hands which hang down, and strengthen the feeble knees"[43] of those less fortunate than ourselves.

As we develop compassion, the scales of indifference, self-righteousness, and selfishness fall from our eyes. We see and feel—perhaps for the first time—the suffering of others. We weep with them and for them. We weep, too, for our own weaknesses and imperfections. We reach out to help the less-fortunate as best we can. We think less of ourselves and more of others. We set different priorities, eschewing the tawdry materialism that has claimed so much of our attention heretofore. We set aside "our consuming selfishness," our "love for comfort and ease"[44] and seek to aid those less fortunate than ourselves.

But be careful how you spell "service." As President Packer has noted, some spell it as though it were "serve-us," the very opposite of those consecrated actions which express the highest degree of Christian stewardship.[45]

6. *Safeguard Your Physical, Mental and Emotional Health.*

As a general rule, as you grow older, you'll find that physical activity is harder to do than when you were younger. Activities which used to be easy become increasingly more difficult and take longer to accomplish. Your endurance is less than it used to be. Perhaps you can't work or walk as easily or for as long as you once could. You may suffer one or more of the debilitating symptoms of the degenerative diseases which plague mankind, and always have. But you need not—and *should* not—hasten that day of your demise by foolish or neglectful actions on your part.

Put in place a daily exercise regimen. Get outside for at least 30 minutes a day and spend at least half an hour daily enjoying a fun, affirming and/or creative activity. What and how much you eat are vitally important. Be certain to include generous amounts of whole-grain foods, vegetables and fruits in your diet. Go easy on the amount of red meat or other foods high in saturated fat, such as some dairy products.

Maintain and even expand your commitment to learning as an eternal goal. Be involved in positive ways with the lives of others, and "spread your net" as widely as possible, such that you include a diverse group of people in your circles of friendship and love.

It is vitally important that you maintain a life of your own. You owe that to yourself, to other family members who are sick (either physically or mentally), to other family members who are not sick, and to the person primarily involved, as well as to friends, business associates, and even to God Himself. You must find time, amidst all of the burdens of stress and toil, of worry, of time, and financial constraints, to recharge and renew your own reserves of strength. Pray for courage, fortitude, and enhanced understanding. Walk with a beloved family member. Be slow to judge and quick to forgive. Spend a few minutes with a good book or give an hour of service to others. What you choose to do is of lesser importance than the realization that nurturing and protecting one's personal wellbeing is essential to the health of *all* those you love.

It is not uncommon for mental illness to afflict you, or someone you love, during one or more phases of mortality. If you or a loved one suffers from the torment and tears involved in the terrible constellation of afflictions that is mental illness, know that much can be done by dedicated professional caregivers, including psychiatrists and psychologists. Medications may be prescribed, and unhealthy ways of thinking corrected. That is the subject of other presentations, where this and other mental health issues are discussed in greater detail.[46]

Eventually, sooner or later, you—and everyone else—will die. That is as it should be. If we have lived as we should, sorrowing over our deficiencies and trying to overcome them, recognizing and accepting Christ as our Savior and Redeemer, with all that implies in terms of sacred covenants, then have no fear. All will be well. You will be welcomed Home, in His good time, to be cradled in His loving arms and reunited with others you love who have passed through the veil of death before you.

Notes

1. Job 14:2.
2. Psalm 103:15–16.
3. Ecclesiastes 3:1–2.
4. Isaiah 40:8.
5. *English Romantic Poetry and Prose,* Ed. Alfred Noyes (New York: Oxford University Press, 1956), 327–328.
6. Joseph Smith, *History of the Church* (Salt Lake City: Deseret Book, Co., 1991), 1:19.
7. For additional details about the Great Apostasy, read Alexander B. Morrison, *Turning from Truth—A New Look at the Great Apostasy* (Salt Lake City: Deseret Book Co., 2005).
8. Moses 6:62.
9. Alma 12:33, 22:13.
10. 2 Nephi 9:6.
11. See Robert L. Millet, *The Mormon Faith: A New Look at Christianity* (Salt Lake City: Deseret Book Co., 1998), 43–48.
12. 1 Peter 2:25.
13. 1 Peter 1:19.
14. See Mosiah 5:7.
15. See "The Family: A Proclamation to the World," published in Sept. 1995 by the First Presidency and Council of the Twelve Apostles.
16. See Moses 1:39.
17. 1 Corinthians 15:22.
18. Hebrews 5:9; emphasis added.
19. Alma 11:40.
20. See D&C 19:18.
21. *Hymns of The Church of Jesus Christ of Latter-day Saints* (Salt Lake City: The Church of Jesus Christ of Latter-day Saints, 1985), no. 86.
22. John 14:21.
23. D&C 43:20.
24. Millet, *The Mormon Faith: A New Look at Christianity,* 63.
25. Ezra Taft Benson, "To the Elderly in the Church," *Ensign,* Nov. 1989, 4ff.
26. "Our Kindred Family—Expressions of Eternal Love," *Ensign,* May 1989, 60.
27. "To the Elderly of the Church," *Ensign,* Nov. 1989, 5.
28. Ibid.
29. See D&C 109:7.
30. See www.alex-haley.com/about_alex_haley.htm.
31. Joseph Smith, *History,* 6:313.
32. "Hallmarks of a Happy Home," *Ensign,* Oct. 2001, 5.

33. D&C 88:118.
34. "True to the Faith," *Ensign,* June 1996, 7.
35. D&C 88:77, 79.
36. "True to the Faith," *Ensign,* June 1996, 8.
37. *Teachings of Gordon B. Hinckley* (Salt Lake City: Deseret Book Co., 1997), 299.
38. *The Neal A. Maxwell Quote Book* (Salt Lake City: Bookcraft, 1997) 185.
39. "To Be Learned Is Good If . . .," *Ensign,* Nov. 1992, 72.
40. 2 Nephi 9:28–29.
41. "To Be Learned Is Good If . . .," *Ensign,* Nov. 1992, 72.
42. Mosiah 4:19.
43. D&C 81:5.
44. "Our Mission of Saving," *Ensign,* Nov. 1991, 52.
45. See Boyd K. Packer, *Mine Errand from the Lord* (Salt Lake City: Deseret Book Co., 2008), 167.
46. See Alexander B. Morrison, *Valley of Sorrow: A Layman's Guide to Understanding Mental Illness* (Salt Lake City: Deseret Book Co., 2003).

2

PLANNING FOR RETIREMENT: EMBRACING THE FUTURE

Roy A. Prete

Many people struggle with the issue of when to retire. Some, where circumstances permit, may decide not to retire at all! Some retire early for health reasons or to escape an unpleasant workplace. Other faithful saints have taken an early retirement in their 50s or early 60s to devote themselves to full-time missionary or other voluntary service. While there should not be any retirement from service in the Lord's Church,[1] most people who are gainfully employed will at some time decide to retire from full-time employment.

The issue of when to retire may be fraught with considerable difficulty, as major considerations affect planning and decision-making. Questions of health, job satisfaction, life expectancy, financial preparation, family circumstances, and expectations for the future are primary considerations. To *what* do we wish to retire? The response to this, as with all major life decisions, will depend on our basic values and beliefs and require us to plan our later life in light of them. Our most basic

Roy A. Prete, a recently retired history professor at the Royal Military College of Canada, Kingston, Ontario, has published widely on Anglo-French military relations in World War I. He is editor or co-editor of five books including, *Window of Faith: Latter-day Saint Perspectives on World History* (2005). The question of the divine purpose in aging and his personal struggle about when to retire provided the motivation for this book.

question as Latter-day Saints may be, "What are our spiritual goals, and how can we organize our temporal affairs to attain them?"

What we wish to retire to is fundamental. As Latter-day Saints, we may wish to prepare for enhanced future service and spiritual growth and development, raising the issues of whether we wish to serve a mission or relocate to be nearer family members or a temple. Do we wish to cash in on the availability of more discretionary time to pursue new interests and activities? What plans have we made to maintain a vibrant and fulfilling lifestyle? How many of our dreams do we wish to pursue? To assure that future decisions will be mutually acceptable, good communications between spouses is required. The nature of one's life's work is the platform from which all retirement planning must take place. Whatever you decide, make a retirement plan early enough to allow you to accomplish the desired outcome.

BROAD TRENDS/MULTIPLE CONSIDERATIONS

A four-decade trend toward earlier retirement culminated in the 1990s. The most recent trend is for people to work longer and retire later. The numbers are startling. According to the US Bureau of Labor Statistics, the median age of retirement between 1950–1955 was 66.9 for men and 67.7 for women. From 1990–1995, the age had fallen dramatically, to 62.7 for men and 62.6 for women—a 4.2-year reduction for men and 5.1-year reduction for women![2]

During the late 1990s, the trend stabilized and has since moved significantly in the opposite direction, mirroring the deferment of Social Security benefits and deeper penalties for early retirement at age 62 (the first age of eligibility) and the tendency toward watered-down retirement and health coverage by businesses.[3] By 2010, the average age workers began to claim Social Security had risen to 63.9.[4]

Many people still working have anticipated later retirement as a result of the 2008 economic crisis, with its resultant loss of savings and more doubtful economic prospects. A major concern for many is preparing adequate resources for longer life expectancy and extended health care, so that "life doesn't outrun savings." In a 2010 survey, more than half the respondents expected to still be working at age 65.[5]

In 2005, my wife and I attended a very helpful retirement seminar sponsored by my employer, which raised our awareness to a wide range of issues related to the decision for retirement. Such classes will normally provide precise information on deferred taxation programs, Social Security, and other pension programs, and also specific information on health benefits available for seniors both federally and in each jurisdiction. To engage in hands-on retirement planning, you will probably be invited to prepare a retirement plan and to work up a future budget in light of your goals and expectations. A retirement seminar will prompt you on matters of estate planning and succession and may broaden your awareness of other issues involved with retirement and the transition to a new phase of life.

In the light of your personal, family and spiritual goals, such a re-appraisal will enhance your decision-making process. I recommend that you attend such a seminar in your mid-to late-fifties—not at 62, as I did—to allow enough time to implement an effective retirement plan.

HEALTH AND JOB SATISFACTION

Health-related issues and those of one's spouse may be basic considerations in the decision for retirement. Diagnosed illnesses or disability of either oneself or one's spouse may force early retirement. Unduly stressful or unpleasant employment may be the underlying cause of serious health issues. In a study tracking the relationship between health issues and early retirement, it was found that "In 2002, almost 30% of those who retired between the age of 50 and 59 indicated their health as the reason."[6]

The level of job satisfaction may be a major consideration for when we retire. Unhappiness with management, strained relations with work associates, unpleasant or uninteresting tasks, the accumulation of stress or fatigue, or other dissatisfactions may precipitate early retirement. In a recent study, women tended to be more adversely affected by stress in the workplace as opposed to men who were more apt to retire early because of management issues.[7]

One's continuing ability to perform required tasks may also be a deciding factor. For example, a professional athlete may need to look to retirement by age 40, while an attorney, who has control of his time and workload, may find it fulfilling to continue to go to his office until age 75.

LIFE EXPECTANCY

Another major factor to consider is life expectancy. As it is not possible for people, even those in reasonably good health, to predict how long they or their spouse will live, we need to consider life expectancies based on aggregate data to form a general expectation. As we age and outlive many of our generation, individual life expectancy increases. According to an October 2005 period life table, in Canada, life expectancy at birth for male babies is 74.14 years and for female babies is 79.45 years. But by age 62, male life expectancy increases to 80.21 and female life expectancy increases to 83.43.[8]

Because life expectancy at age 62 for males is another 18 years and 21 years for females, we need to make provisions for adequate income to cover these later years. This is particularly true for members of The Church of Jesus Christ of Latter-day Saints, as their life expectancy is longer than for the non-LDS population—in Utah, Latter-day Saints live an additional 7.3 years for males and 5.8 years for females, according to BYU demographer Ray Merrill's 2005 analysis.[9] While approximately half of the increased lifespan is associated with living the Word of Wisdom—notably, not using tobacco and alcohol—recent studies show that the other half of the increase is related to satisfying social relationships with family and friends.[10] Numerous studies show that people who regularly attend church live longer.[11]

While various personal risk factors need to be considered in an assessment of your life expectancy, the general view would suggest that the longer span of life after retirement will require more careful financial preparation and planning to enjoy the lifestyle you desire.

Quality of life. Baby boomers—individuals born between 1946 and 1964—are likely to live a long time. An important question for them to ask is: "Will a decline in my health and that of my spouse limit our physical activity enough to curtail our enjoyment of an active lifestyle?"

No one can answer this question with any degree of certainty, although a significant trailing off in physical activity appears likely past the age of 75.

As Lyndsay Green, author of a recent book on retirement planning, has pointed out, we are not only living longer, but we are "dying longer." That is to say, if we do live to a very old age, the chances of having significant health problems increase too. She explains: "According to statistics, by age 65 one in three of us will have a disability, and by age 75 that number will increase to half. These disabilities will likely be mobility and agility limitations, often accompanied by pain. Many of us will have difficulty with our hearing, some form of visual impairment and memory loss. And once we're over 75, nearly a quarter of us will need home health services to help us with the activities of daily living."[12]

One health-care specialist advises that as many as 40 percent of people currently over 65 will eventually require care in a nursing home.[13] We need to make provisions in our financial planning for very old age, likely with infirmities and possibly institutional care.

The pattern in North America is for men to be somewhat older than their wives—three years on average. As women live on average several years longer than men, the chances of a wife surviving her husband as a widow for several years are considerable. Be sure to make adequate provisions to cover that possibility.

Health patterns. In an appraisal of illness among the aging in the 21st century, Dr. Frank D. Ferris noted a pattern from 1940–1980s, in which onset of serious illness in seniors was frequently followed by death. This trend is illustrated in Graph 1.

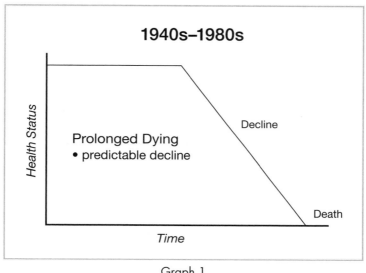

Graph 1

This trend has been altered by advances in medicine. With improvement in the diagnoses of disease and its treatment or control, the pattern of later life may be one of gradual decline, with intermittent onset and remission of serious disease (see Graph 2). Another observable pattern is that of slow decline, resulting ultimately in death without major intervening illness, as indicated in Graph 3. Some people will stay healthy and well until very old age. We now have four observable patterns, as indicated in Graph 4.[14]

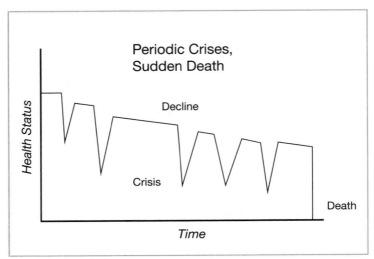

Graph 2

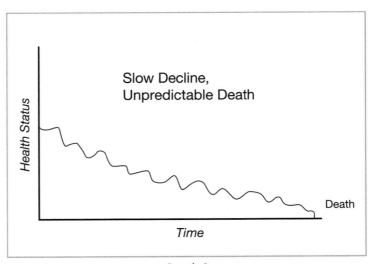

Graph 3

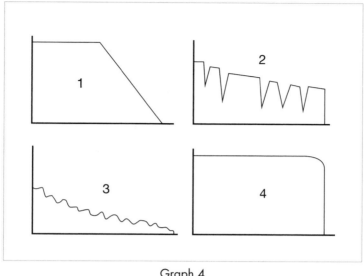

Graph 4

The notion of an ideal demise—a life of health and vigor to age 87 or later with the onset of a sudden terminal illness, preferably a heart attack and with little suffering, is not terribly likely. Rather, the most likely pattern is one of serious illness and impairment in very old age. As a result, consideration needs to be given in your financial planning to healthcare and medical coverage over the course of later years. While good health—or a degree of health allowing the continuation of an active lifestyle—is a tremendous boon in later life, not all of us will enjoy it. Both best-case and worst-case scenarios need to be taken into account.

FINANCIAL PREPARATION

The next issue as we plan our future is that of financial planning in regards to our needs and expectations after retirement. In the next chapter, Stephen R. Callister, drawing on his experience both as an attorney and as a bishop, has underscored the importance of early and disciplined financial planning so as not to have to depend on the bare minimum provided by government programs. Do we anticipate a level of economic wellbeing equivalent to that which we have enjoyed through our productive years? Or are we prepared to downsize and live under more modest circumstances? The tendency in the United States and Canada to extend or remove a mandatory age for retirement means that we have more options available to us. Also the possibility of phased-in retirement, open to the self-employed and offered by many employers, provides added flexibility. Do you wish to pursue any of these options? These are questions we need to address.

I have compiled a checklist of items of particular interest to Latter-day Saints. It includes complementary suggestions that will assist you in financial planning. For example, have we made adequate provision for the educational needs, missions and marriage expenses of dependent children? Have we made provisions for the care of elderly parents and close relatives older than ourselves? Do we want to serve a mission or engage in other voluntary service? What are our expectations in regards to travel and possible relocation? If I am the principal breadwinner, have I made adequate provision through life insurance, savings, accumulation of property, and by other means, for the maintenance of my spouse should I die before her (or him)? What provision is made for our own healthcare and/or possibly assisted living and nursing care in case of disability or extreme old age? What government resources are available in our circumstances? We need to take all of these aspects into consideration in terms of our projected financial needs and expectations.

Also consider the following questions: Have I spelled out in a will or trust how I wish my property to be divided? Have I made provision through an accompanying "power of attorney" documenting who is to manage my financial affairs in case of my inability to do so? Have I determined in a "health-care power of attorney" who will make decisions for my health and wellbeing in my incapacity? Do I have an accompanying "living will" spelling out what measure of resuscitation and treatment I wish in case of terminal illness?[15] All of these things need attention to avoid difficulty later, when we may not be able to manage our own affairs.

Conventional wisdom. There are numerous get-rich schemes of doubtful value, which are to be avoided. Wise investors have typically relied on balanced mutual funds—a portfolio with both bonds and equities—as a good way to prepare a sufficient "nest egg" for the future. The best conventional wisdom says to find a reliable and experienced broker to help manage an investment portfolio.

Many countries allow you to defer payment of taxes pending retirement in a variety of savings and investment plans. In the US, there are tax-deferrable 401Ks, IRAs and various CDs. In Canada you'll find RRSPs (Registered Retirement Savings Plans) and deferred taxes on pension contributions. In some cases, employers will match employee contributions to retirement funds, or they'll make a significant contribution.

Be sure to plan for possible loss of job or financial loss in this topsy-turvy world, in which many secure moorings have been undermined. Also calculate for inflation.

The huge loss in value of mutual funds which many experienced in the 2008–09 market crash following on the heels of the housing and real-estate market collapse merits careful consideration. To guard against such disruptions in the marketplace, it may be advisable to put that portion of retirement savings necessary to cover basic retirement needs into less aggressive, but more secure instruments, and to diversify investments and properties.

Home ownership is crucial. Paying off one's home provides an accrued sense of security and will serve as a hedge against many unforeseen circumstances.

Seniors should also be aware of various extravagant—and sometimes abusive—demands that may be made on them by children or grandchildren who try to make large or improper demands on the hard-earned resources of their elders. In addition to the drain on resources, there is sometimes an excessive drain on time. Beware of charities that prey on seniors for support and all manner of scams and money-making schemes addressed to seniors. Guard against all of these.

Balancing financial and spiritual goals. How much money do you need? The amount may vary considerably from person to person according to individual needs and expectations. You can find estimates online to calculate the amount of funds necessary for your retirement income. Only when you make realistic and accurate projections of present and future accumulation of resources can you determine what is reasonably possible. In times of personal economic reversal or economic hardship, expectations may have to be scaled back. For example, if you don't have the resources for it, the dream of retiring to a lakeshore cottage and owning a boat, or buying a condo in a sunny clime, may have to be reconsidered.

Expectation is largely a function of priorities and value systems. Assessing what resources are required must be balanced against your retirement objectives. The amount of value you place on leisure time and a less-demanding lifestyle, along with your level of desire for future service—as opposed to greater financial security—may determine whether you opt for an earlier or later retirement. In many cases, economic reality has eroded the prospects of early retirement.

On the other hand, it may not be advisable to exercise undue concern for the ongoing uncertainties of the future. Perhaps sufficiency—to have adequate resources for our needs—is a more satisfactory concept than *total* security. Every stage of life has risks. To delay retirement and missionary or other service out of undue concern for greater financial security may be unwise. The need is to find an acceptable balance. In some cases, the issue may ultimately be how much we wish to leave to our children and grandchildren.

Planning. The next step is to inventory, in detail, existing resources.

Then make up a realistic plan for managing those resources in the future and accumulating additional financial resources. Your plans should be consistent with your employment and other circumstances. Then estimate as accurately as you can necessary expenditures for the lifestyle you desire. Expectations may have to be adjusted if resources are insufficient. Preparing such a budget will require effort and reflection, but it is well worth the effort, as it will allow you to put your financial planning on a much firmer basis, and allow you to make realistic choices as to future lifestyle.[16]

If we begin this process early enough, we can fill in the holes in our financial planning through savings or improved resource management to better accommodate our future needs, hopes and expectations.

The need for good communications between husbands and wives in such circumstances is crucial. Establishing a successful retirement plan will depend on close consultation between marriage partners, so that each spouse exercises the necessary discipline and makes the needed sacrifices. As in many instances of married life, both spouses may need to compromise to accommodate the needs and interests of the other. Any departure from the long-term existing arrangements is apt to raise differences of opinions and expectations, given that we all come from different backgrounds and patterns of living. Ultimately, perhaps the best answer is for one to consider the happiness of his or her marriage partner to be a greater priority than his or her own. The prayerful application of gospel principles in this matter—as in all human relations—will bring huge dividends.

PSYCHOLOGICAL PREPARATION AND RELATIONSHIPS

Another significant consideration is psychological preparation for retirement. Those who have worked for many years in a career have made a huge investment in terms of emotional commitment. They've developed habits and relationships focused on their work experience. Their home and family relationships have been shaped by their work.

They may find the psychological loss of a career, with its sense of purpose and meaningful associations, more daunting than they had supposed. Men in particular, whose social interactions tend to center on the workplace, may have more difficulty than women, who tend to have broader social networks.[17]

Retirement provides many wonderful advantages in terms of freedom of time, and it opens up many opportunities for meaningful and satisfying activities. But it also involves a significant change of lifestyle. As marriage counselor James M. Harper points out in a later chapter, retirement requires many personal adjustments and practical adaptations with one's spouse. The ultimate goal has been outlined in Ecclesiastes: "Live joyfully with the wife whom thou lovest all the days of [thy] life."[18] The quality of relationships with family members and associates is one of the most important determinants of happiness in later life.[19]

TAKING THE LORD INTO PARTNERSHIP

In all our retirement planning we should take the Lord into partnership. The payment of tithes and offerings carries with it significant blessings. For those who faithfully pay tithing, the promise is that the windows of Heaven will be open to them, whether for temporal or spiritual blessings,[20] and they have been promised that they "shall not be burned" at the Lord's second coming.[21] Generous contribution of fast offerings will open the path to better communication with God in times of need.[22] Sabbath day observance and worship, coupled with keeping the commandments, carry rich promised blessings of material prosperity, even "the fulness of the earth."[23] Following the counsel of the living prophets in matters of food storage will provide a hedge against personal and collective disaster. Following counsel to get a good education will lay the foundation for a better economic situation. Saving regularly for a rainy day from early on will also shore up our resources for later life. Above all, we need to get out of debt!

In a world fraught with natural calamities such as tsunamis, earthquakes, hurricanes, and social and economic disruption, the one sure defense is in the Lord Himself, for He has declared that, "I, the Lord, am bound when ye do what I say." But, He has carefully spelled out, "when ye do not what I say, ye have no promise."[24]

The decision as to when to retire is highly individual. Only when all of the relevant considerations are weighed and appraised, will it be possible to decide what retirement date will best maximize our own happiness and the future wellbeing of our family. A systematic approach, based on the gathering of all the necessary information, and an in-depth consideration with one's spouse of various options in relationship to spiritual and family goals, is preferable to a whim decision—to just wake up one morning and to say, "Today I need to retire!" Seeking the Lord's guidance at every step of the way and receiving confirmation of our final decision is of paramount importance.

The Lord's injunction to "organize yourselves; prepare every needful thing,"[25] takes on particular significance in connection with retirement. While unforeseen events and circumstances may require us to alter our plans, we may find assurance from the promise that "if ye are prepared ye shall not fear."[26] Adjusting a well-conceived plan may require flexibility and be attended with some angst, but is more likely to produce favorable results than no plan at all![27]

EMBRACING THE FUTURE: EXCITING NEW VISTAS

Retirement from gainful employment opens up many new vistas. Providing that economic resources have been adequately safeguarded, retirement will provide enhanced opportunities to render greater service and pursue exciting activities, including meaningful travel. It is also a time to build relationships with close and extended family members and others, and to enjoy the fulfillment and satisfaction of a life well-lived. Later life can be a time of great realization and fulfillment.[28] The

Psalmist said it best: "They shall still bring forth fruit in old age; they shall be fat and flourishing."[29]

The availability of that most precious of commodities—increased discretionary time—provides many new possibilities. We can choose what we wish to do with it. We may withdraw into sullen survival, living out our days with a sense of impending doom and withdrawing from new challenges. "It's too late to learn the computer," some may say, or, "Why bother making new friends or engaging in new and productive activities?" As we close in more and more upon ourselves, later life may take on a dismal prospect and become a trial but to be endured.

On the other hand, we can embrace the future with enthusiasm, welcoming the chance, upon retirement, to engage in productive activities and accomplish many things not possible before because of the heavy demands of work. Various authors in this volume explore some of these opportunities in the area of family relations, with tips for better grandparenting, extended family interaction, and the preservation of family heritage, including the writing of personal and family histories. Others comment on the joys of volunteer service in a host of venues, including missionary service, with all the varied possibilities open to seniors; still others reflect on the deep fulfillment associated with family history research and temple work. Opportunities for service are available to couples and singles alike.

A complete volume could be written on the need for embracing an active lifestyle and reaching out in new endeavors. Only a few possibilities can be treated here. They may sometimes stretch us beyond our comfort zone, but they'll keep our lives vital and active. Length of life is, in fact, related to its quality.

Both Elder Alexander B. Morrison and Dr. Donald B. Doty emphasize in their chapters the importance of maintaining physical health in later life. If an exercise plan is not already part of your life, retirement may provide the signal to initiate one. "Regular exercise helps seniors maintain health, boost energy, and improve confidence. . . .Walking is a perfect way to start exercising. It requires no special equipment, aside from a pair of comfortable walking shoes, and can be done anywhere."[30] Couples may find walking together equally invigorating to their marriage. All will enjoy a sense of physical wellbeing and a reduction of stress. Many have found exercise time, whether in the gym or elsewhere, to be a time of meditation and reflection, or of choice interaction with their companion. The more venturesome may find later life to be a time to take up a new sport, whether golfing, swimming, cross-country skiing, tennis or horseback riding. Former U. S. president George H. W. Bush found his eightieth birthday the occasion to jump from an airplane!

Others have found later life the time to develop a new skill such as woodworking, or to develop a new talent such as learning to play an instrument, of to improve their existing musical skill; or the occasion to take voice lessons or join a choir, to learn a language, or to complete an educational goal. My sister completed a university degree at age 67. Most communities offer programs of later life learning. Developing skills and talents not only brings deep satisfactions as we follow the divine injunction to "be fruitful," but it allows us to develop capacities and gifts for later service, whether in this world or in the world to come.[31]

Social interactions bring many rewards. Seniors, with the reduction or loss of association with workplace associates, may need to make a special effort to maintain those kinds of connections, whether in a formal or informal way. Those who move to a new location to be near family, or who choose to winter in a more southerly location, may need to reach out to make new friends and associates. One of the sweetest parts of missionary and other volunteer service may be the association with new friends and acquaintances. Those living in assisted-living facilities or nursing homes, or who are otherwise away from family and friends, may find in the cultivation of new friendships and associations a balm to their isolation and loneliness.

Where means permit, retirement may also offer an opportunity for meaningful travel. I personally would like to visit the Holy Land. My wife and I, and my siblings and their spouses, have had wonderful family experiences on two cruises. I know people who have found that a trip to South America, Europe or China is the fulfillment of a life dream that could not be realized earlier.

And, of course, many may find the development of new hobbies and avocations particularly meaningful. Later life may be a time to take up scrapbooking, needle craft, quilt making, creative writing, or even painting, as in the case of Winston Churchill. Some may decide that they, too, can learn to use the computer, communicate with their children on Skype, or enjoy the benefits of a GPS. The possibilities for self-improvement and the development of skills and abilities are nearly limitless and far exceed these few suggestions.

None of these activities should become a "hobby-horse" or an obsession that distracts from our higher family and spiritual goals, but in the right perspective, such activities can contribute significantly to satisfaction in later life and can help keep our lives active, cheerful, and rewarding.

PURPOSE AND ATTITUDE

As I have reflected on the purpose of aging in the divine plan, I have come to the conclusion that later life, with all its opportunities and challenges, represents a window for the accelerated development of those divine attributes required for the next stage of our journey in the eternal worlds. Whether it is our lot to enjoy many of the wide-ranging possibilities outlined above, or to have much suffering, sorrow, and pain—or both—we must recognize, as the Lord told Joseph Smith, that "all these things shall give thee experience, and shall be for thy good."[32] Each challenge may be uniquely designed by a loving Heavenly Father to meet our particular needs.[33] As we develop that triad of divine attributes, faith, hope and charity, increased hope—to see beyond the here and now to a better future, whether in this life or the next—will be of immense value.

Whatever our circumstances, an "attitude of gratitude" and a cheerful, affirmative approach in later life will contribute to our own well being and that of those around us. In the words of President Gordon B. Hinckley, "Age is more a matter of how you feel, how you think, and what's going on in your head than what's going on in your feet."[34] The challenges that one may face, such as ill-health, disability, bereavement, financial struggles, and ultimately death, also have purpose and will help prepare us for the next stage of our eternal existence. In every instance, the circumstances of our lives can be seen either as stumbling stones or building blocks. Preparation and planning, a good attitude, observance of gospel principles, and full trust in the God of our salvation will undoubtedly make our later life better, whatever vicissitudes may confront us. In happiness or in misery, in life or in death, we should remember that "All things work together for good to them that love God."[35]

CONCLUSION

If this chapter has done no more than bring to the reader's attention a number of factors to consider as we plan our retirement, it will have accomplished its purpose. Retirement is a very personal decision. The most that can be offered is a method: gather all of the essential information, consider it all in light of our spiritual and other priorities in consultation with our spouse, and ultimately, as with all other important decisions, take it to the Lord in prayer. His counsel, if followed, will be even better than our own planning. If we prepare properly, our retirement may open the door to even greater opportunities for service and personal fulfillment. To a large degree, we have within our volition the capacity to make of it what we will.

Go forth rejoicing! "The future is as bright as your faith."[36]

Notes

1. Dieter F. Uchtdorf, "Two Principles for Any Economy" *Ensign*, Nov. 2009, 57.

2. Lyndsay Green, *You Could Live a Long Time: Are You Ready?* (Toronto: Thomas Allen Publishers, 2010), 21–60.

3. See "Ebri.org, Employee Benefit Research Institute, July 2001, Trends in Early Retirement" at http://www.ebri.org/publications/facts/index.cfm?fa=0701fact (consulted Dec. 2, 2010).

4. Cathy Herold, Feb.16, 2011, "Average Retirement Age in America," *Retirement Planning@suite 101*, at http://www.suite101.com/content/average-retirement-age-in-america-a348497 (consulted Sept. 9, 2011).

5. AkitoYoshkane, "Working in These Times, April 28, 2010," "Goodbye Golden Years: Americans Planning Late Retirement Poll Finds," http://www.inthesetimes.org/working/entry/5917/gallup_poll_finds_americans_are_planning_to_retire_later/ (consulted Dec. 2, 2010)

6. Jungwee Park, "Health factors and early retirement among older workers," *Perspective*, June 2010, 5, at http://www.statcan.gc.ca/pub/75-001-x/2010106/pdf/11275-eng.pdf (consulted Oct. 1, 2011).

7. Ibid, 10.

8. See "Period Life Table," Updated Oct. 4, 2005, Department of National Defense, Retirement Seminar, Canadian Forces Base Kingston, Dec. 12–13, 2005.

9. See Brittany Karford, "Studies Say Religion Increases Life Expectancy," *The Daily Universe* (BYU), May 25, 2005, Department of National Defense, Retirement Seminar, Canadian Forces Base Kingston, Dec.12–13, 2005.

10. See "Social Relationships Key to Survival, Study Says—Paging Dr. Gupta—CNN.com Blogs, July 27, 2010," at http://pagingdrgupta.blogs.cnn.com/2010/07/27/social-realtionships-key-to-survival-study-says/?hpt+T2 (consulted Aug. 2, 2010).11.

11. See Mark Stibich, PhD, "Religion Improves Health: Religion Might Add Years to Your Life," 2008, http://longevity.about.com/od/longevityboosters/a/religion_life.htm (consulted Dec. 7, 2010).

12. Green, *You Could Live A Long Time*, 14, 145–46.

13. See Janet O'Connor, quoted in "Senior Long Term Care" at http://www.squido.com/care4elderly_(consulted Oct. 26, 2010).

14. See Frank D. Harris, MD, Institute for Palliative Medicine, San Diego Hospice, "Meaning, Value, Quality of Life," courtesy the author, Oct. 14,

2010 (brought to my attention by Nurse Practitioner Diane Batchelor, Kingston, ON).

15. See chapters by Layne T. Rushforth and Daren K. Heyland.

16. On preparing a budget and developing a financial retirement plan, see chapter by Stephen R. Callister.

17. Insight furnished by Svitlana Karavay, Financial Planner, Bank of Montreal, Main Office, Kingston, Ontario, Sept. 9, 2011.

18. Ecclesiastes 9:9.

19. See Green, *You Could Live a Long Time*, 21–60.

20. See Malachi 3:10.

21. D&C 64:23.

22. See Isaiah 58: 6, 9.

23. D&C 59: 9–20.

24. D&C 82:10.

25. D&C 88:119.

26. D&C 38:30.

27. After gathering relevant information, reviewing the options with my wife, Carma, and prayerful reflection, I decided in line with the current trend to take a late retirement at age sixty-seven (in the fall of 2011, just prior to the publication of this book). A prime consideration was to remain employed long enough (thirty-five years with the Canadian government) to maximize my pension. As our children and extended family are widely spread out in places as far flung as New York City, Alberta, Idaho, Utah, Nevada, and Arizona, periodic visits involve major travel expense. I also wished to make better provision for my wife in case I should pass away before her. Another consideration was the desire to complete two major book projects on World War I, on which I had worked for many years. My hope was that our health would be good enough upon retirement to serve one or more missions and to engage more fully in family history research and temple work. I continue to serve as a counselor in the district presidency.

28. See chapter by Lloyd D. Newell.

29. Psalm 92:14.

30. "Senior Exercise and Fitness Tips," Helpguide.org, at http://helpguide.org/life/senior_fitness_sports.htm (consulted Sept. 9, 2011).

31. See Genesis 1:28, D&C 131:18–19. Idea developed by friend, Stephen R. Elliott.

32. D&C 122:7.

33. See Isaiah 28:23–29; Craig J. Ostler, "Earthquakes, Wars, Holocausts, Disease, and Inhumanity: Why Doesn't God Intervene?" in Roy A. Prete and others, eds., *Window of Faith: Latter-day Saint Perspectives on World History* (Provo, UT: Religious Studies Center Brigham Young University, 2005), 200–01.

34. Gordon B. Hinckley, *Stand a Little Taller: Counsel and Inspiration for Each Day of the Year* (Salt Lake City: Eagle Gate, 2001), 267.

35. Romans 8:28.

36. President Thomas S. Monson, "Be of Good Cheer," April 2009 General Conference, available at www.lds.org.

3

FINANCIAL PREPARATION

Stephen R. Callister

*Organize yourselves; prepare every needful thing; and establish a house,
even a house of prayer, a house of fasting, a house of faith, a house of
learning, a house of glory, a house of order, a house of God.
(D&C 88:119)*

INTRODUCTION

Many aspects of our lives deserve preparation and organization. Very few, however, will bring us greater peace or freedom as we age than good financial preparation. Being prepared financially for retirement frees us from the burden of debt, forced reliance on family members, anxiety over limited resources, and unnecessary stress. With enough financial resources available in our retirement years, we can pursue happier and more productive lives without the manacles of hard and unpleasant choices. The challenge, however, is in achieving the necessary level of preparation.

Stephen R. Callister, a graduate of the J. Reuben Clark School of Law at BYU, practices law in Glendale, CA, as partner in the firm Callister and Broberg. His principal area of practice includes probate, acquisitions and sales, estate planning, healthcare organizations, and tax law. He serves as bishop in his ward.

FINANCIAL SECURITY THROUGH GOVERNMENT PROGRAMS

Governments often mandate some financial preparation. These measures generally provide for some monetary benefits to replace wages no longer earned during retirement and healthcare benefits to cover increasing medical costs associated with aging. However, government programs generally provide only limited benefits and won't guarantee a satisfactory lifestyle during retirement. Moreover, these programs are subject to possible modifications made necessary by financial hardship and political expediency.

United States. The United States has two such basic programs: Social Security and Medicare. These programs are intended to directly benefit retirees in a number of ways, none of which was ever intended to be the only source of benefits for retirees.

Social Security. In the United States, Social Security provides benefits not only to retirees but also to disabled persons, survivors of retired workers, and to dependents of beneficiaries. The Social Security program is intended to be self-sustaining by having you, during your years of employment, pay into the program through deductions in your wages in the form of payroll withholdings. These withholdings, or payroll taxes, are then deposited into trust funds that, in turn, provide benefits to retirees and disabled persons. Approximately 85% of payroll withholdings are deposited into a trust fund that benefits retirees and their families, while the remaining 15% goes to a trust fund that benefits people with disabilities and their families.

Benefits are typically paid by way of monthly checks or by direct deposit into personal accounts. The expectation is that you will receive benefits when you retire while other, presumably younger, workers will continue to pay into the trust funds for your benefit. Employees in the United States pay a Social Security tax of 6.2% on their earnings below the fixed amount of $106,800 (for 2010), and their employer also pays 6.2%. The self-employed pay 12.4% of their net earnings.

As an income earner, you accrue Social Security credits as you work. In 2010, workers were entitled to one credit for each $1,120 in earnings—up to a maximum of four credits per year. Generally, 40 credits (or 10 years of work) are required to become eligible for benefits. These credits are used in calculating the amount of benefits you will receive at retirement.

Social Security benefit payments were never intended, however, to be the only source of your retirement income, but were designed to replace only a percentage of your income. To help you plan for retirement, the Social Security Administration sends out a yearly statement, which shows your earning history and provides an estimate of the benefits that you and your family may receive. This annual statement is an estimate only. Still, it is a useful guide that will assist you in planning for retirement. A benefit estimate can be obtained at any time by visiting the Social Security Administration's website at www.socialsecurity.gov.

Benefits. Social Security benefits may also vary depending upon the timing of your retirement. At present, depending upon your date of birth, eligibility for full retirement benefits will fall somewhere between age 66 and 67. If you extend your retirement beyond that age, your benefit will be increased by a percentage. Similarly, you can elect to retire as early as age 62, but your benefits will be reduced by a percentage.

The average monthly benefit for 2010 for a retired worker was $1,164. For a retired married couple, the monthly benefit was $1,892. Benefits may also be payable—and they vary as to the amount—for disabled workers, surviving or divorced spouses, and their families. You should apply for Social Security benefits about three months before you want to begin receiving them.

In recent years, concerns have been raised over the long-term viability of the Social Security program. Periodically, adjustments have been made in the program to maintain adequate funding levels. Such adjustments have included increasing the Social Security tax and delaying the age for full retirement. Some estimate that the Social Security trust-fund reserves will be exhausted by 2037. If taxes are maintained at the present level, it is projected that by then, the incoming taxes will pay only 76 percent of the scheduled benefits. The Social Security Administration makes many assumptions when it comes to estimating future benefits and funding levels, including retirement ages, the number of employees in the workforce capable of paying taxes into the system, and the investment return on the trust fund's assets, among others.

Generally, baby boomers reaching retirement are expected to place a heavy burden on Social Security resources. Conversely, the drop in birth rates following the baby-boom generation will result in fewer workers paying Social Security taxes to provide benefits to an increasing number of retirees.

Consequently, the precise amount of benefits, and the retirement age, may change in the coming years to keep the program on secure footing. While some level of benefit should be available at your retirement—and the benefits will play a key role in your financial preparation—avoid relying exclusively on Social Security as the main source of your future retirement income.

Medicare. For those who are over age 65 or who are disabled, Medicare is the United States' basic health insurance program. It consists of four parts: Hospital Insurance (Part A), Medical Insurance (Part B), Medicare Advantage Plans (Part C), and Prescription Drug Coverage (Part D). Generally, you will be eligible for Medicare coverage when you turn 65. There is an initial seven-month enrollment period, which begins three months before you turn age 65. If you do not sign up during the initial enrollment period, you can sign up during the annual open enrollment period between January 1 and March 31 of each year. Early sign up is important, as coverage is not immediate. Earlier coverage may be available if you become disabled or suffer from certain medical conditions.

Generally, Parts B through D are optional and require the payment of additional premiums. Medicare has many choices associated with its coverage that are beyond the scope of this piece. More information on Medicare and its coverage options is available at www.medicare.gov.

Suffice it to say, however, that although Medicare will pay for many of your healthcare costs, it will not pay for all of them. Additional insurance is available, sometimes known as "Medigap" coverage, to help cover the deficiencies in Medicare's coverage. Generally, plan to purchase Medigap coverage within the six-month period that begins on the first day of the month you turn age 65.

One significant gap in coverage not covered by either Medicare or Medigap insurance is the cost of long-term care in the event that you become unable to care for yourself. Long-term care insurance has become increasingly difficult to purchase, and many policies have significant restrictions on the range or duration of benefits.

Like Social Security, the future viability of Medicare has also been questioned, particularly since it's anticipated that aging baby boomers will put an added strain on the system, making it increasingly difficult to maintain the current level of benefits. For this reason, and because not all medical costs may be covered, when you plan for your own financial future, it's important that you consider these costs—and the potential reductions in coverage.

Reliance on either Social Security or Medicare as the sole source of your financial and medical stability in your retirement years would be a serious mistake, and one not to be easily rectified when you are no longer earning an income.

Canada. As in the United States, Canadian government plans are not intended to replace all of one's preretirement income. Since Canadian demographics mirror those of the United States, the same kinds of concerns are shared about the future viability of these plans. But they are structured somewhat differently. Canada has two pension plans.

The first is Old Age Security, for which everyone over age 65 is eligible, and which is fully supported from tax funds. In 2010 this plan paid approximately $500 per month, and had a supplemental benefit for those with limited resources, of approximately the same amount, plus various allowances for dependents. If your annual retirement income is over $66,500, however, the Old Age Security payment is progressively clawed back until it disappears altogether at an annual income of $108,000.[1]

The Canada Pension Plan (Quebec Pension Plan, in Quebec) is very similar to Social Security in the United States in that both employees and employers make contributions, and that the self-employed may also contribute to it. The payment is graduated according to years and amount of contribution, and according to the age at which payment is begun (with an option for as early as 60). Maximum payment for 2010 was $934 per month.[2] Many will receive much less. As in the United States, these programs will provide only a bare maintenance for seniors and will not sustain the lifestyle many are used to or hope to have in retirement. Information on how to apply for these programs can readily be obtained on the Service Canada page of the Government of Canada website.

Under the Canada Health Act, Canada has universal hospital and medical coverage for people of all ages. The services provided vary slightly from province to province as the program, though sustained by federal funding, is administered by the provinces. Prescription drugs, glasses, and dental expenses are not covered. The standard coverage continues after age 65, except that prescription drugs are normally covered for seniors, with some restrictions. In Ontario, for example, there is an initial co-payment of $100 annually and a minimal service fee for filling prescriptions, which are charged to the patient. Specifics in each province may be found on provincial websites. With an aging population, the funding for universal health coverage is a source of concern in Canada, as in the United States, and there are frequently significant wait times for elective surgeries, such as knee and hip replacements.

FINANCIAL SECURITY BEYOND GOVERNMENT PROGRAMS

If anything, the foregoing discussion should make clear the importance of not relying on government programs to provide you with a satisfactory lifestyle on retirement. These programs all fall short, and uncertainties in the future may result in changes to these programs that are more likely to result in fewer, not more, benefits available to you. Ultimately, planning for your future comfort and security begins with you. Speaking of self-reliance, the Apostle Paul taught: "But if any provide not for his own, and specially for those of his own house, he hath denied the faith, and is worse than an infidel."[3]

Financial security through personal planning. Financial security—or in other words, your ability to meet future expenses and maintain a desired lifestyle—begins with planning. Today's workers need to save and plan even more extensively than past generations. In the present economic climate, average workers between the ages of 18 and 38 can expect to be employed by approximately ten different employers during their work years. Only 43% of those workers will be able to retain their retirement plans by rolling them over into an IRA or a new employer's plan as they change jobs. In addition, small-business owners are increasingly unlikely to offer any type of retirement plan, because it's too costly for them. Yet small-business owners are responsible for creating 70% of new jobs in recent years. Given these factors, workers are increasingly left to their own planning and determination to save.

Studies show, however, that despite the need to plan for future retirement, workers are consuming more, saving less, and acquiring more debt. The recent economic crisis has brought some correction to this trend, but not enough to bring saving levels to a point where workers will be able to retire in a manner matching their desired lifestyles.

Analysts estimate that you should plan to have 70–80% of your preretirement earnings to maintain a comfortable lifestyle. Retirement savings needs to be a priority.

Get started. There is no magic solution to planning for retirement;

it is a simple formula of planning and discipline. Getting started is the key—and as early as possible. The later you begin, the fewer options and less time you'll have to achieve your retirement goals. If your goals cannot be met, you may be forced to live on less, or to retire much later than planned. The Department of Labor has noted that each 10 year delay in saving for retirement requires three times as much money monthly in savings to catch up. The Department of Labor pointed out that even small savings can make a difference: $100 saved at age 20 might be expected to grow to more than $1,900 by age 65. No matter when you start saving for retirement, even if it is late, any savings at all will result in an improved lifestyle.

With motivation and increased vision, you can meet your retirement goals. Many tools are out there to help you. The internet has many financial-planning resources. Perhaps even more invaluable is locating and working with a reputable financial planner or accountant. They can help you create a budget and discuss investment strategies. Some hands-on financial advisors will monitor your budget, pay your bills, and otherwise ensure that you meet your planning goals.

Again, however, the most important thing is to get started—and do so as soon as possible.

Gather information. To move forward with financial planning for retirement, you'll need to gather information and consider your future needs. A complete discussion of all of the elements of financial planning for retirement is beyond the scope of this chapter. On a basic level, however, consider several important questions:

Where will you live?

What expenses do you anticipate having?

What do you want to do with your retirement years?

Review your current expenses and consider how those might be adjusted up or down when you retire. Since inflation has always been a factor historically, factor it into your future costs. To meet your future needs, you will need to know what resources you have available, or will have available at retirement. This includes the equity in your home, the value of your investments, any pension income, Social Security benefits, and other expected sources of future income.

If you are uncomfortable with analyzing your present financial situation, estimating your future needs, and making budget decisions to help you meet your retirement expectations, consider working with professionals such as a financial planner or accountant.

Set goals. Whether you make your own plans or seek the advice of a professional, it is important to assess your present situation and compare it with where you need to be financially to retire comfortably. This requires that you set personal savings goals. It is not enough to say that you want to save an additional $200,000 before retiring. Make the goal real by breaking it down into smaller, achievable goals. A monthly budget with an investment plan makes achieving such a goal easier and makes it realistic rather than theoretical. One goal worth setting might simply be to meet with a professional who can help you plan.

Meet your goals. Setting goals is one thing. Meeting them is another. No one wants to face the idea of what life would be like if we become old *and* poor—a compelling image. No one wants that as his or her experience late in life. Setting and meeting your goals will help you avoid that outcome.

REAPING THE BENEFITS OF SUCCESSFUL PLANNING

If you are successful in planning for your retirement, you'll find many benefits to reap. Proper planning will enable you to enjoy those years and find a greater sense of personal fulfillment. It will give you more flexibility for where you live, provide you with time to spend with your family, afford you with more enriching life experiences through travel and education, open up opportunities for you to serve others (including serving a mission), free you from the burdens of debt, grant you with the means to meet your expenses—including unexpected ones—without undue stress, present you with the means to improve your health and lifestyle by having the ability to afford your care, and generally grant you with the resources to live life to its fullest rather than at a meager level.

As a professional and as a bishop, I've seen clients and ward members who have planned well. When they retire, they have opportunities and happiness in their new stage of life. Reaching that point took discipline and planning. They had to set and meet goals, and the end result has been rewarding. They are enjoying their families, sometimes traveling to distant places to see grandchildren. They serve in the temple and on missions. They are, in short, enjoying their later years.

On the other hand, I have too often heard the complaints of both older and younger clients and members who feel that they cannot—or will not be able to—afford to enjoy their retirement and families because they must work or do not have the means available. Many do not think that they will be able to serve a mission for the Church—even though that is their desire. If you examine their concerns closely, however, you will frequently see that the root of their problem lies in their not having planned for retirement.

Certainly, in the test of life there is no guarantee of being spared trials as we age. Yet when we have set goals and worked to reach them, the words of Section 38 of the Doctrine and Covenants, as contained in verse 30, are comforting: "If ye are prepared ye shall not fear."[4]

Planning, as promised by the Lord, brings comfort and opportunities.

BLESSINGS OF FOLLOWING THE COMMANDMENTS

The final section to this chapter might be seen as an afterthought, but it should be viewed more as a forethought against which the entire concept of financial preparation should unfold. That is, in any financial preparations, remember that there are blessings to be had in following the commandments. More specifically, there are real blessings—even financial blessings—in obeying the law of tithes and offerings and in living the Word of Wisdom.

With respect to tithes and offerings, as well as in financial planning in general, Elder Joseph B. Wirthlin offered these goals as a means of achieving financial blessings and security: (1) pay your tithing, (2) spend less than you earn, (3) learn to save, (4) honor your financial obligations, and (5) teach your children to follow your example.[5]

I have noted that the first and most important principle he taught was to pay your tithing. Speaking of tithing's significance, Elder Wirthlin stated: "Do you want the windows of heaven opened to you? Do you wish to receive blessings so great there is not room enough to receive them? Always pay your tithing and leave the outcome in the hands of the Lord. Obedience to God's commandments is the foundation for a happy life. Surely we will be blessed with the gifts of heaven for our obedience. Failure to pay tithing by those who know the principle can lead to heartache in this life and perhaps sorrow in the next."[6]

Elder Wirthlin's mention of the windows of heaven being open when we pay tithing is a direct reference to a scripture in Malachi which beautifully illustrates the Lord's promise: "Bring ye all the tithes into the storehouse, that there may be meat in mine house, and prove me now herewith, saith the Lord of hosts, if I will not open you the windows of heaven, and pour you out a blessing, that *there shall* not *be room* enough *to receive it.*"[7]

Paying tithing and expecting the blessings promised is an integral part of financial planning. When we pay our tithing and plan for our future, we are worthy to receive the Lord's promised blessings. Moreover, budgeting and paying our tithing has, as a direct consequence, the added blessing of requiring us to have discipline to meet our financial needs and goals. Paying tithing not only brings blessings from the Lord, it also brings needed discipline to financial planning and savings.

Interestingly enough, there are also financial blessings to living the

Word of Wisdom, Section 89 of the Doctrine and Covenants. Studies have shown that healthcare costs are a major financial concern for elderly households. Poor health results in an increased risk of out-of-pocket healthcare expenditures for retirees. It results in reduced assets through paying expenses from the retiree's financial resources and in lost income due to a reduction in financial resources. Conversely, good health permits these financial resources to remain intact. It enables healthier individuals to devote more time to managing their finances, and it makes them cognitively more capable of making better investment decisions.

The Word of Wisdom provides an inspired guide to achieving and maintaining good health by teaching us basic elements of healthy living. Given as a revelation to Joseph Smith in 1833, it still resonates today as a guide to good health by teaching us to refrain from the destructive habits associated with smoking and addictive substances while maintaining moderate eating habits. We are promised that if we follow its wisdom, we will be blessed to "run and not be weary" and "walk and not faint." Moreover, the Lord promises better health by noting that the "destroying angel shall pass by [us]"[8] if we follow this commandment.

CONCLUSION

Each of us desires the happiness, and hopes for the blessings that come from, financial independence. Achieving the goal of financial security, however, requires planning and dedication. We cannot rely on government programs to provide us with a lifestyle that will be conducive to happiness. More than ever, there is a need for us to take personal responsibility for our futures by saving more.

This principle is one which the Lord has repeatedly taught through scripture and modern prophets. Secular experts have also advocated the need for increased retirement planning. Great blessings come from following these teachings. If we are prepared, our future will be brighter and open to many more opportunities. With opportunities comes an increased hope for happiness and satisfaction.

Notes

1. See "Service Canada, Old Age Security (OAS) Payment Rates, Oct.–Dec. 2010," at http://www.servicecanada.gc.ca/eng/isp/oas/oasrates.shtml (consulted Dec. 1, 2010).
2. "Service Canada, Canada Pension Plan," at http://www.servicecanada.gc.ca/eng/isp/pub/factsheets/ retire.shtml#generaion_info_cpp (consulted Dec. 1, 2010).
3. 1 Timothy 5:8.
4. D&C 38:30.
5. "Earthly Debts, Heavenly Debts," *Liahona*, May 2004, 40–43.
6. Ibid.
7. Malachi 3:10; emphasis added.
8. D&C 89:21.

4

PLANNING FOR BETTER HEALTH
Donald B. Doty, M.D.

When we are young, life and time seem to have no end. As time passes, we eventually come to the realization, often suddenly, that life is finite and the years of life remaining are numbered. For me, it happened at age 48.

I was practicing as a heart surgeon at LDS Hospital in Salt Lake City. I was busy, productive, and at the peak of my career. I had operated on a patient to create a venous bypass graft to bypass the superior vena cava, the large vein that returns blood from the head, neck, and arms to the heart. A new, fast CT scanner had just been acquired by the hospital that allowed detailed imaging of blood vessels and the heart. I was eager to see what this new machine could do to show the new vascular graft I had created for my patient. I accompanied the patient to the radiology department and was most pleased to be able to see the graft, open and functioning, on the monitor screen.

The radiologist, seeing my excitement regarding the new technology, asked if I would like to have my coronary arteries imaged. He was looking for "normal" subjects. So I went into the donut hole of the

Donald B. Doty, M.D., is a renowned thoracic and cardiovascular surgeon, and author of over 250 scientific articles and chapters and 4 textbooks. While Chief, Department of Surgery, LDS Hospital, Salt Lake City, UT, he also served as an Area Seventy. Since retiring in 2004, he has served as Chairman of Missionary Health Services for The Church of Jesus Christ of Latter-day Saints.

scanner, and the images were quickly acquired. As I sat with the radiologist watching the images appear on the monitor screen as they were processed, I was horrified. I saw calcifications in both the right and left coronary arteries, including at the "widow maker" position in the left anterior descending artery—clear evidence that I had degenerative coronary artery disease.

I stumbled through the rest of my responsibilities at the hospital and went home early. I sat in a chair and dropped my head against the cushion behind me. What was to become of me? Why me? I was too young to have coronary artery disease. Had I done something to deserve this? I had a wonderful wife and two great sons, one on a mission and the other about ready to go. What if I died? Who would be there to take care of my family? This and many other thoughts left me depressed and paralyzed in that chair for hours.

Finally, I thought, *What must I do?*

My wife found me and inquired what was wrong. After we talked, I decided that moping around wasn't going to change anything. I had to do something about this. I called a cardiologist whom I respected and made an appointment for the next day. (Only doctors can do this!) He checked me over and scheduled a stress test with thallium imaging for the following day. The stress test was negative, meaning that none of the calcium in the plaques seen on the CT scan was obstructing blood flow through the coronary arteries. What a relief! But it was a clear wake-up call to me to do something about planning for better health and healthy living.

Fundamentals We All Should Know

As Chairman of Missionary Department Health Services, I see applications for missionary service from many of our seniors whose health records demonstrate deterioration and a lack of attention to preservation of health. As a heart surgeon, I cared for hundreds of patients with coronary artery disease and performed coronary artery bypass operations on them. Invariably, as they recovered from the operation and were ready to go home, they asked: "What can I do so I never have to return for another operation for coronary artery disease?"

I had a rote speech: "You need to live healthy. This means a more healthy diet with less red meat and more fish and poultry, less eggs, cheese, butter, and saturated fats, much less sugar, more fruit, vegetables, and whole grains, and, for sure, smaller portions, because you need to lose some weight. You will lose 20 pounds due to this operation. Keep it off and lose some more. You need to exercise every day, starting today, gradually working up until you can walk, run, bike, or swim for at least 30–60 minutes without stopping for rest. No bad habits. If you are smoking, stop now. Get control of high blood pressure and get your cholesterol levels to normal or below normal, which may mean taking some medicine. Do what you can to relieve stress in your life."

When I gave this little speech, I wondered if anyone would actually do anything to help themselves. I had added some real stress to my life as I labored over them for several hours in the operating room, giving them a new lease on life, but would they make the effort to do the things that were required to prolong their lives? Doesn't everyone already know this little speech? It's all public knowledge. It wasn't anything new or revolutionary. The only thing new was for each of us to make the lifestyle changes necessary to live healthy.

At 48, *I* was the one that needed this speech and actually did something about it. I began regular exercise and worked at running until I could run for at least an hour or even two hours. I have continued to exercise ever since (I'm now 73 years old). This was not difficult for me, because I had always been active and enjoyed running, biking, swimming, and hiking. It was the commitment to finding the time to exercise every day that was difficult. It was making time for myself when I was busy serving others. Encouragement from my wife was most helpful.

Exercise helped reduce my blood pressure and cholesterol levels for a time, but eventually medications were required. I took them absolutely as prescribed by my physician. I tried to eat better foods, and I have controlled my weight to what it was at age 18. It's been 24 years since I learned that I had degenerative coronary artery disease, and I continue to be well—after many stress tests, an active lifestyle with hard physical work, and a vigorous professional life.

Will symptomatic coronary artery disease strike me sometime in the future? Probably. But I will know that I have done what I could to delay the onset of symptoms. I feel some accomplishment that I am personally doing what I advised my patients to do.

Of course, everyone has heard the little speech from a doctor or can find information on planning for better health—there are countless books on the subject. Books promoting the latest diet are available for purchase and are reviewed in the newspapers or magazines. Literature and testimonials regarding the latest miracle pill, diet supplement, or vitamin are ubiquitous. Pharmaceutical companies market directly to the consumer with encouragement to "Ask your doctor for . . ." Alternative medical practices are advertised everywhere. What are we to believe, and where do we turn for reliable information? The internet, of course, is the source that most seek. While the internet has a lot of useless and misleading information, there are also many sites on aging and health sponsored by government health agencies and by reputable medical institutions. Since the internet is likely where you, the reader, will go for information, I sorted through several of the best, most reliable sites, referencing the information to guide you in planning for better health.

Living a long and healthy life is a wish we all have. To know the factors that help us remain healthy, vigorous, and disability-free at older ages, we need solid evidence. For this we look to the Okinawa Centenarian Study, which helps identify the major factors of longevity.[1] This evidence-based gerontology study examines over 900 Okinawan men and women who have reached the age of 100 years or more. The findings indicate that (1) genetic factors are important to human longevity and (2) Okinawan lifestyle provides many reasons why older Okinawans are so remarkably healthy far into their senior years.

OKINAWA CENTENARIAN STUDY: FACTORS IN
HEALTH, AGING AND LONGEVITY

1. Genetics: About a third of human lifespan may be heritable. Genetic phenotypes that suggest slower aging, such as survival to 90+ years, may have an even stronger genetic basis, explaining why centenarians and near-centenarians tend to cluster in families. Okinawan centenarians have HLA genetics that place them at lower risk for inflammatory and autoimmune diseases.

2. Caloric restriction and metabolic damage: The free-radical theory postulates that damage from unstable molecules, generated mostly from metabolizing food into energy, damages vital body tissues and cellular microstructures (such as DNA). Damage accumulates over time, causing aging. Eating fewer calories reduces free radicals and, in theory, increases lifespan. Okinawans practice caloric restriction by a cultural habit known as *harahachibu* (only eat until 80% full).

3. Cardiovascular health: Elderly Okinawans have impressively young, clean arteries, low cholesterol and low homocysteine levels compared to Westerners. These factors reduce risk for coronary heart disease by up to 89% and keep stoke frequency low. Their healthy arteries appear to be due to their lifestyle, diet, regular exercise, moderate alcohol use, avoidance of smoking, blood-pressure control, and a stress-minimizing, psycho-spiritual outlook.

4. Cancer: Okinawans are at extremely low risk for hormone-dependent cancers, including cancer of the breast, prostate, ovaries, and colon. Some of the important factors that protect against these cancers include low-caloric intake, high vegetable/fruit consumption, higher intake of good fats (omega-3, mono-unsaturated fat), a

high-fiber diet, high flavonoid intake, low body-fat levels, and high levels of physical activity.

5. Osteoporosis: Okinawans have about 40% fewer hip fractures than Americans, while bone density studies are similar. Protective life-style factors include high-calcium intake in food and drinking water, high Vitamin D levels from exposure to sunlight, increased physical activity—especially at older ages—and high dietary flavonoid intake from plants.

6. Exercise: Okinawans participate in dance, soft martial arts, walking and gardening for their entire lives.

The Okinawa Centenarian Study provides solid data as to what is presently known about aging. It shows that the Okinawans have the good genes for long life. We can't do much about our genes; we are what we are when we receive our genome from our parents. Lifestyle and diet, however, we can do something about, and this fact forms the basis of planning for better health. It all boils down to a simple formula: *Move more, eat less (and better)*.

WEIGHT GAIN AND AGING: THE VALUE OF EXERCISE

Why do we gain weight as we age? Physical ability begins to decline about age thirty and continues throughout the rest of life.[2] The rate of decline varies with individual fitness and lifestyle. Cardiovascular function declines approximately 0.5% per year, manifest by decreasing heart rate achievable at maximal exercise. A young conditioned competitive bicycle rider can maintain a heart rate of 160 beats per minute for prolonged periods (hours), while I can only manage 120 beats per minute. Muscle mass may be reduced 40–50%, with similar decline in bone mass. Metabolic rates also decline with age. Body fat increases as a result of imbalance of caloric intake and physical activity (eating more than we burn).

Most women gain weight during their 40s or 50s, coinciding with menopausal transition.[3] On average, this amounts to about a pound a year, adding inches around the abdomen rather than on hips and thighs. But changing hormone levels aren't entirely to blame. Lifestyle factors of exercising less, eating more, and the resultant burning of fewer calories are probably the major factors. Most women know how to "do the math" (eating more calories without exercise = weight gain), and it is more difficult to keep the math in balance with aging.

Men also gain weight for the same reasons.[4] In a study of nearly 5000 male runners between the ages of 18 and 50 years, the average six-foot-tall man gained about 3.3 pounds and ¾ inches around the waist each decade. Over the years, the weight gain added up, until 30% were overweight in spite of consistent exercise. The only way to compensate for middle-aged weight gain for these runners was becoming even more active, that is, to run more miles.

Both the Surgeon General of the United States and the Centers for Disease Control recommend 30 minutes of moderate physical activity for everyone on most days of the week. It's no wonder that weight gain comes with aging, when you take into account the need for substantial increases in activity over time. A recent study (2010) of over 34,000 women with the average age of 54 years, published in the *Journal of the American Medical Association,* showed that 60 minutes a day of moderate intensity activity (twice the amount of previous guidelines) is required to maintain normal weight over a thirteen-year period while on a usual diet.[5] *Moderate intensity activity* means that it makes you sweat. It is *not* strolling around the neighborhood and chatting with your friends. So the answer is in: increase the exercise time to 60 minutes most days in the week. My personal experience would confirm this. I don't get enough exercise in 30 minutes to maintain cardiovascular conditioning; 60 minutes is just about right; more than one hour spent exercising gains little physical conditioning, may be harmful to joints, and is probably just selfishness for further enjoyment of the activity and the environment.

Healthy Diet

The whole diet thing is just too complicated. It needs to be simplified to fit the older person's life. Most of us are living as a couple or alone, without anyone depending on us. We like "comfort food," meaning food that tastes good and is simple to prepare. A healthy diet can fit our needs by adhering to some basic principles. Below are the basic objectives for a healthy senior diet:[6]

1. Reduce sodium (salt) intake to favorably affect high blood pressure and fluid retention.

2. Reduce fat- and cholesterol-containing foods to diminish coronary artery plaque.

3. Increase calcium and vitamin D for bone health.

4. Increase fiber-rich foods or use fiber supplements to prevent constipation.

5. Increase protein, reduce carbohydrates (sugars) to help control weight gain.

6. Increase water intake for better body hydration.

Anti-aging Diet. Every time I read a list of foods that slow the aging process, I get the feeling that these lists are made by young diet experts that really know little about the preferences of older people. Anti-aging diets seem to be for younger women worried about a few wrinkles and want the snob appeal of "eating healthy." Here is the list of the usual top ten foods to prevent aging from *Women Fitness:*[7]

1. Avocado: monounsaturated fat (good fat, vitamin E, potassium)

2. Berries: flavonoids (antioxidants that protect against free radicals and aging)

3. Cruciferous vegetables: cabbage, cauliflower, broccoli, Brussels sprouts, etc. to fight cancer.

4. Garlic: one clove per day cooked or raw to protect against colon cancer and heart disease.

5. Ginger: for arthritis, digestion, and circulation.

6. Nuts: particularly walnuts for minerals, digestion and immune system.

7. Soya: to help maintain estrogen levels.

8. Whole meal pasta and brown rice: for the fiber.

9. Watermelon: a good source of fluid, and it tastes good. When blended, the seeds are supposed to be nutritious.

10. Water: for hydration and elimination of toxins. Two quarts per day suggested.

There are some problems with these anti-aging diet foods for older people, and the nutritional value of some of the foods is questionable. Personally, I like avocados, but some people don't. I think most people like berries. While very popular with many, some simply do not like cruciferous vegetables. Covering them with cheese or some other sauce to make them more palatable sort of defeats the healthy purpose. If eaten raw, they can be tough on the intestinal tract of some older people. Eating a clove of raw garlic would be difficult for me, but it is kind of good when roasted. Many just do not like ginger. I like nuts of most kinds, but I don't think that salted nuts would be considered health food, because of the high sodium salt content. Walnuts irritate my mouth. Tofu is an acquired taste but is good for women. I prefer pasta made from refined grain and white rice, as do most people everywhere in this world. There are other ways to get fiber. I don't eat watermelon seeds. No one drinks enough water. If you are worried about chlorine added to water from municipal sources, buy a pitcher with an advanced filter that will remove contaminants.

Will we continue to eat things we are familiar with and like? Of course we will, but in sensible portions rather than in gluttonous portions that result in weight gain and obesity. And we will base our diet on the six basic objectives of a healthy diet for seniors and include some of the top ten anti-aging foods for their added benefits. Keep it simple and avoid the fads.

But you ask: where are the meat, potatoes and gravy that we were raised on and thought to be good for us? Sorry, they are not recommended anymore for good health. The most recent advice by the US Surgeon General is to reduce animal products and increase plant products in our diet.[8] The Word of Wisdom, which suggests we should eat meat sparing and base our diet on "wholesome herbs," cereals, and fresh fruits and vegetables, remains the best guide, with its promise that we shall "run and not be weary, and shall walk and not faint."[9] Recent nutritional advice points in the same direction.

Several years ago, I had the misfortune of alighting from my bicycle over the handlebars head first. This resulted in a jaw fracture repaired by arch bars on my teeth to stabilize and immobilize the jaw. I spent eight weeks on a liquid diet because I was unable to open my mouth or chew. I lost weight rapidly drinking milk shakes from McDonald's that were mostly sugar and a little milk. I needed protein to sustain myself. It was then that I discovered the high-protein fruit smoothie, my ultimate health food.

HIGH-PROTEIN FRUIT SMOOTHIE

In a big blender jar, place:

1 cup plain yogurt

1 cup 1% low fat milk

1 cup orange juice

$\frac{1}{4} - \frac{1}{2}$ cup pure egg white (processed liquid egg)

2 scoops whey protein, chocolate, vanilla, or other flavor

1–2 Tbsp Metamucil (prevents constipation from the dairy products)

Berries or other fruit, frozen, about a handful

Ice, cubes or crushed

Blend, and drink when you can. Store the rest for later.

This high-protein drink will prevent hunger for hours, because protein is digested and metabolized slowly. Protein metabolism is actually an energy-consuming process, so that the calories ingested are not all converted into energy. After my jaw healed, I continued to use this drink for my breakfast instead of the usual pure carbohydrate meal of orange juice, sugar-laced cereal, toast and jelly, or muffin that lasts about two hours until you're looking around for something else to eat. Anything you can do to get a breakfast high in protein and low in carbohydrate helps control weight gain.

SLEEP

As people age, they tend to have more difficulty falling asleep and staying asleep than when they are younger.[10] The idea that older people need less sleep is a misconception; sleep needs remain constant throughout adult life. What happens is that older people spend more time in lighter stages of sleep than in deep sleep and may wake more frequently during the night. Older people become sleepy earlier and go to bed earlier than when they were younger—hence they tend to wake up earlier in the morning after the usual seven or eight hours of sleep.

Insomnia, however, has a higher prevalence in older people. Snoring is the primary cause of sleep disruption and affects millions of people. Snoring is often related to being overweight, and it becomes worse with age. Loud snoring, especially when accompanied with periods of silence, when there is no breathing, suggests obstructive sleep apnea. This may be associated with daytime drowsiness that impairs daytime function. Sleep apnea requires prompt medical attention, because of the risk for cardiovascular disease, headache, memory loss, and depression. Obstructive sleep apnea is a serious disorder that is easily treatable.

MENTAL HEALTH

It is estimated that 20 percent of people age fifty-five years or older experience some type of mental-health disorder.[11] Depression, a type of mood disorder, is the most common mental-health problem among older adults. Other common mental-health issues include anxiety and cognitive impairment.

Depression is a treatable medical condition, not a normal part of aging.[12] Older adults, however, are at increased risk, because it is more common in people with chronic health conditions, such as heart disease or cancer, or in those who become functionally limited. Older adults are often misdiagnosed and under treated for depression, even though they respond to treatment as well as younger people. Older individuals may not see depression as something that should be treated, and therefore do not seek help.

Late-life anxiety is not well understood but is probably as common as it is in younger age groups. Similar to depression, anxiety is less likely to be reported to physicians, and older people are more likely to emphasize the physical complaints associated with anxiety. Anxiety at any age is related to stress, and at the top of every list of ways to manage stress is regular exercise.

Losing cognitive mental function is the most feared aspect of aging.[13] While the ability to learn continues throughout life, older people often require more time and effort to assimilate new information. They may need to read instructions more carefully and repeatedly. They tend to avoid learning things that are not meaningful or rewarding. Learning requires linking the new information to other senses, such as sight and hearing. As a result, when these senses decline, so does the ability to learn. Short-term memory also tends to decline with aging. Long-term memory, based on information collected through a lifetime of education and experience, is much more permanent. Long-term memory increases from age 20 to 50 and remains the same until well after age 70.

Adaption to age-related changes in learning and memory is accomplished by slowing down, doing things more carefully, thinking a little longer to remember, and avoiding new or strange environments. Memory loss may not even be noticed until there is a major life change, such as moving to a different home or the death of a spouse. Information processing slows down with aging, so it takes a little longer to figure things out and to make decisions. Whether intelligence itself declines is debatable. Older people may be slower to respond, but because older people value correctness, their answers tend to be more accurate. Older adults gain support, respect, status, and a sense of purpose by interacting with younger people, who, in turn, benefit from the experience, stability, and continuity of older people.

Dementia is another type of mental problem related to age. "Dementia is significant loss of intellectual abilities, such as memory capacity, severe enough to interfere with social or occupational functioning."[14] Dementia occurs in as many as one percent of adults age sixty, and the frequency doubles every five years after age sixty. Alzheimer's disease is the most common form of dementia, but there are other causes.[15]

Staying involved in activities that require mental effort—such as reading, board games, playing a musical instrument, dancing, crossword puzzles, and learning a new hobby—is thought to reduce risk of dementia. Staying active in church, community activities, or support groups also helps. Other preventive strategies include medical control of high blood pressure and cholesterol levels in the blood, weight control, exercise, reducing salt in diet, and, of course, not smoking.[16]

PROPER MEDICAL CARE

A core set of recommended preventive services are very effective in preventing and detecting disease early when treatment is most effective. "Despite the effectiveness of these potentially life-saving preventive services, only 25 percent of adults aged 50 to 64 years in the United States, and fewer than 40 percent of adults 65 years and older, are up-to-date on these services," according to the Centers for Disease Control.[17]

Screening Tests Recommended for
All Adults Ages 50–70[18]

- *High blood pressure* (Hypertension). 120/80 or lower is normal, 140/90 or higher is high blood pressure, and between 120 and 139 (80–89) suggests high probability for eventually having hypertension.

- *Cholesterol and lipids.* High levels of cholesterol and lipids measured in blood increase risk for coronary artery and other vascular disease.

- *Diabetes.* Related to insulin deficiency. Type 1 diabetes usually occurs in young people and requires insulin therapy. Type 2, primarily a disease of older people, is more common and may be related to prior diet, obesity, and lifestyle. Traditionally diagnosed by levels of sugar in blood; new evidence indicates that HgA1C test is better.[19] Diabetes is associated with heart disease, stroke, amputation, loss of vision, kidney failure, impotence in men, and death.

- *Osteoporosis.* One-half of women and a quarter of men older than 50 will suffer bone fracture due to osteoporosis. Diagnosis is by bone density test and vitamin D levels in blood.

- *Colorectal cancer.* This cancer can be prevented by removal of precancerous polyps from the colon. Everyone over age 50 years should have a colonoscopy periodically.

- *Coronary artery disease.* A stress test is recommended for those with three or more of the following risk factors for coronary artery disease: over 50 years of age, male, family history of coronary artery disease, hypertension, diabetes, and elevated blood cholesterol or lipids.

SCREENING TESTS RECOMMENDED FOR WOMEN AGES 50–70

- *Cervical cancer.* Vaginal examination with Pap test annually until age 65.
- *Breast cancer.* Mammogram every two years.

SCREENING TESTS RECOMMENDED FOR MEN AGES 50–70

- *Prostate cancer.* Rectal digital examination and prostate specific antigen (PSA) in blood. Strongly recommended annually. Some consider this optional because PSA may be elevated by prostate conditions other than cancer.

IMMUNIZATIONS

- Diphtheria-Tetanus+Pertussis (Td/Tdap)—booster every 10 years.
- Zoster (shingles)—one time at age 60.
- Seasonal Influenza—at age 50 then annually.
- H1N1 Influenza—one time as available.
- Pneumococcal vaccine—one time at age 65.

Following these guidelines is just good, common-sense, preventive medical care and will go a long way toward maintaining good health. Since estrogen levels diminish in women and testosterone levels drop with age in men, it is also good to have these levels checked. Hormone replacement can make an enormous difference in retaining physical strength. Your doctor will usually guide you in obtaining these screening tests and immunizations. If not, ask for them.

SPIRITUAL WELLBEING

Well over a thousand studies show a connection between spirituality and aging successfully.[20] Looking to the academics is difficult, because, in an effort to remain objective and ecumenical, they get bogged down in their explanations of the relationship between spiritual wellbeing and graceful aging. One such commentary refers to spirituality as the "Forgotten Factor" in successful aging.[21] It is clear, however, that religion helps older people maintain morale, overcome difficulties, and protect against depression. When illness or injury results in a disability that cannot be cured by usual medical treatment, or when the end of life is approaching, palliative care and hospice resources may be summoned to assist.

Hospice and palliative care involve a team-oriented approach to expert medical care, pain management, and emotional and spiritual support expressly tailored to the patient's needs and wishes. Support is provided to the patient's loved ones as well.[22] Note the pivotal requirement for specifically *spiritual* support at life's end. It should be obvious that attention to religion will be accompanied by spiritual wellbeing during aging.

The best place to look for recommendations on spiritual wellbeing during aging for members of The Church of Jesus Christ of Latter-day Saints is in the words of the living prophets. President Boyd K. Packer, President of the Quorum of the Twelve Apostles, provides the pattern to follow in an address titled "The Golden Years." Following are excerpts from that address:

> When the Presidency and the Twelve meet together, we combine 1,161 years of life with an astonishing variety of experiences. And we have 430 years, cumulatively, as General Authorities of the Church. Almost anything we talk about, one or more of us has been there, done that—including military action!
>
> We live now in troubled times. In the lifetime of our youth, the troubles will never be less and will certainly be more. Old folks offer a sure knowledge that things can be endured. . . . We are old now, and in due time, we will be summoned beyond the veil. We do not resist that. We try to teach the practical things

we have learned over the years to those who are younger—to our family and to others.

We cannot *do* what we once did, but we have become more than ever we were before. Life's lessons, some of them very painful, qualify us to counsel, to correct, and even to warn our youth.

In your golden years there is so much to *do* and so much to *be.* Do not withdraw into a retirement from life, into amusement. That, for some, would be useless, even selfish. You may have served a mission and been released and consider yourself as having completed your service in the Church, but you are never released from being active in the *gospel.* "If," the Lord said, "ye have desires to serve God ye are called to the work."[23]

You may at last, when old and feeble, learn that the greatest mission of all is to strengthen your own family and the families of others, to seal the generations.[24]

SUMMARY

The principles of planning for better health include moderately active exercise for 60 minutes daily. A healthy diet should be taken, with emphasis on controlling caloric consumption to avoid weight gain (and to lose weight as needed) and to include some foods that may promote longevity. Sufficient rest should be obtained, correcting things that disturb sleep.

Everyone worries about mental health and dementia associated with aging. Use interventions that can improve mental health and cognition. The importance cannot be over-emphasized of receiving proper medical care, following established screening guidelines for prevention and early detection of disease, and immunization to prevent disease. These actions will relieve suffering and prolong life.

And finally, attention to spiritual wellbeing associated with consistent religious practice and Christ-like service to others will provide for a more meaningful life in the golden years.

Notes

1. See "The Okinawa Centenarian Study: Evidence Based Gerontology," http://www.okicent.org/study.html.
2. See "Why Do We Gain Weight as We Age?" http://www.hughston.com/hha/a_15_2_4.htm.
3. See "Weight Gain After Menopause," http://www.mayoclinic.com/health/menopause-weight-gain/.
4. See "Middle-Age Weight Gain: Men Unlikely to Outrun It," http://www.lbl.gov/Science-Articles/Archive/spare-tire.html.
5. See "Physical Activity and Weight Gain Prevention," Mar. 24/31, 2010, 303 (12): 1173, http://jama.ama-assn.org/cgi/content/abstract/303/12/1173.
6. See "Nutrition for Seniors: Health Eating Tips for Older Adults," http://helpguide.org/life/senior_nutrition.htm.
7. See "Top 10 Anti-Aging Foods," http://www.womenfitness.net/anti_aging_food.htm.
8. See "Extracts of the Surgeon General's Report on Nutrition and Health, US Department of Health and Human Services, Public Health Service," http://www.mcspotlight.org/media/reports/surgen_rep.html.
9. D&C 89:10, 20.
10. See "Aging and Sleep," http://www.sleepfoundation.org/article/sleep-topics/aging-and-sleep.
11. See "The State of Mental Health and Aging in America," http://www.cdc.gov/aging.
12. See "Depression Is Not a Normal Part of Growing Older," http://www.cdc.gov/aging/mentalhealth/depression.htm.
13. See "Aging in the Know: Psychological and Social Issues," http://www.healthinaging.org/agingintheknow/chapters.
14. "Dementia Prevention: Brain Exercise," http://www.medicinenet.com/script/main/art.asp?articlekey=23705.
15. Ibid.
16. See "Alzheimer's disease health center: Dementia—Prevention," http://www.webmd.com/alsheimers/tc/dementia-prevention.
17. "Aging—Clinical Preventive Services," http://www.cdc.gov/aging/services/indes.htm.
18. See "Health Screening," http://nlm.nih.gov/medlineplus.

(HealthMaintenance Guidelines: Ages 50–70.
http://www.pamf.org/preventive/section4.html).

19. See "Expert Committee Recommends Use of A1C for Diabetes Diagnosis,"
   http://www.medscape.com/viewarticle/704021.
20. See "Spirituality: 'Forgotten Factor' in Successful Aging?"
   http://www.agewell.com/spiritual/04-parker-forgotten-factor.aspx.
21. Ibid.
22. See "What Is Hospice and Palliative Care?"
   http://www.nhpco.org/i4a/pages/index.cfm?pageid=4648.
23. D&C 4:3.
24. Boyd K. Packer, "The Golden Years," *Ensign*, May 2003.

5

YOU AND YOUR SPOUSE IN
RETIREMENT
James M. Harper

When people make the transition from working full time to what we call retirement, their lives undergo many obvious changes. However, one change that receives little attention is how retirement affects a person's marital relationship. While we often think simply in terms of individuals adjusting to retirement, research has shown that retirement has a strong impact on a couple's marriage.[1] Couples assume their marriage relationship will continue as it always has, but, in fact, retirement is one of life's major transitions, and like all transitions, it requires that both spouses make adjustments individually and in their marriage relationship.

Retirement requires emotional preparation, a spirit of adventure, and increased flexibility from both husband and wife. The focus is often on what a person is *retiring from*. As emphasized in other chapters in this book, it is more important to focus on what one is *retiring to*: a new era with new opportunities for learning, adjusting, and a new stage for marriage. While women often struggle with the transition of launching

Dr. James M. Harper, Zina Young Williams Card University professor in the School of Family Life at Brigham Young University, has authored four books and published extensively in professional journals. A former stake president, mission president, and branch president, he currently serves in the high priest leadership in his ward.

the last child to become "empty nesters," men more often struggle with retirement from employment.

During employment years, men tend to focus on being good providers, and women on being good nurturers while raising the couple's children, though in recent years, increasing numbers of women are also retiring from employment. Consequently, the change in roles and the need to form new identities present struggles for retiring men and women and new challenges for their marriage as they seek meaning in new endeavors and activities that retirement affords.

Since work often structures how people spend their time, retirement involves learning how to structure one's own time as an individual as well as one's time with a spouse. Retirement almost always means that couples will find themselves having more time together than before.

One wife observed that men who have worked all their lives suddenly have a lot of time on their hands. In her case, he was suddenly always there. Neither knew what to do with all the time together. They had planned on serving a mission, working in the temple, and spending more time with adult children and grandchildren, but this was the first time in their married life when they had so much time to spend with each other. Because he didn't leave for work and arrive back home, their normal leaving and greeting routines involving a hug and a kiss disappeared. It required some adjustment and attention on their part to decide together how to structure their lives.

Elder Marvin J. Ashton of the Quorum of the Twelve Apostles visited the Pusan Korea Mission when I was serving as a mission president. After a good visit, he gave the following counsel to me and my wife: "When you have finished your assignment and are ready to get on the airplane to return home, you will not take even one of these missionaries home with you, but you will return with your spouse and children. Remember that your relationship with them is the most important relationship you have, both in terms of returning and in terms of every day of your life." This should be our primary consideration as we embark on this new adventure.

A MAJOR MARRIAGE MILESTONE

Every couple will experience change in their marriage following retirement, because it is a new stage for their marriage. Couples who have a good marriage prior to retirement can generally expect to experience more of what is good in their relationship.[2] However, couples who may have struggled with prior conflict in their marriage may experience increased conflict and will struggle with desires to spend less, rather than more, time together. Retirement may have an especially negative impact on a marriage if the wife experiences her husband as intruding into her domain.[3]

Retirement can actually be thought of as a series of stages, each requiring a transition or adjustment period.[4] The first two years of retirement require more adjustment and see more relationship changes than later retirement.[5] In later retirement, changes in health and a decreased ability to volunteer require even more adjustment. Retirement has at least six stages: retirement planning, retirement event, honeymoon, disenchantment, reorientation, and routine.[6]

Retirement planning can last anywhere from a few days to years. A friend of mine planned financially for years, but in a matter of a week or two, he decided to actually retire, and his wife cried for days. While they had planned financially, they had not planned psychologically, at least not in a shared way, and his sudden decision affected their marriage.

The retirement event can last from a day to a few months. This period is often marked by the formal announcement of retirement, and it often then ends with a formal event, such as a dinner or celebration.

The honeymoon period lasts from several months up to one year. During this time, both partners feel free and somewhat relaxed.

However, in time, a couple begins to realize that they need to change some of the patterns in their relationship and in their life.

The disenchantment period begins when both partners realize that the realities of retirement are different from their expectations. This is an important time to work together to find new ways to negotiate the marriage relationship rather than blaming each other for not meeting expectations. It is during this period that a couple realizes they need to set new goals, structure their time, renegotiate parts of their relationship, and work through the grief associated with loss of work, the productivity associated with work, the loss of relationships with associates, loss of identity or status at work, and loss of structure that work provides.

The reorientation stage overlaps some with the disenchantment phase. It is the time when new changes are negotiated and implemented. It is an especially good time to revitalize a marriage.

The routine period is eventually established as the couple develops a new pattern that meets their marital and personal needs.

As changes in health and new activities, such as missionary service, occur, the couple will again find themselves responding to changes which, in turn, lead to new interpersonal patterns in marriage. Couples who cannot be flexible with change will typically experience more distress in retirement and will take longer to navigate these stages. Couples should assume that the psychological and marital adjustment through these stages will change many aspects of the relationship they had enjoyed before retirement.[7] These changes will be experienced as negative only if partners are desperately trying to hold on to the ways they used to do things rather than viewing this as a new stage that exposes couples to new adventures, requiring new ways of relating that build on the established foundation of a successful marriage.

What Can Couples Expect?

Changes that can be expected include more time together, negotiating a new separation-togetherness balance, changes in how financial decisions are made, negotiating a different set of rules for your relationship, and desires to pursue new activities that require couple decisions. They also include renegotiating how you both relate to children and grandchildren, developing new friends as a couple and new individual friends, changes in perceived status, changes in roles in the household and in couples volunteer work.[8] It is important to work together as a couple in these transitions, because the quality of retirement affects marital satisfaction.[9] Retirement should not be thought of as an important event in an individual's life. More accurately, it should be thought of as a major milestone for both partners in the marriage.[10]

Expect changes in how you structure your time. Work fosters a sense that time is valuable and that life is meaningful. Men seem to have a more difficult time adjusting to unstructured time as they enter retirement,[11] but both partners experience change as they have more opportunity to share time together. This increased time together upsets the routine of the separate-together balance that has been established prior to retirement. Sometimes wives complain that their newly retired husbands are not giving them enough "room to breathe."

Things have changed, and she has to negotiate a new pattern of time together. Her husband needs to realize that while increased time together is an opportunity, it will be tainted if a couple cannot also establish time apart. Couple togetherness is most appreciated when partners also experience time away from each other to do their own separate activities. Too much time together is usually associated with increased couple conflict.

Expect changes in perceived status and in financial decision making. One consistent research finding is that pre-retirement gender patterns continue into retirement.[12] Work provides meaning and satisfaction for both men and women, and positions at work are often perceived as part of a person's social status. Husbands who are in the midst of the transition from retirement to new work roles may feel they have lost their status, which threatens their sense of wellbeing. Their consequent irritability may lead to more conflict-filled interactions, especially when the change is unanticipated and not discussed between husband and wife.

Retirement creates financial changes to which couples must adjust. If retirement is viewed as a period of loss and a constraint of resources, people usually respond with frugality and control. But control and power issues regarding financial decisions may surface. In these days, when retirement investments are constantly changing and often taking dips, husbands or wives may respond by attempting to exert greater control over the other.

For example, a couple had successfully negotiated finances through-out their marriage by the wife taking care of paying bills. This left her husband free to focus on his work. He believed that she was better qual-ified for that role anyway, because she was more frugal than he was. When they retired and their retirement investments took a dip, he no longer felt in control, as he was unable to rely on his next paycheck. He focused more on where the money was going and became more aware of what things cost. He responded by accusing her of not being frugal enough. Feeling that money was symbolic of his self-worth, he handled this threat by passing the blame to her. Not understanding the under-lying feelings he was experiencing, she became more withdrawn, and they talked less and less.

Retirement often upsets the power balance between wives and hus-bands. No longer able to rely on a feeling of importance by making decisions at work, he may attempt to make more decisions at home, which she perceives as stepping on her toes.

Expect to negotiate new rules. Repetition in relationships leads to an implicitly understood set of rules. Each partner learns to predict what the other will do. Retirement changes some of these patterns, so couples should expect to negotiate new rules in the first few months to two years.

Prior to retirement, Martha frequently talked to her adult children on the phone in daytime hours. When Jack retired, he expected her to spend her time with him, and Martha's time on the phone got in the way. He also listened in to her calls on the other line. After all, they were his children, too, he reasoned, so he had a right to listen in on the conversations. In this case, what had been an acceptable rule—Martha talked to their children—changed to an intolerable condition for both of them. This situation required each of them to talk and negotiate new circumstances under which she could make calls, and he would respect her privacy by not listening in. He had to learn to develop his own relationship with his children rather than riding on the coattails of Martha's calls to them.

In another case, Jim and Barbara gladly accepted a mission call to serve in Italy and found themselves in the Missionary Training Center studying together several hours a day and being together most of the time. Being used to autonomy in his work setting, Jim failed to include Barbara in some of the decisions he made about their study and how he perceived they would do missionary work. Barbara had to negotiate new rules about sharing information related to the work they were both involved in, and Jim had to learn to seek more of Barbara's input. These are just two examples of numerous rules that may change.

Expect changes in how you relate to your children and grand-children. Wives are often better than their husbands at keeping family connections with adult children and their families. Retirement presents an opportunity for fathers and grandfathers to forge new ways of connecting to their children and grandchildren, and being a grandparent may become even more meaningful in retirement.

However, retirement may threaten the routine that wives have developed in relating to grandchildren and their parents. If she expects that the way these relationships are maintained to be entirely her domain, she will feel threatened, and he may never take the opportunity to be involved in new ways with extended family. Children and grandchildren also have to respond to these changes. At first they may be uncomfortable, but open discussion and negotiation will help everyone make a successful transition.

Expect changes in friendship patterns. Prior to retirement, friendships for men often occur in the context of work. Women tend to have more friends outside of work settings. In this sense retirement requires that husbands develop new friends. A husband expecting his wife to be his sole friend after retirement will likely create tension and stress for her and eventually for him as well. Forging new individual and couple friends is an important part of adjustment to retirement.

Missionary service and volunteer work at Family History Centers often afford an opportunity to develop new and lasting couple friendships. Couples who successfully negotiate the transitions in retirement develop new couple and individual friendships, while partners who rely solely on their spouse for friendship often experience depression.[13]

Expect changes in household roles. While research shows that pre-retirement roles in terms of household chores are likely to continue into retirement,[14] wives are happier when they perceive their husbands as willing to help more with household tasks and chores after they retire.[15] Women often give their husbands a break in terms of household chores before retirement, reasoning that he is working hard and providing which, in turn, compensates for what he may not be doing at home.

However, when paid work is no longer part of the pattern, wives typically resent it when the pattern of her performing more household chores remains the same after retirement. Studies indicate that doing household chores the same way as before retirement often leads to marital conflict.[16]

The transitional period into retirement is a perfect time to renegotiate a different division of labor. Regular couple councils provide time for discussing and brainstorming how to adjust workloads. For retired husbands, expect to be more involved in helping with household chores. Making this expectation explicit between you and your spouse by talking about it will add to your marital satisfaction in retirement years.

Transitions in life require couples to respond with flexibility, and the transition into retirement is no different. Husbands and wives will thrive in retirement when they anticipate and even welcome the changes, are not surprised when these changes occur, when they feel that together they can be in control rather than have circumstances controlling them, and when they show faith by viewing these changes as adventure and opportunity for personal development and progression rather than a threat.

Making Marriage Strong and Vibrant After Retirement

Make the Atonement a central part of your marriage. The Atonement gives all of us hope that we can be better marriage partners than we currently are. Seeing a marriage partner through Heavenly Father's eyes helps us realize that the Atonement is as applicable to them as it is to us. Jesus Christ can redeem everyone—even spouses who may annoy us at times.

Realizing that it is the Atonement that opens the possibility of forever marriage as eternal companions, and applying it to daily stresses of living, teaches husbands and wives to forgive. Our ability to forgive our spouse is very much dependent on a personal sense of our own forgiveness.[17] If we hope that Christ's act can pay the cost that justice demands because of our personal mistakes, our eyes are then opened to understanding that Christ can do the same for our spouse. Christ's infinite Atonement thus applies to our failures as well as to the failures of our spouse. Studies have shown that spouses who develop forgiving temperaments increase their satisfaction with their marriage.[18]

Be accessible, responsive, and engaged. The best way to make marriage strong and vibrant through and after retirement is for both partners to be determined to be accessible, responsive, and engaged. *Accessible* means that a partner is available to his or her spouse and can share their deepest and even vulnerable feelings. *Responsive* means that a person hears and acknowledges his or her partner's feelings, needs, and experiences with acceptance and without being defensive. *Engaged* means that a person's whole being exhibits caring for their partner and an attitude of enjoying being together, and that the person does not emotionally withdraw from his or her partner.

Retirement affords more time than ever before for couples to share dreams and expectations. Studies show that sharing dreams and talking about meaningful things with each other is related to marital satisfaction in later years.[19]

These behaviors (accessibility, responsiveness, and engagement) are the foundation of a secure marriage.[20] When these qualities are exhibited by both partners, women and men both are healthier physically and emotionally, are more resilient in the face of stress and challenge, experience a calming effect by being with their partner, and exhibit more confidence in their lives.[21] The development of these qualities in marriage requires that each partner develops expressiveness, or the ability to share feelings and meaningful experiences and ideas. It is through daily friendship, expressing things close to the heart, and practicing accessibility, responsiveness, and engagement, that couples form a strong companionship in which they express less negativity and more affection than younger couples.[22]

Forgive and let go of the past. The retirement transition provides the chance to forgive old wounds and hurts and develop more positive marital patterns. Forgiving and letting go of past marital disappointments is one of the first key tasks for couples at this stage.[23] No relationship is more meaningful than marriage, but spouses also hold the greatest capacity to hurt each other. All marriages are nurtured by forgiveness and letting go on a daily basis.

Family Therapists Terry D. Hargrave and Suzanne M. Hanna

found that forgiving was as beneficial for the person offering forgiveness as it was for the person receiving it. They describe a process where
both marriage partners come to a general agreement of what the hurt
involves, acknowledge to each other their responsibility in doing wrong,
and make a verbal apology. [24] Prayer is also a vital ingredient in this
process of letting go. These processes of forgiving and letting go are
part of the needed life review in later marriage,[25] and they help couples
better prepare for missionary service.

Let your spouse influence you. Both husbands and wives should seek influence from one another on a regular basis. This capacity to let your
spouse influence you is strongly related to happy, enduring marriages,
especially when husbands allow their wives to influence them.[26] Of
course, this requires the ability to be humble and seek feedback. It requires that pride be avoided, and a knowledge that our partner cares
deeply about us even when she or he sees our weaknesses.

Resolve conflict. One marital researcher found that happily married older couples had on average 13 conflict-filled, unresolved topics
in their relationship, but they had determined that none of them was
worth damaging their relationship.[27] One of the differences between
older and younger marrieds is that older couples have less outward conflict.[28] It may be that couples entering retirement know how to avoid
"hot" topics, so they have less conflict. Yet the increased togetherness
and the desire to find meaning in this marital transition may bring unresolved issues to the surface.

If a couple has a successful conflict-resolution pattern in their relationship, then issues that surface during the transition to retirement
will likely be resolved smoothly. If a couple has not learned how to
effectively resolve conflicts and differences, retirement is a perfect time
to learn. Everyone can improve the way they resolve conflicts. The
following suggestions may prove helpful.

Criticism and blame only serve to fuel conflicts in marriage. Elder
Lynn G. Robbins, of the First Quorum of the Seventy, pointed out

that being intolerant, ill-tempered, critical, and cranky in our marriages is not the Lord's way. Tone of voice and beginning statements with the word "you" are sure markers of criticism. Critical spouses become so focused on their partner that they have difficulty hearing their own voice.[29]

Spouses who are prone to criticizing their partners would do well to avoid their first tendencies to speak. Self-reflection and trying to understand what about the issue is upsetting is almost always more helpful. Reflecting about what underlies anger is also a good antidote to being critical. Usually more vulnerable, tender feelings—such as anxiety, fear, or even sadness—lie deeply under the anger. Learning to express these more vulnerable feelings will be far more helpful in resolving marital conflict than impulsively expressing anger.

Defensiveness is often the quick response to criticism from a spouse. An antidote to defensiveness is really learning to listen. The first step to good listening, of course, is not talking. While one can still be defensive without speaking, it is more unlikely. Avoid interruption—a companion of defensiveness and an enemy of good listening. Where true listening helps diffuse anger and blame, interruption, whether to make a point or to correct a seeming misperception, usually results in the other person getting more frustrated and feeling like they will never be listened to.

Continue to build spiritual practices. A couple's spiritual and religious practices are just as important in retirement as at any other time. In some ways, they take on added importance as family history, temple work, and missionary work become part of the retirement lifestyle.

Couples family home evenings provide the opportunity to study the gospel together and have enjoyable activities, do family history together, or do service for adult children and their families.

Sometimes retired couples get together with other retired couples in their ward once a month to hold a combined family home evening. The other weeks of the month, they have their own family home evening activities. The principles behind family home evening are as important for a retired married couple as they are for a couple with children still in the home. Family home evening helps strengthen marriages just as it strengthens families.

Councils are also an important part of our heritage, and family councils help families function better.[30] President Spencer W. Kimball explained that the purpose of a family council is to "discuss family matters, family finances, make plans, and support and strengthen family members."[31] Retired couples are a family unit, and counseling together as a couple to coordinate and plan, to determine how to deal with challenges, and to determine how to have more meaningful influence, will help couples more effectively reach their goals.

President Kimball taught that "listening, honest communication, and respect for the opinions and feelings of each other" are vital ingredients for success in holding a couples council.[32] A couples council should involve looking ahead to prevent or minimize problems that could arise from a lack of planning. Such councils help couples bond as they work together to accomplish their goals. Faithful family home evening practices and couples councils help you prepare for senior couple missionary service.

Strive to be flexible and avoid "premature hardening of the categories." In terms of spiritual knowledge, there are absolute truths, but in most human interactions, there are multiple perspectives, and research has shown that one person's view is not necessarily more accurate than another's.[33] We all have our own filters and blind spots. Married partners who quickly form opinions and then stick to their own views and judgments of situations make it difficult for other family members, especially their spouses. This propensity to quickly make judgments and then hold rigidly to one's ideas without considering additional input and feedback from others is often referred to as "premature hardening of the categories."

Along with its associated partners of rigidity and judgment, premature hardening of the categories is related to a person feeling he is right and that others, including his spouse, are wrong. Humberto R. Maturana, a Chilean biologist, once defined violence as "holding an idea to be true such that another's idea is untrue and must change."[34] People who have rigid beliefs find it harder to successfully adjust in retirement.[35]

In contrast, people who strive to be flexible, by considering what others see and feel, create safe havens where both marital partners can enjoy sanctuary with each other.

What to Expect as a Couple on Your Mission

Retirement is a time when couples think more seriously about the possibility of church service or volunteer work in their community. Numerous studies have found that volunteering after retirement is associated with greater life satisfaction, which, in turn, is related to better marital satisfaction. Volunteering is also related to better physical health and lower death rates for both men and women, compared to older adults who do not volunteer service in their community or church.[36] Those who serve find new meaning and identity, which replaces the identity and status many feel they lose when they retire from the workforce.[37]

While couples who have served missions recount tremendous blessings and spiritual as well as marital growth, contemplating a mission often brings up many uncertainties and fears. Grandmothers especially are reluctant to leave their children and grandchildren for an extended period. People may fear having to learn a new language or live in an unknown environment. Missionary service, like retirement, entails a significant readjustment. In any life transition, people tend to try to hold on to what they know and continue what is comfortable for them. However, such a strategy gets in the way of adjustment. The following qualities help couples thrive in missionary service: taking charge of your life, accepting responsibility, planning together what you want as a couple, letting the missionary department know your desires, exhibiting faith that the Lord will support you in whatever calling you receive, and understanding that this is a new period of growth in your spiritual progression.

What can you expect as a couple missionary? Regardless of whether you serve and live in your current home or whether you leave home, you can expect change. A three-pronged attitude helps— that change is good, that you have choice and control over how you approach change, and a commitment to adjust. Such an attitude will help you acquire more hardiness and the capacity to thrive even in stressful experiences.[38] Learning a language, learning new programs, working in a different setting, working with different people, and working together as a couple for a sustained time, are all types of change you may encounter.

Missionary service as a couple will certainly provide a context in which differences will inevitably arise, just as they do in missionary companionships of young elders and sisters. Serving a mission may present new demands on a couple and new situations in which the couple has to establish new roles.

Julia and Robert had been called as senior couple public affairs missionaries. As they learned to teach together, Julia noticed Robert interrupting when she talked. She eventually asked him if he saw himself as knowing more than she did or if he saw himself as having more spiritual experience than she did. They hadn't previously experienced this kind of teaching together, and it required them to develop new roles.

The good news about serving missions is that couples cannot possibly retain all of their old role patterns. This requires them to talk and discuss how they will work together, which helps them more successfully accomplish the transition—and that then revitalizes their marriage.

Elder David B. Haight, a member of the Quorum of the Twelve Apostles, promised, "Though you may have had many years of married life together, you will never work so closely and so intensely with one another in such a rewarding effort. Your love will deepen and you will discover wonderful new dimensions of your companion's inner soul. You will have a greater feeling of unity and a heavenly relationship will be strengthened."[39]

You can also expect to experience some stress, but if you will put into effect the counsel in the early section of this chapter about making your marriage strong and vibrant, you will weather the stress together, and your marriage will become even stronger. It is only when a couple is not talking and sharing, not being accessible, failing to be responsive to each other, and not being engaged, that stress can create feelings of isolation and conflict. You can expect to do things that are hard. But if you will turn to the Spirit for direction and guidance, these circumstances will allow you to live the experience exemplified in the scripture: "And inasmuch as they follow the *counsel* which they receive, they shall have power after many days to accomplish all things pertaining to Zion."[40]

For those called to serve on the Lord's errand, "He shall *prepare* a way for them that they may accomplish the thing which he commandeth them."[41]

Expect to develop new relationships regardless of what type of missionary service you are engaged in. You will most likely be serving with other missionaries and will often be serving other people. Remember that research has shown that developing new friends as an individual and as a couple is an important process for successful retirement. Elder Dallin H. Oaks related that you will have opportunities to become friends to missionary couples who are serving their third, fourth or fifth missions.[42]

You can expect to find more meaning in your life, which will include strengthened testimonies of the Atonement and the Lord's Church. You will need to rely on the Spirit, on each other, and on the strength of your family. That type of dependency yields spiritual experience. Finding meaning in life and mastering new knowledge and practice is crucial to good adjustment in retirement.[43]

While you will miss your children and grandchildren, you will discover that their testimonies are strengthened by your service. They will admire you and cherish your experiences. With today's global communication technology, you will find ways to have an influence in their lives even if your mission is far from where they live. Elder Russell M. Nelson related the experience of one couple who was worried about leaving their children and grandchildren. They said that while they were gone, other people stepped in to perform parenting functions and help grandchildren. This couple suggested that serving a mission might be considered as a way to help a family problem that has not yielded to prayer and fasting.[44]

In conclusion, retirement is not only an individual event. It is a major milestone in a marriage relationship. Understanding the issues and adjustments in behavior discussed in this chapter will help you pump vitality into your marriage in the important retirement transition and will lead to greater happiness and fulfillment in later life.

Notes

1. See Maximilliane E. Szinovacz and David J. Ekerdt, "Families and Retirement," *Handbook of Aging and the Family,* edited by Rosemary Bleiszner and Victoria H. Bedford (Westport, CT: Greenwood Press, 1995), 375–400.
2. See Adam Davey and Maximilliane E. Szinovacz, "Dimensions of Marital Quality and Retirement," *Journal of Family Issues* 25 (2004): 431–63; Tanya R. Fitzpatrick, Barbara H. Vinick, and Suzanne Bushfield, "Anticipated and Experienced Changes After Husbands Retire," *Journal of Gerontological Social Work* 46 (2005): 69–84.
3. See Davey and Szinovacz, "Marital Quality and Retirement," 431–63.
4. See Claire Allison Stammerjohan, Louis M. Capella, and Ronald D. Taylor, "Retirement and Transition Phenomena in the Family Purchase Process" *Psychology and Marketing* 24 (2009): 225–51.
5. See Jeffrey Dew and Jeremy Yorgason, "Economic Pressure and Marital Conflict in Retirement-Aged Couples," *Journal of Family Issues* 31 (2010):164–88.

6. See Sara Yogev, *For Better or Worse. But Not for Lunch: Making Marriage Work in Retirement* (New York: Contemporary Books, 2002).
7. See Froma Walsh, "Normal Family Processes: Growing Diversity and Complexity" (New York: Guilford, 2003).
8. See David Arp, Claudia Arp, Scott Stanley, Howard J. Markman, and Susan Blumberg, *Fighting for Your Empty Nest Marriage: Reinventing Your Relationship when the Kids Leave Home* (San Francisco, CA: Jossey-Bass, 2000); Allison Blurton, "A Qualitative Study Exploring Maritally Satisfied Retired Couples in Early Years of Retirement" (Ph.D. diss., Alliant International University, 2004); P. Moen, J. E. Kim, and H. Hoffmeister, "Couples' Work/Retirement Transitions, Gender, and Marital Quality," *Social Psychology*, Quarterly 64 (2001): 55–71.
9. See Davey and Szinovacz, "Marital Quality and Retirement;" Susan F. Higginbottom, Julian, Barling, and E. Kevin Kelloway, "Linking Retirement Experiences and Marital Satisfaction: A Mediational Model," *Psychology and Aging* 8 (1993): 508–16; Moen, Kim, and Hoffmeister, "Couples' Work/Retirement Transitions."
10. See Liat Kulik, "The Impact of Men's and Women's Retirement on Marital Relations: A Comparative Analysis," *Journal of Women & Aging* 13 (2009): 13–27.
11. See Szinovacz and Ekerdt, "Families and Retirement."
12. See Karsten Hank and Hendrick Jurges, "Gender and the Division of Labor in Older Couples: A European Perspective," *Journal of Family Issues* 28 (2009): 399–421.
13. See Yogev, *Making Marriage Work in Retirement.*
14. See Maximilliane E. Szinovacz and Paula Harpster, "Couple's Employment/Retirement Status and the Division of Household Tasks," *Journals of Gerontology* 49 (1994): S125–S136.
15. See Maximilliane E. Szinovacz, "Couples' Employment/Retirement Patterns and Perceptions of Marital Quality," *Research of Aging* 18 (1996): 243–68.
16. Ibid.
17. See James M. Harper, "Seventy Times Seven," Brigham Young University Speeches (Provo, UT: Brigham Young University, 1997), http://speeches.byu.edu/reader/reader.php?id=2947 (accessed June 20, 2010).
18. See Frederick A. Diblasio and Brent B. Brenda, "Forgiveness Intervention with Married Couples: Two Empirical Analyses," *Journal of Psychology and Christianity* 27 (2008): 150–58; Andrea J. Miller and Everett L. Worthington, "Sex Differences in Forgiveness and Mental Health in Recently Married Couples," *The Journal of Positive Psychology* 5 (2010): 12–23.

19. See John M. Gottman, *The Marriage Clinic: A Scientifically Based Marital Therapy* (New York: W. W. Norton, 1999).
20. See Susan Johnson, *Hold Me Tight* (New York: Little, Brown, and Company, 2004).
21. See Kiecolt-Glaser and Newton, 2001; Johnson, *Hold Me Tight*; James A. Coan, Hillary S. Schaefer, and Richard J. Davidson, "Lending a Hand: Social Regulation of the Neural Response to Threat," *Psychological Science* 17 (2006): 1032–39; Jonathan G. Sandberg, Richard B. Miller, and James M. Harper, "The Impact of Marital Conflict on Health and Health Care Utilization in Older Couples," *Journal of Health Psychology* 14 (2009): 9–17.
22. See Laura L. Carstensen, John M. Gottman, and Robert W. Levenson, "Emotional Behavior in Long-Term Marriage" in *Close Relationships: Key Readings*, edited by Harry T. Reis and Carl E. Rusbult (Philadelphia: Taylor and Francis, 2004).
23. See David Arp, and Claudia Arp, *The Second Half of Marriage* (Grand Rapids, MI: Zondervan, 1996).
24. See Terry D. Hargrave and Suzanne M. Hanna, "Aging: A Primer for Family Therapists," *The Aging Family: New Visions in Theory, Practice, and Reality*, edited by Suzanne M. Hanna and Terry D. Hargrave (Philadelphia: Brunner/Mazel, 1997), 39–58.
25. See Jeffrey Dean Webster, Ernst T. Bohlmeijer, and Gerben, J. Westerhof, "Mapping the Future of Reminiscence: A Conceptual Guide for Research and Practice," *Research and Aging* 32 (2010): 527–64.
26. See Gottman, *A Scientifically Based Marital Therapy*.
27. Ibid.
28. See Carstensen, et al, "Emotional Behavior in Long-Term Marriage."
29. See "Agency and Love in Marriage," *Ensign*, Oct. 2000, 16.
30 See M. Russell Ballard, "Counseling with Our Councils," *Ensign*, May 1994, 24.
31. See Spencer W. Kimball, and Edward L. Kimball, *The Teachings of Spencer W. Kimball, Twelfth President of The Church of Jesus Christ of Latter-day Saints* (Salt Lake City: Bookcraft, 1995), 343.
32. Ibid.
33. See Carol Travis, and Elliot Aronson, *Mistakes Were Made (But Not By ME): Why We justify Foolish Beliefs, Bad Decisions, and Hurtful Acts* (Orlando: Harcourt, 2007).
34. Humberto R. Maturana and Francisco J. Varela, *The Tree of Knowledge: Biological Roots of Human Understanding* (New York: Shambhala, 1992), 246–47.
35. See Maximilliane E. Szinovacz, "Changes in Housework after Retirement: A Panel Analysis," *Journal of Marriage and the Family* 62 (2000): 78–92.
36. See H. Cox, T. Parks, A. Hammonds, and G. Sekhon, "Work/Retirement

Choices and Lifestyle Patterns of Older Americans," *Journal of Applied Sociology,* 18 (2001): 131–149; M. A. Musick, A. R. Herzog, and J. S. House, "Volunteering and Mortality Among Older Adults: Findings from a National Sample," *The Journals of Gerontology* 54B (1999): S173–S180; R. L. Jirovek and C. A. Hyduk, "Type of Volunteer Experience and Health Among Older Adult Volunteers," *Journal of Gerontological Social Work,* 30 (1998): 29–42; N. Morrow-Howell, J. Hinterlong, P. A. Rosario, and F. Tang, "Effects of Volunteering on the Well-Being of Older Adults," *The Journals of Gerontology,* 58B (2003):S137–S145; D. Schmotkin, T. Blumstein and B. Modan, "Beyond Keeping Active: Concomitants of Being a Volunteer in Old-Old Age," *Psychology and Aging* 18 (2003): 602–07; Marieke Van Willigen, "Differential Benefits of Volunteering Across the Life Course" *Journals of Gerontology,* 55B (2000): S308–S318.

37. See Greenfield and Marks, 2004.
38. See Thomas F. Holcomb, "Transitioning into Retirement as a Successful Life Event," *Handbook of Stressful Transitions Across the Lifespan*, ed. Thomas W. Miller (New York: Springer, 2010), 133–46.
39. See David B. Haight, "My Neighbor—My Brother!" *Ensign,* Apr. 1987.
40. D&C 105:37; emphasis added.
41. 1 Nephi 3:7; emphasis added.
42. See Dallin H. Oaks, "I'll Go Where You Want Me to Go," *Ensign*, Oct. 2002, 67.
43. See Michael A. Melton, Michel Hersen, Timothy D. Van Sickle, and Vincent B. Van Hasselt, "Parameters of Marriage in Older Adults: A Review of the Literature," *Clinical Psychology Review* 15 (1995): 891–904; Moen et al, "Couples' Work/Retirement Transitions," 55–61.
44. See Russell M. Nelson, "Senior Missionaries and the Gospel," *Ensign*, Oct. 2004, 79.

6

GRANDPARENTING

Carma Prete

My father's mother died before I was born, so growing up, I had only one living grandmother, my mother's mother, Grandma Carpenter.[1] She and Grandpa lived on a farm in Osgood, Idaho, about an hour's drive from our home, so we saw them quite frequently. Some of my mother's siblings lived even nearer to Grandma than we did, and lots of aunts and uncles and cousins were often there when we came to visit. We had big family gatherings for all the major holidays and for birthdays, baby blessings, missionary farewells and homecomings. Christmas Eve at Grandma's was the highlight of the year.

I always loved going to Grandma's house. There was always plenty of good food, interesting things to do, and fun people who loved to tease and tell jokes. There was lots of space for us energetic grand-children to run outside and play games. But looking back, I think the main reason I loved to go to Grandma's was because I knew she loved me and that she was always so excited to see me. I firmly believed (and maybe I still do) that I was her favorite grandchild. I'm quite sure that all the other grandchildren felt the same way about themselves.

Being the oldest child in my family, I was the first to get married

---

Carma Prete is the mother of six and the grandmother of eighteen. A BYU graduate and former teacher, she has written extensively on local Church history. She has served in numerous church callings, including multiple times as Primary president at the ward/branch and stake/district level.

and the first to have children, making my parents into grandparents. I watched my mother in her new role as a grandmother. My husband and I have always lived a substantial distance from my parents, so I learned from my mother's example that it's possible to be a wonderful grandmother even from very far away. She wrote letters, sewed and crocheted lovely gifts, made quilts, and always remembered birthdays. When we made the long journey to Idaho for a visit, about every three years, she made each of our children feel so loved and welcome. On two occasions my parents came to our home in Kingston, Ontario, for a visit, and from there we went on lengthy car trips together. My mother was a wonder, sitting in the back seat with the children, telling stories, doing finger-plays, singing songs, and generally keeping them happy and entertained, mile after mile, hour after hour.

MY TURN

As our six children grew older and we started having weddings, I knew that before long I, too, would be a grandmother. I wasn't sure how good I would be in that role, so I started to reflect on the role models I have had—my own grandmother, my own mother—and to observe a number of other grandmothers in my circle of acquaintances. I found that there are many admirable qualities that grandmothers have and many wonderful things that grandmothers do, many of which I might want to incorporate into my own grandmotherly persona, but I also concluded that no one person could do and be all things. There are innumerable ways to be a good grandmother, and each grandmother develops a unique combination of grandmotherly qualities to fit her circumstances.[2]

My first three grandchildren were born within 2½ months of each other, so my grandparenting learning curve was quite steep. But the feeling of love that swept over me when I held those beautiful babies in my arms helped me to know that these were truly children of God, and they are connected to me through powerful genetic, spiritual, and emotional bonds. It has been such a delight to get acquainted with each of our grandchildren (we now have eighteen and expect more), to feel the overwhelming love for each new baby and to feel that love grow as our grandchildren grow and develop. It is exciting to discover each little personality emerging, to see talents and abilities blossoming, and to recognize characteristics in them that we have seen in previous generations. Being a grandparent is an adventure that just keeps getting better. No wonder there is hardly a grandmother who does not carry photos of her grandchildren in her purse!

NURTURING LOVING RELATIONSHIPS

Grandparenting is quite different than parenting. Parents provide food and shelter, give day-to-day structure to the lives of their children, love, teach, train, establish family rules, and impose discipline. Frequently, though, with the demands of work, family, and church service, parents may not always have as much time as they would like to devote to each child to meet his or her needs. Grandparents can often supplement parents' efforts, filling in the gaps, nurturing and encouraging their grandchildren, and building relationships of love and trust.

One thing I admire about the grandparents I see around me is that they make an effort to attend their grandchildren's special events—not only baby blessings, baptisms, and weddings, but also school concerts, soccer games, graduations, piano recitals, science fairs, spelling bees, courts of honor, even talks in Primary. Grandparents who live too far away to frequently attend such events can still follow the fortunes of a grandchild's little-league baseball team and call to congratulate him on a good report card or a successful musical performance. Through careful listening, a grandparent can cultivate an awareness of what grandchildren are interested in, what activities they participate in, and what is important to them.

Not all grandparents play the same role in their grandchildren's lives. If grown children live close by, some grandparents host regular family dinners, gathering the extended family together for special occasions and/or weekly Sunday meals. Some grandparents provide regular or occasional childcare for some or all of their grandchildren. Some grandmothers bake cookies, create scrapbooks or make quilts. Some grandparents invite their grandchildren to visit one at a time to enjoy one-on-one time with each child. Some grandparents even have a "grandparents' retreat" where all the grandchildren over eight years come to a special place where they can stay overnight and spend a day or two with only their grandparents.

Some distant grandparents not only send cards and letters, but utilize various alternate forms of communication, such as telephone, email, and webcams, to maintain relationships with grandchildren. Whichever methods you use, the important thing is that grandparents make the time and effort to stay connected with their grandchildren and to communicate their love and interest to them and their faith and confidence in them.

We live over 2000 miles from most of our grandchildren, so one important element in building and maintaining relationships with them is to visit them as often as possible. We have set a goal to see each family at least twice each year. This traveling takes a significant slice out of our annual budget, but we feel that it is well worth it to spend time in each home, interacting with the grandchildren on their own turf, playing games, helping them do household chores, going for walks, attending Church together. For many distant grandparents, visiting so frequently may not be possible, but the essential idea is to do all we can to reach out and nurture the relationships with our grandchildren.

FOSTERING MEANINGFUL TRADITIONS

One tradition we enjoy is selecting and sending grandchildren gifts for birthdays and Christmas. We usually invite the parents to make suggestions of what gifts might be of interest to each child, but we make the final selections and find great satisfaction in trying to send just the right gift. (Amazon.com has been a considerable help in our long-distance shopping.) Sometimes we have followed the examples of my own mother and mother-in-law, who, years ago, often sent our own children gifts of a spiritual nature, such as Bible story books, Book of Mormon stories, and books about baptism. We have given copies of scriptures, pictures of temples, "My Gospel Standards" posters, church videos such as *Mountain of the Lord*, and even Book of Mormon action figures. Such items enrich the gospel environment in each home and build faith.

My husband had a precious grandparenting experience two years ago. Two granddaughters, aged four and six, made it very clear that they wanted Grandpa to take them fishing. So Grandpa gathered together some fishing poles, tackle, and some worms, and they went out. They fished and fished, but the fish just weren't interested. Our six-year-old granddaughter said, "Grandpa, we ought to say a prayer." Grandpa was hesitant, not wanting to risk her faith on the lack of a catch. But, after an encounter with brambles which led the younger girl to go home, the six-year-old still wanted to fish and insisted they pray. They said a prayer together. After that, they caught two fish. What a beautiful example of a grandfather-granddaughter bonding experience that strengthened faith.

Family reunions have been a wonderful vehicle for strengthening family ties. Since our family is so widely scattered geographically, it is a considerable challenge to get all of us together. It has been gratifying to see our children involve themselves enthusiastically in planning and preparing these reunions and to observe the sacrifices they are willing to make to attend and participate. One tradition that has evolved in our family is "Happy Land for Babies," which comes into being each time we all get together. The older grandchildren, led by one precocious granddaughter, organizes a daycare program for the younger grand-children. The administrative skills involved are astonishing. They not only provide wholesome and educational programs for their younger cousins, but they create registration forms and hold parent-teacher interviews and graduation ceremonies. Without our family reunions bringing all the cousins together from time to time, such memorable and bonding activities would not take place.[3]

Family newsletters can be a great strength to family relationships. There are many different formats and parameters for family newsletters.[4] In our family, we have a publication called *Bridges,* which builds bridges of communication between various parts of the family who are separated by many miles. This newsletter always features a thoughtful article by my husband (Grandpa) and another by me (Grandma), sometimes featuring faithful ancestors. Then, each family submits one or more articles and lots of pictures. The newsletter often contains a list of upcoming birthdays, and sometimes includes drawings and poems by the grandchildren. We take turns editing and producing the newsletter, which we send around electronically so each family can print out a hard copy. Although we haven't produced new issues of *Bridges* as often as we first intended, this has been a unifying activity for us, and the newsletters are an important permanent record of the unfolding history of our family.

Role Model and Example

The example of grandparents can be a powerful influence in the life of a child. Knowing that Grandma and Grandpa pay tithing, attend the temple, and go to church every Sunday can be a constant in their universe. Hearing grandparents teach principles of the gospel during everyday associations, listening to their wise counsel and hearing them bear testimony, builds faith in the hearts of young grandchildren. Knowing that grandparents have found happiness and fulfillment in a lifetime of faithful church service can be an anchor to younger family members surrounded by worldly influences and eroding societal values. Seeing beloved grandparents prepare for and go on a mission sends a stirring message to children that the gospel is true and that the Lord's work is worthy of sacrifice.

Love of learning can be effectively fostered by grandparents. Having a home filled with good books and other wholesome reading materials can provide a stimulating and exhilarating environment for visiting grandchildren. Reading stories and books together can be an important shared experience. Sharing interests and hobbies with grandchildren can kindle curiosity and broaden their experience.

For example, I have always been interested in astronomy. It has been a pleasure to show grandchildren the planets and the constellations. One of my cherished memories is with my granddaughter, watching and identifying the space shuttle move across the sky one evening at twilight. My husband seeks for activities that both he and the grandchild will enjoy, such as camping, fishing and canoeing. Even working together can be greatly beneficial. I have had some very rewarding experiences outside pulling weeds with my grandchildren. Talking together as we worked, it was surprising how quickly the job was finished, and it was satisfying to see how our work had improved the garden.

As it is now fairly common for people to live into their 80s and 90s, grandparents frequently become caregivers for their own aged parents. Grandparents set an important example by the way they treat and care for their elderly parents. As we honor, love and respect our elderly parents, we teach our children and grandchildren in a powerful way to value and cherish their elders.[5]

SUPPORT IN TIMES OF NEED

Grandparents can be a vital resource to children and grandchildren in times of challenge or difficulty. Sometimes grandparents can provide financial help or provide a temporary home to family members in need. Sometimes they can be a vital help in times of illness or crisis. Sometimes, they can give understanding and a listening ear.

Like many grandmothers, I have provided meaningful service by staying with our children when new babies are born, whenever possible. This has given me an opportunity to see and cuddle each new baby and begin the process of grandparent-grandchild bonding, but I have also been able to be of some assistance to the new mothers, helping to strengthen relationships with our children, their spouses, and the baby's siblings. On one occasion after my daughter and her family were involved in a serious traffic accident, I was able to spend a few weeks with them during a highly stressful period of their lives. Whatever challenges our children may encounter, we can provide moral support, a listening ear, encouragement, and/or other hands-on support, as the situation requires.

BRIDGING THE GENERATIONS

A grandparent is a crucial link in a family between the past and the future. Most of us grandparents, when we were children ourselves, knew our own parents, grandparents, and perhaps even great-grandparents, along with siblings, aunts, uncles, and cousins, some of whom have now passed away. Many of the names on the family tree are not just names to us, but are real people in our living memories.

Grandparents are in a unique position to transmit this knowledge to the next generation. When we tell grandchildren about what it was like when we were young, when we tell stories about our parents, grandparents, brothers and sisters, it can be a powerful tool in helping a child formulate his or her own identity. Share stories of how you or your ancestors first heard about the gospel. Testify about how important that conversion has been in the lives of the entire family.

A grandparent can teach children to love their ancestors and can share feelings about the importance of family history and temple work. In fact, grandparents are in a unique position to provide a significant leadership role in organizing and encouraging family history and temple work among members of the extended family. For example, my husband has given each of our children a 12-generation pedigree chart of his ancestors, compiled by his mother years ago. My husband has then invited each of our children to select one name on that pedigree chart, many lines of which run out at the fifth generation, and to do further research on that line. With the New FamilySearch website (soon to be merged with a revamped version of familysearch.org), our children can more easily identify what work has been done and what still needs to be done.

I am fortunate to have some towering figures on my family tree—ancestors who joined the Church in the early years, some of whom knew the Prophet Joseph Smith, and many of whom endured persecutions and made great sacrifices for the gospel's sake. Many crossed the plains and labored faithfully to build up Zion in the West. These ancestors have been a significant influence in my life, as my personal identity has been formed, to a large extent, by my awareness of their faith and example. Transmitting this awareness, this sense of identity, to my grandchildren and great-grandchildren is an important focus and objective of my life.

One project that I have been working on in this regard began three years ago, when I gave each of our children a binder called "Our Noble Ancestors." The binders had biographies of four of my pioneer ancestors. Each binder contained a pedigree chart with the corresponding ancestor names highlighted. Their biographies were relatively short—1½ to 2 pages, single-spaced—so as to be more accessible when reading them. I have since added pages to the binders, including additional biographies and pictures. My intention is to produce more pages on other ancestors to build a more extensive resource with which our children can transmit this important sense of heritage and identity to their own children. I have been delighted to learn that our children are using this material for family home evening lessons to teach about their pioneer heritage.

Writing a personal history is an important way to reflect on one's life and record significant events and experiences for posterity. My father passed away recently at the age of 90. I shall be forever grateful that, more than 20 years ago, he took the time to record, in some detail, the events of his life up to that time, his childhood, his education, his family, his military service, his marriage to my mother, his work, his children, his travels and interests. During my father's last years, his mind became confused, and his memories were clouded and lost, so I cherish the memories he recorded when his mind was still clear. What better legacy can grandparents leave to their posterity?

JOY AND REJOICING IN YOUR POSTERITY

My Grandpa Carpenter used to tell us frequently, with a wry smile, referring to his happy and numerous posterity, that being a grandparent is great. "You get an increase every year," he would say, "and you don't even have to pay any taxes on it." This humorous musing revealed the deep love he had for his family and the rich sense of satisfaction and rejoicing he felt in his posterity.

Fulfillment in later life is very much a function of family associations. That fulfillment comes through knowing that our lives have been well-spent, as we gain a greater appreciation for the significant contribution we have made in rearing our families. One of the greatest divine blessings are "joy and rejoicing in our posterity." There is peace in looking back on a life well-lived and great joy and satisfaction in seeing our children and grandchildren grow, develop, and build homes where the gospel is taught and where the Spirit is felt in abundance.[6] As John the Revelator said, "I have no greater joy than to hear that my children walk in truth."[7]

As members of the Church, with our knowledge of the plan of salvation, and through the ordinances of the temple, being grandparents has a rich dimension of happiness far beyond enjoying the cute things our grandchildren say and do. We understand that we can be sealed for eternity, not only to our spouses, and to our parents, and to many generations of ancestors, but to our children and our children's children and going onward into the future forever.

Among the choicest blessings the Lord promised Abraham was to have posterity more numerous than the stars of the heavens,[8] and that through his posterity, all the nations of the earth would be blessed.[9]

Abraham and Sarah, who longed for children, had been childless for many years, but, having faith in the Lord and His promises, they eventually had a son, Isaac, in their old age, who brought them great happiness. Isaac did not marry until age 40, and he was 60 years old when Jacob and Esau were born, but Abraham was blessed to live to age 175, long enough to see these two grandsons. What joy he must have felt to see the promised blessings begin to be fulfilled.

As physical and spiritual heirs of the blessings of Abraham, Isaac, and Jacob, we grandparents stand at the head of a posterity that stretches onward into eternity. Our earthly experience as grandparents can be rich and fulfilling, an integral part of the peace "which passeth all understanding,"[10] but it is only a glimpse of what awaits us in the eternities. The perspectives of the gospel deepen our understanding and expand our vision. Like the two mirrors in the temple whose reflection is never ending, so we, like them, are the links between those before and the untold multitudes who will follow after us.[11]

Notes

1. I also had two very elderly great-grandmothers still living when I was a child, but for simplicity's sake, I do not discuss them here.
2. There have been some wonderfully helpful *Ensign* articles on grandparenting. See Bernice McCowin, "Being Grand Grandparents," *Ensign*, Oct. 2002, 72; Mildred Barthel, "Now That I'm a Grandmother . . .," *Ensign*, June 1982, 67; Caroline Eyring Miner, "Makers of Moons and Testimonies," *Ensign*, Sept. 1978, 68.
3. See the chapter by L. Lionel Kendrick.
4. Ibid.
5. See Boyd K. Packer, "The Golden Years," *Ensign*, May 2003, 82.
6. See Ezra Taft Benson, "To the Elderly in the Church," *Ensign*, Nov. 1989, 4.

7. 3 John 1:4.
8. See Genesis 15:5.
9. See Genesis 12:3.
10. Philippians 4:7.
11. See Gerrit W. Gong, "Temple Mirrors of Eternity: A Testimony of Family," *Ensign*, Nov. 2010, 36.

7

FAMILY RELATIONSHIPS AND HERITAGE

L. Lionel Kendrick

Before we began our telestial trip through mortality, principles were taught, counsel was given, cautions were expressed, and a support system was established to assist us in returning to the presence of the Lord. Heavenly Father provided us with a means for staying in touch with Him through a divine communication system. This support system includes the Light of Christ in the form of our personal conscience, the companionship of the Holy Ghost, a prophet, personal revelation, the sacred scriptures as a means of continuing counsel, and our earthly family.

As parents in mortality, we should pattern our earthly responsibilities much the same as Heavenly Father taught us, by precept and example. As we follow His pattern, we will be blessed as parents. Just as He taught us, we should teach our children powerful principles, and give them inspired counsel and wise words of caution.

When our children leave home to establish their own homes, we should provide a means for them to stay in touch with us and with each

L. Lionel Kendrick is an emeritus member of the First Quorum of the Seventy. He served as president of the Asia North Area, Philippines Micronesia Area, and Dallas Texas Temple. Elder Kendrick was a professor of Health Education at East Carolina University. He is the author of one book and chapters in four books.

other. This becomes their earthly support system that is an addendum to the one provided by Heavenly Father.

As parents, we can provide this family support system by focusing on the eternal perspective as we share our family heritage and traditions through family reunions, family projects that promote family history, journals and personal histories, and as we establish a communications network adapted to the needs of our family.

ETERNAL PERSPECTIVE

Our sacred responsibility as parents is to always keep the eternal perspective in our families. Our foremost goal is to teach and guide each family member in their journey home to the presence of Heavenly Father and to help them to be spiritually prepared to receive the gift of "eternal life, which gift is the greatest of all the gifts of God."[1] To receive this gift, one must be worthy to enter into, and be faithful to, sacred covenants with the Lord. These covenants include baptism, the priesthood, endowment, and sealing.

Family governance. The family is the most important unit of the Church and should be organized and governed following the pattern of Church governance. The principle of presidency is the guiding principle for governance in the Church as well as in the family.

The Prophet holds the Holy Melchizedek Priesthood and all the keys of the kingdom. This gives him the authority to preside over the Church. In the eternal family unit, the husband holds the Holy Melchizedek Priesthood. This priesthood gives him the authority and sacred responsibility to preside over his eternal family in righteousness. Fulfilling his sacred responsibility in this co-equal eternal relationship must be done based upon principles of righteous priesthood leadership as found in Doctrine and Covenants 121:34–46.

The President of the Church has been given two counselors to sit with in council. Decisions are to be made by "the unanimous voice of the same."[2] The husband has been given only one counselor, his wife and eternal companion. I believe that the daughters of God have been given a special sensitivity to the Spirit. While the husband presides, husbands and wives are to counsel together in making decisions. In fulfilling their sacred family responsibilities, the Proclamation to the World on the Family affirms that "fathers and mothers are obligated to help one another as equal partners."[3]

Patriarchal responsibilities. A father's patriarchal responsibilities and a mother's nurturing responsibilities are eternal in nature. They never cease and will be in effect even on the other side of the veil. President Joseph F. Smith counseled in a letter to his missionary son, "I believe that our departed kindred and loved ones are far more mindful of us and solicitous for our salvation day by day than they ever were in the flesh, because they know more."[4]

Challenges of wayward children. The plan of salvation allows us to experience challenges in mortal life as a part of the proving and perfecting process exercising our moral agency. In the grand council, the Savior said, "And we will prove them herewith, to see if they will do all things whatsoever the Lord their God shall command them."[5] The Savior gave the reason for this proving process: "My people must be tried in all things, that they may be prepared to receive the glory that I have for them."[6]

The Lord, through His prophets and apostles, gave many sacred and special promises to those who are born or sealed into the new and everlasting covenant. Even when a family member is not faithful to these sacred covenants, there is still hope from a loving Savior and a forgiving Father. Speaking of wayward children, President Boyd K. Packer counsels: "We cannot overemphasize the value of temple marriage, the binding ties of the sealing ordinance, and the standards of worthiness required of them. When parents keep the covenants they have made at the altar of the temple, their children will be forever bound to them."[7] President Brigham Young likewise affirmed: "I care not where those children go, they are bound up to their parents by an everlasting tie, and no power of earth or hell can separate them from their parents in eternity; they will return again to the fountain from whence they sprang."[8]

SHARING FAMILY HERITAGE AND TRADITIONS

As part of the divine support system, God has instructed that his word should be written and that the people should be brought into frequent remembrance of his love and mercy and the great things that He has done for them. The righteous traditions of the people will thus be transmitted from generation to generation and be a substantial strength to the next generation. Likewise, as parents following the divine pattern, it is our obligation to transmit to our descendants that part of our family heritage and traditions which will best bless their lives. When we pass through the veil, we take with us only three things: our knowledge, our personality and our relationships. The remainder we leave behind. Included in the things we leave behind are our heritage and our traditions.

Heritage is the legacy that a person leaves upon death that is remembered by others and has an impact on their lives. It may be a remembrance of the life of values one has lived, beliefs one has cherished, principles one has taught or counsel one has given. A man who impacted my life shared with me the family heritage that had shaped his life: "I stand for certain things because my father and his father stood for those things. I will not do certain things because my father and his father would not do those things. My family name is important."

Our family has embraced these family proverbs:

"We can do hard things."

"Purity equals power."

"When in doubt, don't."

"A crisis never comes at a convenient time."

"Leaders lead, and they lead best by example."

A *tradition* is a practice or custom that is passed from one generation to another. Traditions give each generation a sense of security, a sense of wellbeing and a sense of worth. A great tradition recording form can be found on line at *Family Tree Magazine*. Family traditions can be daily rituals, annual events, religious activities, vacations, patriotic events, reunions, birthdays and holiday celebrations.

One of the great works of this dispensation is the development of righteous families, reaching back to past generations and extending to our descendants to form an eternal chain back to the beginning. The feeling of family is in our spiritual DNA. Focusing on our eternal relationships and our earthly heritage is a part of our preparation for eternal life. There are several ways in which we as parents and grandparents can our share family heritage and traditions with our generational family.

FAMILY REUNIONS

Family reunions strengthen family relationships and perpetuate family traditions—outcomes essential in the ever-increasingly secular world in which we live and in the wicked world in which our posterity will live. The strengthening of family relationships can result in increased love for each other, increased unity, increased testimonies, an increased sense of who we are, and an increased desire to live the gospel. Reunions do not need to be expensive or elaborate gatherings. They should be adapted to the needs and circumstances of each family. Where family member are widely dispersed geographically, family reunions may be less frequent, and perhaps longer events than where families live in close proximity.

The impact of a reunion can be reflected in comments made by family members. Our six-year-old grandson wrote a class paper about what he would be doing for the summer. He described some of the activities that had been planned for the family reunion. At the end he wrote, "The best part is I get to be with the whole Kendrick family." His family ties have been strengthened, reunions have become an important part of his family traditions, and he has fond memories of his extended family and their traditions.

Themes. Family reunions are often more effective when they have a theme that strengthens family relationships and traditions and makes lasting memories of the event. One year our theme came from the ancient African word *UBUNTU,* which means, "I am what I am because of who we all are." This theme prompted a wonderful discussion and reinforced the synergistic power that comes from family. Planning around a theme can have a powerful effect on building a strong eternal family united in a great bond of love and support.

Shared Responsibilities. Each adult child can, on a rotating basis, take the lead responsibility for a reunion, such as site selection, theme, meal assignments, activities and family home evenings. Multiple details must be given attention for the reunion to be a success. Among these are invitations, scheduling dates and places, accommodations, tickets to events, logos, theme shirts, budgets, group pictures, meals, etc. Do an internet search for "Family Reunions" to see books and other resources that are helpful with organizational details. Family Reunion Organizer is a very useful software program for planning successful reunions.

Sharing Time. This may involve stories of ancestors, mission memories, childhood memories, memories of parents or grandparents, faith-promoting experiences, ancestor pioneer stories if applicable, testimonies, and mission reports from recently returned missionaries. Missionary reports at family gatherings can affect generations of family members. Grandparents, who have known earlier ancestors, can also share their knowledge and love of them, helping form a bridge with previous generations.

Fun Time. A significant part of any reunion is to have fun, fostering happy memories. Fun activities are determined by the site selected for the reunion and the family's preferences for activities. The oft-repeated platitude has some truth to it: "Families who play together, stay together."

Grandparents' Time. It's important for grandparents to take personal time with each grandchild. Individual time is a great blessing not only for the grandchildren but for the grandparents. This time will bring some of the greatest memories from the reunion. Memories of grandparents can be a source of strength during difficult days that children will have in the future.

Teaching Time. Never overlook the opportunity to teach sacred principles. This may be a scheduled time, or teaching moments may occur during other activities. Some of the most effective teaching is done by the examples we set before our family. Grandparents who serve missions can be a powerful example for their children, grandchildren and even great-grandchildren.

Father's Interviews and Blessings. When children are living long distances from their parents, the family reunion offers the opportunity for father's interviews and blessings, where a father takes time to interview each of his children in keeping with his patriarchal responsibility. He can listen to his children's successes as well as their challenges, and when impressed or asked, give a priesthood blessing. Expressions of gratitude and love are effective in this private setting.

Recording. For the preservation of the family heritage, remember to take photos and make video and journal records of the reunion events. These can be an important part of the history of the extended family. In addition, the reunion is an excellent time to video parents and grandparents telling their life histories and their feelings about specific items of interest. Where possible, appoint a family photographer and historian as well as someone to spearhead and coordinate family-history research.

Follow-up. After the joyful occasion is over, the official family photographer (a family member—or perhaps a small committee of family members), can produce a DVD or other record of the reunion to be given to each family. A bound photo book of the reunion would be a valuable gift for each family member, including grandchildren and great-grandchildren. These will be a valuable part of their personal family histories and a recorded part of their family traditions.

FAMILY PROJECTS FOSTERING FAMILY HISTORY

One of the challenges for family history is how to interest the younger generation in the process of seeking after their kindred dead. Societal changes have contributed to this challenge. In his keynote address at the 2010 BYU Computerized Genealogy Conference, David Rencher indicated that the younger generation (ages 13 to 29) is not likely to go to the library, search microfilm or un-indexed data, but needs a technical experience to use their social networking and computers skills.[9] We must design family history projects that will interest our computer knowledgeable family members with the foremost goal to design projects to turn the hearts of our children and grandchildren to their ancestors.

Grandparents can play a major role in fostering this activity. A gift of a family-history notebook, including a pedigree chart, family group sheets, historical timelines and maps can motivate youth to become involved in searching for their ancestors.

Research trips with children and grandchildren can be motivational, including trips to cemeteries, ancestral homes, courthouses and to older extended family members for interviews, documents, photographs and video recordings. When the younger set participate in research trips, collect data, take photo images, geo-map the locations where the information was found, and input this into the computer, they are not only motivated, but they utilize their technical skills. All of this information can be copied with a handheld scanner and then uploaded to computers.

Having children and grandchildren participate in appropriate ordinance work and creating both meaningful and memorable temple experiences can turn their hearts to their ancestors. We have family members sign the back of the family file temple cards, adding the ordinance they acted as proxy for. This has generated interest and motivation for them. Our children have expressed that when their families attend the temple together using family names, they have their most rewarding temple experiences.

Consider giving lessons during family home evenings on family history, family traditions, family heritage, personal journals, personal history and temple work. These teaching experiences on family-history related subjects can be both motivating and enlightening.

Celebrate a family-history week or month and focus on selected subjects, such as sharing stories about family lines, grandparents, and parent's childhood experiences, each child's childhood experiences, and spiritual experiences involving family history. Give each child or grandchild an assignment to research an ancestor. Other activities and experiences could be used to celebrate family history or the family.

JOURNALS AND PERSONAL HISTORIES

Time endures, but can never fade the memories that love has made.

As members of the Church, we are a record-keeping people. A significant part of Church history has been gleaned from personal journals of the early members. The scriptures are the personal writings of inspired prophets who have distilled the essence of their spiritual experiences for their family, the saints of their day, and future generations.

Journals. Journals provide a means of recording memories, thoughts, feelings, motivations, insights, significant events, spiritual experiences and spiritual impressions. Entries may be made in a written book or in a digital format.

We should encourage journal keeping at an early age. Even young children in elementary school should be encouraged to keep a journal. Our son gave his children journals and challenged them to write daily for thirty days on how they saw the hand of the Lord in their lives each day. At the end of that period, he asked them to share with him their feelings about the experience.

President Henry B. Eyring recorded in his journals how he saw the hand of the Lord in his children's lives each day and later printed and bound these volumes to give to each child.

A personal history is dynamic in nature. It's never complete until after the person has passed through the veil. Perhaps the final segment should be written by a descendent to include everything that was not written by the departed. No significant detail should be left unrecorded. In writing our personal histories, we do so hoping to bless the lives of our posterity. The record of our lives may become a source of strength for them during their struggles. It may be a means to strengthen their testimonies. Personal histories bridge the gaps between generations even for some who are yet unborn.

Personal histories are just that—personal—and they should be written in one's chosen format. The following are suggestions for categories that may be included: Early Beginnings, Parents, Spouse and Children, Education, Military Service, Profession, Church Service, Civic Activities and Boards, Publications, Impact Scriptures, Impact Thoughts, Family Traditions, Holidays, Awards and Achievements, Spiritual Experiences, Testimony, and Counsel for Posterity. An appendix may include significant documents, important letters, certificates, patriarchal blessings, newspaper articles, and photographs.

Parents should encourage and assist their children to begin collecting and organizing significant information, which will form the foundation for a written personal history. This can be an exciting project. A good method for collecting, organizing and publishing limited quantities of personal histories for distribution to other family members may be found at CherishBound.com.

Communications Networking

The capacity to communicate with each other is a priceless gift. Where families live close together, much communication between family members and between generations may take place by personal visits, family meals at Grandma and Grandpa's house, in various other family gatherings and activities, and in attendance at a variety of functions and events. In the wonderful information age in which we live, we also have the ability to communicate personally or long distance through the marvels of technology. The technology of our time is of particular benefit to families who are widely spread out geographically, as it allows them to maintain a close personal relationship even when travel may not be economically feasible. A family's continued communication serves as a strong spiritual support system. It is the vehicle through which we as parents and grandparents continue to teach, counsel, support and encourage our family even when we live far away.

The telephone is an old standby, and now that long-distance rates have fallen sharply and numerous low-cost plans are available with generous allotments of minutes, the phone remains a staple of inter-family communications. Where distances prevent a personal visit of a grandparent, grandchildren love to receive phone calls on their birthdays and other important occasions. Sunday afternoon and evening conversations with far-away children are a regular occurrence in many homes. The cell phone makes it possible to call anytime from almost anywhere.

The use of computer technology, with its amazing possibilities, need not become a challenge in a negative manner. As older people, we may struggle with even the rudiments of computer know-how, but with perseverance *we can* learn to appreciate and become competent, using it to our advantage. If we are hesitant, we can seek help from our computer-savvy grandchildren. We have a variety of technologies available to foster communications networking such as, blogs, photo services, video blogging, social networking, telephone internet services, internet chat services, instant messaging services, family web sites, and electronic family newsletters. Our grandchildren can surely teach us about each of these.

Blog sites. A *blog* is a website where you can make entries (like a journal entry) that are recorded, usually in a reverse chronological order. Blogs are simply *web logs,* essentially online journals. They provide a way for families to keep connected and current on the extended family activities, experiences, photos, travels, and future plans. Most blog sites are free and contain a feature allowing users to be automatically notified when new content is posted. The following are frequently used blog sites: Bloglines.com, Blogger.com, Blogster.com and Wordpress. com.

Photo and video sites. With the following websites, one can share photos with other family members or friends: Flicker.com and Picasa. A popular site for sharing videos is YouTube.com, which has become a popular way to share the experience of young people and couples opening their mission calls. Caution should be noted that less than desirable videos might be found on this site.

Social networking sites. These internet-based sites provide means for communications over the internet using messages and e-mails. The following are some of the more popular sites: Facebook, Twitter, MySpace and Nexopia (primarily used in Canada). Some care should be exercised to ensure that personal information is protected. Each site allows the user to establish individual privacy settings.

Internet telephone services. Free telephone contacts can be made over the internet using one of the more popular services. Vonage has a small monthly fee but unlimited local and long-distance calls to most parts of the world at no extra charge. Skype offers most of their services free of charge.

Chat services and instant messaging. Several good free internet chat services allow families to stay connected and communicate with each other, such as Google Voice and Video Chat, Google Talk (Text Chat, Voice Chat, Audio Chat), Facebook Chat, Yahoo!, Windows Live,

Skype, and AOL. Several of these have the advantage of webcam visual interaction. These services appeal to the younger generation, although Skype has a high appeal to the working, middle-age market. There are also many different applications for smart phones (like the iPhone) that can help families stay connected.

Family web sites. Most of the following sites provide free services. Some are pre-designed sites, while others allow you to design your own web site: MyFamily.com, MyHeritage.com, FamilyLobby.com, FamilyPlan.com and Apple.com/ilife/iweb/ (for Mac users only). Many of these sites provide services for blogs, photos, messages, and family history pedigree charts and family group sheets. These and other similar sites are excellent means for communicating valuable family information to family members or to others.

Family electronic newsletters. These are usually edited by one family member and formatted with space for each extended family. Family members email their news, photos or other items of interest to the editor. The editor then cuts and pastes the information into the respective family section and then e-mails the completed newsletter to each family.

CONCLUSION

Our greatest joy, as we approach the golden years, will undoubtedly be found in our families. By maintaining the pattern of leadership and instruction shown to us by our Father in Heaven, we can help bind our families to us and to the Lord, fulfilling the promise of the Spirit of Elijah.[10] The effort that we put into sharing the rich heritage and traditions will bring eternal benefits and help lead our children, and generations that follow, back to their Heavenly Father—and to the enjoyment of eternal family relationships in His kingdom.

Notes

1. D&C 14:7.
2. D&C 107:27.
3. "The Family: A Proclamation to the World."
4. Hyrum M. Smith III and Scott G. Kenney, comps, *From Prophet to Son: Advice of Joseph F. Smith to His Missionary Sons* (Salt Lake City: Deseret Book Co. 1981), 39.
5. Abraham 3:25.
6. D&C 136:31.
7. Boyd K. Packer, "Our Moral Environment," *Ensign,* May 1992, 68.
8. Brigham Young, "Remarks," *The Deseret News* (Weekly), May 10, 1866, 178.
9. David E. Rencher, "Harnessing the Power of the Information Age for Family History," BYU Conference on Computerized Family History and Genealogy, Salt Lake City, Apr. 26, 2010.
10. Malachi 4:6.

Further Reading

Drew Smith, *Social Networking for Genealogists* (Baltimore: Genealogical Publishing Co., 2009).

8

THE JOY OF SERVICE
Ardeth G. Kapp

"Unless we lose ourselves in service to others, there is little purpose to our own lives."[1]

A few years ago, as Christmas drew near, I found myself confronted with a very full schedule. The streets were crowded, my calendar was crowded, and my mind was crowded. There was so much to do and so little time. An invitation to give a brief Christmas message to the residents of a nursing home nearby was one activity I thought I could check off rather quickly and then move to the next pressing matter.

As I rushed past the receptionist at the nursing home door, I was ushered into a large room where I suddenly stopped. Life was moving at a different pace here, if it was moving at all. There were wheelchairs, bent shoulders, gray hair, tired eyes, and an impression of so little going on. Though the room was warm, many of the elderly had knitted shawls draped over rounded shoulders and wooly slippers covering tired feet.

Following my message, one of the visitors, the granddaughter of

Ardeth Kapp served as General Young Women president 1984–92. She also served with her husband, Heber, as he presided over the Canada Vancouver Mission and as matron when he was president of the Cardston Alberta Temple. Author of several books and a lecturer, she has taught Institute and currently serves on several boards.

one of the elderly residents, asked if I had time to visit with her grand-mother in her own private room for just a few moments.

She commented, "She thinks she knows you," indicating per-haps that her grandmother's mind might also be tired. I followed the younger woman as she helped her elderly grandmother shuffle down the narrow hall to her room. When she reached her bedside, this dear elderly woman slowly turned around, let go of her granddaughter's arm, and sat on her bed. Then she raised her head so that I could look into her face. My eyes caught hers.

"Sister Myrtle Dudley!" I exclaimed. "You were my Primary teacher." Her wrinkled mouth formed a smile as she pulled on her granddaughter's jacket and said, "See, I told you she would know me."

I continued, "I remember when you used to lead the singing. You wore that wine-colored dress with the big sleeves that waved back and forth as you taught us the songs."

Again she pulled on her granddaughter's jacket. "I told you she would know me . . ." She reached out her arms and drew me close. I felt like a child once again, back in Primary, in the arms of my teacher, who loved me.

Then she whispered in my ear. "I knew you would know me . . ."

After a time, I reluctantly left the presence of my Primary teacher and walked slowly back to my car. I sat there pondering while the snow-flakes fell gently on the windshield. It was the season of celebration for the birth of Jesus Christ, our Lord and Savior. It was he who asked us to love one another and to serve one another.

He said to each of us, "Inasmuch as ye have done *it* unto one of the least of these my brethren, ye have done *it* unto me."[2]

Yes, I thought, I knew Sister Dudley because she had served me. Then the vision cleared before my eyes. We will know Him, and He will know us, when we serve Him.

I asked myself, *Can I one day say with the same confidence with which Sister Dudley spoke, "I told you He would know me"?*[3]

VOLUNTEER WORK

President James E. Faust reminds us—because we were there—that "In the grand council in heaven, when the great plan of salvation for God's children was presented, Jesus responded, 'Here am I, send me,' and, 'Father, thy will be done, and the glory be thine forever.' And thus he became our Savior."[4] Jesus' magnificent act of service was in volunteering to become the Savior of all mankind. The Son of God volunteered and gave His life to bless every child of God.

A definition of a "volunteer" is someone who works for nothing or who receives no pay. Is it possible to participate in an act of volunteer work and still receive payment? Yes, if the meaning of "payment" comes not in the form of some monetary reward of dollars or cents. Truly, the "pay" (the reward and benefits of volunteer work) is immeasurable. It is priceless—out of this world. These rewards are expressed by President Spencer W. Kimball: "In serving others, we 'find' ourselves in terms of acknowledging divine guidance in our lives. Furthermore, the more we serve our fellowmen in appropriate ways, the more substance there is as we serve others—indeed, it is easier to 'find' ourselves because there is so much more of us to find!"[5]

My dear friend and next-door neighbor, Lois Webster, a mother of four, is an inspiration to all who know her and a blessing to thousands and thousands who do not know her. Her voluntary service over the years has included love and support for over 60 foster-care children, one young woman from the Indian Placement Program, followed by a mission call for her and her husband to serve in Leeds, England. These bonds of friendship, forged in their service to others, continue to be a blessing in their lives.

Lois is now 77. She has had a serious bout with cancer over the past several years, which continues to restrict her mobility, but not her serviceability. While she is not able to accept a regular church calling, from the comfort of her home she reaches out to the world in selfless service. She says she is happy and adds with a smile, "It gives me a good feeling," and quotes the scripture, "Inasmuch as ye have done it unto one of the least of these my brethren, ye have done it unto me."[6] Privately, away from the world with no public acclaim, she ministers to the world. She (with some reservation) allowed me to write down some of the hand-made articles she has made between 2002 and 2009 for the humanitarian cause: shirts, pants, pillows, bears, thousands of blankets, and on and on. At the time of our conversation, she modestly shared with me that the number of items made to date is 34,936. Many others assist by donating some of the fabric needed, which helps Lois provide this remarkable service.

Elder Dallin H. Oaks explains, "This principle—that our service should be for the love of God and the love of fellowmen rather than for personal advantage or any other lesser motive—is admittedly a high standard. The Savior must have seen it so, since He joined His commandment for selfless and complete love directly with the ideal of perfection. . . . Service with all our heart and mind is a high challenge for all of us. . . . I know that God expects us to work to purify our hearts and our thoughts so that we may serve one another for the highest and best reason, the pure love of Christ."[7]

In today's world there are unlimited opportunities to enrich one's life with meaningful service. At the Washington Elementary School in my area, on Monday mornings and other days during the week, you can see a child sitting at a desk in the hallway between classrooms with a volunteer eager to help the student master the essential skill of reading. This person may not be a certified teacher, but with love and patience, she or he can help change a child's life. I was a bit surprised to see a recently retired, very prominent and successful man from our neighborhood serving in that volunteer role. I thought of the hundreds of people he had interacted with over the years in his very successful career. But seeing him sitting with a child, one on one, I was reminded of the Savior's example of ministering "one on one"[8] as He "took their little children, one by one, and blessed them."[9]

The accolades of a crowd in the professional world may be paled by the warmth that can fill one's heart when a child needing additional attention, tutoring, and encouragement is gradually released from limited ability and begins to blossom. And in the process, the return on the investment of one's time is priceless.

The variety and range of opportunities for volunteer service is almost endless. Community organizations, service clubs and healthcare institutions for the elderly and handicapped are in great need of helpers. Prison ministry can be most fulfilling. Civic and political involvement at every level of government is another avenue of service. Hosts of volunteers are required in church-related activities including family history, temple work, welfare, church administration and medical and dental service. And then there are missions, which may be served at home or abroad and may include service, educational, humanitarian aid and other kinds of missions. Each kind of volunteer activity brings its own rewards and satisfactions.

INCIDENTAL SERVICE

Incidental service is that service which is performed unintentionally. It may be at a time when one person who is in tune with the Spirit becomes the answer to another person's prayer. If our daily service includes an effort to be radiant, happy and cheerful, we may find ourselves being an instrument in the Lord's hand many, many times. Just a warm greeting can be of great service to someone needing a lift on a cloudy day.

Following a women's conference in California, where everyone had appeared to be in good spirits, I received a card in the mail that opened my mind to the importance of unintended service. This troubled sister expressed her gratitude: "Thank you for taking your precious time to look at me; so few people care nowadays." I was stunned by the fact that there are sons and daughters of God, our brothers and sisters, that, even surrounded in a crowd, could feel totally isolated, ignored, and overlooked. If just a sincere look could lift a soul, could a warm greeting to a stranger make a difference?

A young man wrote the following account of an experience when someone unknowingly changed his life: "I was at a very low point in my life at the time, having lost my mother, my best friend, to illness. As you came to the counter, and I rang up your purchase, we struck up a conversation. That's when something happened. I don't know what you said to me—if it was unspoken, if you asked my name, or any of the details. But I knew from your demeanor that you sensed a need in me and that you cared about me. There was an unspoken expression of love and confidence and concern. As you left, I remember thinking, *She knew me. She knew how low I am. How could she know that?* I also felt the Spirit of the Lord. After you left, I felt uplifted not just for that day alone, but that little experience, along with some others, gave me the courage to carry on."

Perhaps this experience is evidence of someone who tries to "press forward [with] . . . a perfect brightness of hope, and a love of God and of all men."[10] Hope is expressed in our countenance, our conversation, the tone of our voice, the things we talk about, and the things we choose not to talk about. When we press forward with steadfastness in Christ, with a perfect brightness of hope, our lives have meaning. We begin not only to look, but also to see; not only to touch, but also to feel; not only to talk, but also to communicate. Our otherwise routine activities, our goings and comings, can be filled with meaningful incidental acts of service. We don't just serve—we nurture. We don't just take a loaf of bread—we share the bread of life.

When we strive to share the love of Christ and be like Him, our lives have meaning and purpose at every age.

MENTORING

"The woman saith unto him, I know that Messias cometh, which is called Christ: when he is come, he will tell us all things. Jesus saith unto her, I that speak unto thee am *he.* . . . The woman then left her watering pot, and went her way into the city, and saith to the men, Come, see a man, which told me all things that ever I did: is not this the Christ? Then *they* went out of the city and came unto him."[11]

The account of the woman at the well in Samaria is a powerful example of the blessing and opportunity to mentor. To take something we have come to know and then to eagerly share, teach, advise, inform and help another benefit from what we have learned is to become a mentor.

The words of Elder Neal A. Maxwell suggest we look for opportunities to mentor. "[T]o withdraw into our private sanctuaries not only deprives others of our love, our talents, and our service, but it also deprives us of chances to serve, to love, and to be loved."[12]

When needs and resources are brought together, both the one who is being mentored and the one who is mentoring are blessed. Mentoring is to help another with something we are capable of sharing. "For all have not every gift given unto them; for there are many gifts, and to every man is given a gift by the Spirit of God."[13] The reservoir of gifts and talents is unlimited when we are willing to mentor one another.

Alma and Raya Jones had retired. Their previous work had prepared them to be skilled with computers. They had developed a passion for family history and genealogical work. When they arrived in their mission, the mission president requested that rather than speaking in meetings about the importance of family history, they could share their skills by mentoring individuals one by one. As members received personal tutoring, they developed to the point of not only being able to search their own family lines, but they were prepared to share their skills and mentor others. This activity had a snowball effect on the entire stake. When Elder and Sister Jones were ready to leave their mission and return home, a party was held in appreciation for their service. The stake president announced that they had "been an answer to a prayer we never offered" and expressed gratitude for the impact they had had that would continue to grow. They left behind a small army of well-trained, enthusiastic individuals eager to carry on this important work and to mentor others.

THE HABIT OF SERVICE

Through our tireless service we come to know our Lord and Savior Jesus Christ. When we develop a habit, a pattern, and an attitude of service, we find there is always work to be done. We are on His errand. We become more sensitive to the Spirit pointing the way to our service, from the smallest act to a major mission.

Habit is a behavior pattern that is regular and often unconscious. When service to others becomes an ongoing part of our lives, no matter what our age, stage or situation—physically, financially, emotionally, geographically, or in whatever way—our life gains meaning and purpose.

Dave and Maxine Thompson developed the habit of service in their young lives, and that habit continues today. Maxine writes, "Now we are older [91 and 85], and my health is not the best. My ninety-one-year-old husband is the caregiver. Currently I am involved in Family Search indexing and have cleared several thousand names. This is rewarding now with my limited dexterity."

She continues, "One Christmas we announced to the family that because we were getting older, we were giving them each a picture to remember us by. But before we could give them their gift, they needed to watch a short video first. At the end of the video, there was absolute silence. As the lights were turned on, we could feel how touched they each were. There were many tears." [The video showed recipients of what has, to date, amounted to over 358 wheelchairs donated by the Thompsons to the Wheelchair Foundation in the names of family members. The WCF gives the donor a picture of the person who received the chair along with a certificate in an impressive paper folder with their name on it.] Even the teenage boys said, 'We should do this every year.' And so we have. We have been richly blessed, and it is wonderful to be able to give back in whatever way we can."

The Thompsons have served three missions. They responded four more times to assist in offices temporarily as needed. The habit of service began early in their lives and has become a part of who they are—a truly happy, peaceful couple.

MISSIONS AND TEMPLE WORK

The least of us, the humblest, is in partnership with the Almighty in achieving the purpose of the eternal plan of salvation. . . . In our pre-existent state, in the day of the great council, we made a certain agreement with the Almighty. The Lord proposed a plan conceived by him. We accepted it. Since the plan is intended for all men, we became parties to the salvation of every person under that plan. We agreed, right then and there, to be not only saviors for ourselves but measurably, saviors for the whole human family. We went into a partnership with the Lord. The working out of the plan became then not merely the Father's work, and the Savior's work, but also our work.[14]—John A. Widtsoe.

Missions. Apostle John A. Widtsoe confirms the truth that we came to this earth with a mission. This call to service extends to every season of our lives. When the responsibilities of home and family are less demanding and retirement opens opportunities not previously available, and health and circumstance are in our favor, a mission is a must. A mission provides blessings, challenges, rewards and spiritual growth like no other calling.

A dedicated couple—maybe with some reservation—will close the door to their home, say farewell to family and loved ones, miss the traditional family gatherings and celebrations that will go on in their absence, and volunteer to accept a call wherever the Lord reveals it to those responsible for matching needs and resources. While waiting for the letter that provides the answer to the anxious question, "Where are we going?" they may feel prone to sing: "I'll go where you want me to go, dear Lord," and then add privately, "But please not to_____ or_____ or _____."

Then the call comes, and, in two cases of good friends I am aware of, the call was exactly where they hoped *not* to go! Did they go? Yes, of course they did. But the unexplainable mystery is why, after they had filled honorable missions and returned home to family and loved ones, within a year or so each couple sent in their papers again in hopes of returning to the same locations in the far corners of the world. They returned to the mission field. They continued to expand their circle of influence. Members, nonmembers, the less-active, and those who were brought into the waters of baptism and started on the path to exaltation and eternal life, will bless these couples forever for being willing to leave home and family and come and search for those ready to receive the glorious truths of the gospel.

And what happened to the missionaries' families and their relationships with their children and grandchildren? They reported that they received blessings in abundance, and the reuniting left no empty spaces but provided a powerful example of priorities and faith stronger than any words could convey.

When the allotted time in the mission field comes to a close, and you return home and reluctantly take off your missionary name tag, it is not the end of missionary labors. As members of The Church of Jesus Christ of Latter-day Saints, we carry His name always. When we continue to open our mouths and look for opportunities to share, our missionary labors never end. A member on a recent plane trip took the opportunity to be of service to a fellow traveler. A few days after the trip, this member received an e-mail from a new friend. It read in part: "You allowed me to better grasp an understanding of the foundation of Mormonism that other people have not been able to answer for me.

It has always been important to me to understand the doctrinal differences between Mormonism and Christianity, and I finally got some answers—thanks for your taking time with me. I hope you will be open to my asking a question about your faith if I have need for an explanation." She was sent a copy of the Book of Mormon, which provides the opportunity for continuing contact and answering questions.

There is no end to the opportunities for missionary service. They will continue on and on. We are indeed in "a partnership with the Lord."

Temple work. Service in the temple doesn't seem like work—not if *work* suggests some tiresome, never-ending job to be done. But when we think of work in the context of the Savior's declaration: "For behold, this is my *work* and my glory—to bring to pass the immortality and eternal life of man,"[15] then we see our part at this time in our lives as a wonderful opportunity not to retire, but to continue to work, in partnership with the Lord, as we agreed to do. Our lifespan in our era allows us the blessing of additional years to assist in this great work. In the temple our eyes are opened; our understanding is increased. There we are taught by the Spirit and grow spiritually while serving someone who has been waiting for that glorious day when a faithful member would become like a savior on Mount Zion, doing for them what they could not do for themselves.

Temple work becomes especially satisfying when we are able to do it for and with our own families. Do we understand fully the opportunity that is ours? President Wilford Woodruff taught: "We have blessings that have never been given to any other generation since the days of Jesus Christ and the Apostles. . . . You hold the keys of the destiny of your fathers, your mothers, your progenitors, from generation to generation; you hold the keys of their salvation. God has put that power into your hands."[16]

President Gordon B. Hinckley reinforced the importance of temple work in our day. "We shall continue the great work that goes on in our temples, an unmatched work of love reaching out even to those who have gone beyond the veil of death. Can there be a greater labor of love than this? It comes more nearly of partaking of the spirit of the Lord Himself, who gave His life as a vicarious sacrifice for all of us, than any other work of which I know. It is done in the name of Him whose salvation is universal."[17]

In one's retiring years, one might ponder the question: "How far do I live from a temple?" The distance might be measured in miles or kilometers or hours, depending on the location. In recent years that distance has be shortened with the expanding number of temples built—evidence of this glorious and sacred work. The honest answer to that question may have nothing to do with the measurement of miles, kilometers or hours, but rather how far we live from the temple in relation to our priorities. Is it possible that a family in some remote part of the Philippines, saving for several years to go with their family to the Manila Temple, may actually live closer to the temple than a family living just a few blocks away, even just around the corner, if the draw of the world dims their priorities, and they lose themselves to the glitter of the world in place of the glory of the gospel? Elder Dallin H. Oaks reminds us that, "In sacred temple ceremonies we covenant to sacrifice and consecrate our time and talents for the welfare of others."[18]

Missions and temple work during one's retirement years provide an enormous opportunity for one's spiritual growth. President David O. McKay taught us that, "The development of our spiritual nature should concern us most. Spirituality is the highest acquisition of the soul, the divine in man. . . . It is the consciousness of victory over self and of communion with the infinite. It is spirituality alone which really gives one the best in life."[19]

THE PULL OF MATERIALISM/THE ANTIDOTE OF SERVICE

"Many in the world are focused on self-gratification. They put themselves first, and they love pleasure more than righteousness. They do not believe they are their brother's keeper. In the Church, however, we believe that these stewardships are a sacred trust."[20]

In the world today, we can have more, want more, see more and do more than ever before. The pull of materialism is real. The pressure to accumulate, pile higher and deeper, is ever-present. If one is good, two is better.

Years ago the Mountain States Telephone Company, in an effort to provide sufficient telephone service for everyone, tried to promote the idea that just one black telephone on a 25-foot cord, centrally located in the hall of a home, would be adequate for the needs of the family. We have come a long way since that time. Not only do we have telephones in almost each room, but often every member of the family has their own cell phone, with no cord attachment, free to travel far and near and to communicate instantly. We see multitudes of advancements on every front.

While this can be a great blessing, it can also become a serious distraction if we do not balance and prioritize what matters most at each season of our lives. With retirement comes the option to determine our highest priorities. A natural question in looking to the future might be, "What shall we do?" With such a multitude of enticing choices at hand, the pull of materialism is very strong. A more important question than, "What shall we do?" is a serious reflection on, "What do we want to happen?" as directed by the Spirit. When that objective is clear in our minds, we have an inner court in which to appeal when making decisions.

President Spencer W. Kimball has provided a clear guide for each season of our lives and especially our retirement years. He counseled us, "Since immortality and eternal life constitute the sole purpose of life, all other interests and activities are but incidental thereto."[21] Does this suggest there should be no time for recreation, parties, hobbies, travel or adventure into new experiences? Of course not. But when we have a clear sense of purpose, knowing what we want to have happen, life takes on new meaning. We become future-oriented, with a sense of anticipation by knowing our desired outcome. We can sort our way through the temptations, amorality, and materialism that are almost saturating our society, and we can find our way to those choices that are centered in Christ that bring us joy and peace and fulfillment.

President Marion G. Romney has given wise counsel that remains timeless: "The Lord has said, 'He that findeth his life shall lose it: and he that loseth his life for my sake shall find it.'[22] We lose our life by serving and lifting others. By so doing we experience the only true and lasting happiness. Service is not something we endure on this earth so we can earn the right to live in the celestial kingdom. Service is the very fiber of which an exalted life in the celestial kingdom is made. . . . Oh, for the glorious day when these things all come naturally because of the purity of our hearts. In that day there will be no need for a command-ment, because we will have experienced for ourselves that we are truly happy only when we are engaged in unselfish service."[23]

From my own experience I know that the challenges of life, which are an essential part of our life's mission, can be eased when we lose ourselves in service to others and follow our Savior's example. We can be filled with love and peace as expressed in the words of the hymn, "Lord, I Would Follow Thee," by Susan Evans McCloud:

> Savior, may I learn to love thee,
> Walk the path that thou hast shown,
> Pause to help and lift another,
> Finding strength beyond my own.
> Savior, may I learn to love thee—
> Lord, I would follow thee.[24]

When the time comes for the curtain to fall on our "second act," our earth-life experience, to determine if we have filled the "measure of our creation," it won't matter if our part in mortality has been cen-ter stage, backstage, or in the wings. If Christ is at the very center of our lives, we can look forward to the glorious words of commendation from the only one that really matters: "Well done, good and faithful servant . . . enter thou into the joy of thy Lord."[25]

Notes

1. Thomas S. Monson, "What Have I Done for Someone Today?" *Ensign,* Nov. 2009, 84.

2. Matthew 25:40; emphasis added.

3. Ardeth G. Kapp, *My Neighbor, My Sister, My Friend* (Salt Lake City: Deseret Book Co., 1975), 10–12.

4. James E. Faust, *Liahona,* Nov. 2002, 1.

5. Spencer W. Kimball, *New Era,* Mar. 1981, 47.

6. Matthew 25:40.

7. Dallin H. Oaks, "Who Do We Serve," *Ensign,* Nov. 1984, 12.

8. See 3 Nephi 11:15.

9. 3 Nephi 17:21.

10. 2 Nephi 31:20.

11. John 4:25–26, 28–30; emphasis added.

12. Neal A. Maxwell, *Of One Heart* (Salt Lake City: Deseret Book Co., 1975), 22.

13. D&C 46:11.

14. John A. Widtsoe, "The Worth of Souls," *Utah Genealogical and Historical Magazine* 25, Oct. 1934, 189–90.

15. Moses 1:39; emphasis added.

16. Conference Report, Oct. 1897, 47, as quoted in "Sacred Spires," *Ensign,* Feb. 2007, 20.

17. "Reach Out in Love and Kindness," *Ensign,* Nov. 1982, 76.

18. "Unselfish Service," *Ensign,* May 2009, 94.

19. In Conference Report, Oct. 1936, 103.

20. Quentin L. Cook, "Stewardship—A Sacred Trust," *Ensign,* Nov. 2009, 91.

21. Spencer W. Kimball, *The Miracle of Forgiveness* (Salt Lake City: Bookcraft, 1969), 2.

22. Matthew 10:39.

23. Marion G. Romney, "Celestial Nature of Self-reliance," *Ensign,* Nov. 1982, 91.

24. *Hymns of The Church of Jesus Christ of Latter-day Saints* (Salt Lake City: The Church of Jesus Christ of Latter-day Saints, 1985), no. 220.

25. Matthew 25:23.

9

CHOOSE LIFE: EMBRACING THE FUTURE WHEN SINGLE

Elaine Jack

As Moses led the children of Israel out of Egypt toward the
Promised Land, he made clear what was before them and how to obtain it. He said, "I call heaven and earth to record this day against you,
that I have set before you life and death, blessing and cursing: therefore
choose life."[1]

This choice faces each of us today, married or single, old or young.
Choose life. What a stimulating phrase! This choice is followed by the
promise: "That thou mayest love the Lord thy God . . . and that thou
mayest cleave unto him: for he *is* thy life, and the length of thy days."[2]
We have the positive assurance and blessing that the Lord is our life
and the length of our days if we love Him and cleave unto Him.

Loving the Lord and following His commandments is the objective of every child of God in this church. Following His plan qualifies us to return home to our Heavenly Father regardless of our marriage situation. Each of us must be passionate in our belief and in our
commitment to love the Lord and His gospel plan. We must know

Elaine Jack was born in Cardston, Alberta, and later settled in Utah. She has
served 21 years in general Church service: 11 years as a member of the Relief
Society General Board, 3 years as a counselor in the Young Women General
Presidency, and 7 years as Relief Society General President. She has written one
book and several chapters and articles.

unequivocally that He is with us always, that He will guide and direct us as we work toward our own salvation.

This knowledge is the underpinning for our daily actions at every age and stage of our lives. I am confident that the attitudes and actions we are choosing today set the stage for the happiness and contentment we will reap as we age. What is important is living now while preparing for the future.

"ALL ARE ALIKE UNTO GOD"

Singles occupy a unique place in the Church. At least one-third of the adult Church membership is single. As President James E. Faust has pointed out, we were all single before we were married, and many, due to divorce or death of a spouse, will once again be single. The promise of an eternal family is nonetheless available to all who are worthy.[3]

This concept was illustrated by a friend who wrote: "I plan for my future as if I'll be single until I die. And deep down *I hope* that some-day I'll learn what it means to want to give up everything for someone else. I believe in this family church for a reason. And that reason is it makes no sense to live alone. Nothing makes more sense in my life than being part of a family. So I have hope for the future. I hope that as I go through this single stage in my life, I am learning the important things that will develop within me a caring, thoughtful, insightful, giving, loving individual. And when I refer to 'my life,' I refer to my life through the eternities. I have hope in the big picture."

With this common eternal goal in mind, individual differences and circumstances should be enriching rather than divisive. One of my favorite words is "inclusion." It presents to me an image of the membership of this great church. Paul taught that we are all fellow citizens in God's kingdom.[4] This call encompasses us all in whatever life circumstances we are found, whether single or married. The challenge for all is to worship and serve from the depth of our capacities and to accept the service of others. The blessing is that our individual capacities and strengths can mutually support gospel values and perspectives, each drawing on what is uniquely ours and benefitting from the distinctive contributions of others.

I believe that there are more similarities than differences in the lives of Latter-day Saints, and that understanding the perception of those who are not currently in a traditional family setting will lead to more satisfying interactions. People in all categories can work and live together to promote gospel peace, harmony, love, and service.

Although there are many categories of "singles," each is an individual. One single friend observed, "There is as much difference within the range of married couples as there is between married and single people."

Another commented, "I do not think I am in denial, but I really do not think of myself as single. My perspective is I just have not married yet. I would rather be known as a daughter of God, a disciple of Christ, a covenant child of Israel, one who loves life and chooses a holy walk." These realities describe us whether married or not.

There is a plan for happiness available to Latter-day Saints, and it is available now, during one's lifetime. We learn of that plan in the temple. A main value of temple worship is that it symbolizes the long-range view of things, an eternal view. With the endowment comes a comprehension of the larger purpose of life. This understanding can help diminish many trials and concerns and bring them into a gospel perspective. Participating in the ordinances of the temple increases personal revelation. We receive joy from service, peace from obedience, guidance and direction for the future. Temples chart our course for eternity and provide revelation for our place and time, whether young or old, married or single.

Armed with this perspective and power, we can choose a life today that will bring satisfaction and peace now as we prepare for the future. With the help of many friends who have graciously shared their experiences, I will focus on the particular challenges and opportunities facing single adults within the Church as they age. Many of the opportunities and challenges that face church members as detailed in other chapters in this book—such as financial planning, good health practices and preparation for increased service—are much the same for both singles and married couples as they advance toward later life. Others may be somewhat different. Many of the challenges are merely an extension of those encountered in earlier years, but may be exacerbated by the circumstances of later life.

Being Single in a Family Church

The Church is stronger because of the single men and women, holders of the priesthood and active workers in Relief Society, who are tremendously important to building the kingdom. Although some single people may feel lonely in a church that emphasizes families, it is important to keep our sights fixed on the goal of family living. By making ourselves part of the ward family and extending ourselves in service, we feel connected, needed and valued.

A positive outlook of living singly in a family church was expressed this way: "I am no less a part of a family than anyone else. I have had all blessings promised to me, and it is completely in my control whether I receive them or not." It is often easy for single people in a family church to be reminded of what they don't have—a spouse or children—and lose focus on the compensatory blessings the Lord has given them.

In addition to the ward family, there are many kinds of families to which we can belong: parents, extended family, neighborhoods, professional colleagues, groups with similar interests, and so forth. The associations, connections, and experiences with each can be fulfilling. But when we get discouraged, it may be easy to segregate ourselves, to feel like an outsider or to wait to be noticed.

"I have learned to be very careful who I choose to spend my time with," said one friend. "It is natural for single people to congregate together with a closeness and understanding. But while this association can offer a unique support system that at times can lift and strengthen me, it can also be a trap which drags me down. I know I need to be around people who are positive." Being grouped together merely because "single" is in the marital status column does not automatically create satisfying relationships. Choosing associations by attitude, interests, and disposition rather than marital status can enrich the lives of both those who are married and single.

It is best not to categorize or stereotype ourselves or others based on these external situations. Just as circumstances vary among married couples, each category of single can create limiting perceptions or stereotypes. Those who are single may internalize the stereotypes of others as limitations for themselves. For example, it would be better if single members could help other church members consider their own stereotypes and assumptions, helping them understand the diversity which exists among single members and the commonality shared with married associates.

COPING WITH ALONENESS AND LONELINESS

Feeling lonely is not exclusive to those who are single. As one woman shared, "I find that to be alone as a divorced woman is much less lonely than the loneliness I experienced in a marriage filled with unfulfilled expectations of companionship." However, feeling lonely is more understandable, because people who live alone—the elderly, in particular—may not have the interactions and companionship ideally found in families living together.

Regardless of the circumstance that bring one to singleness— never married, death of a spouse, divorce or abandonment—in each instance, positive solutions can abate loneliness. "Feeling lonely while single," one observed, "is dependent upon personality and situations. As a highly independent single person, I don't feel as lonely as often as others may, because I enjoy having time to myself."

Another instructive insight came from a sixty-year-old divorced father of two: "Singles need . . . to look at themselves as being absolutely, positively no different than any other member of the Church. You are alone. You are not lonely. Lonely people are the ones in the nursing homes, who no one ever visits. The solution to loneliness is not being married. There are millions of very lonely married people. The solution to loneliness is focusing your life outside your own problems."

As Lehi taught, "Men are, that they might have joy."[5] This is as much a commandment as a statement.

"There are many ways to fight off loneliness, but the most important first step is to choose to not be a victim of self-pity," observed one friend.

For many, the realities of life itself—family, church, work—keep them so busy they have little time to be lonely. As a woman who just turned fifty explained: "My life has been so busy that I have rarely struggled with loneliness. I have found my Heavenly Father to be my companion. Another way I cope is surrounding myself with wonderful friends who inspire me. My close circle of friends, both single and married, are very driven, positive, high-functioning, confident individuals. They are rarely sad and depressed. They are busy, physically active, involved, goal-oriented, and gospel-focused. There is such a strength that comes from surrounding myself with good friends. Most of all, I truly trust the Lord. I trust His timing and *I know* His timing is best."

For most people, periods of loneliness are customary. Another of my single friends explained: "Wow! I still struggle with this. It's a great tactic of Satan to make you feel like you are all alone in the world and that no one understands what you are feeling. If you keep busy with lots of activities, it can help, but you are still going to hit bottom from time to time. It's cyclical for me. Sometimes I'm way cool with it; sometimes it's unbearable."

Another shared this insight: "I have noticed that when I'm not good with my relationship with God, or I feel like I'm not doing my part and communicating with Him, I'm *so* messed up in the head about my singleness. However, if I'm doing what I can—studying the scriptures, going to the temple, fulfilling my calling, praying sincerely—that is when I have the most faith. That is when I have the most trust that God *does* want me to succeed and that He really isn't tormenting me or being mean to me. That's how I deal with the loneliness—I keep working on my relationship with God."

Being involved with others helps. Many stay involved with extended family.

Whether these interactions are with actual family or with "adopted" or ward family, the benefits can be the same. Attending any social gathering with friends on a regular basis makes things like loneliness melt away.

A divorced woman explained it this way: "Coping with aloneness and loneliness is the hardest adjustment to make. My husband left me, and I think the death of a spouse would be so much easier to deal with than divorce. I do remember how difficult it was to walk into church alone, especially the first few weeks. Fortunately I have often enjoyed the quiet and privacy of being alone, and I tried right away to make it a positive thing. I have become much more independent. A single woman can learn to extend herself to others who also crave companionship, and I find others readily accept my lead in such activities."

Sharing, talking about coping, and analyzing one's experience to find insights is not the same thing as complaining or being discouraged. It helps to seek out and nurture relationships where you can share your feelings and also help each other build and grow.

There are elderly single people, nonetheless, many of whom have lost their companions, who, because of infirmities or otherwise, are shut-ins, or confined to assisted-living or nursing homes. For them loneliness takes on a special challenge. One elderly gentleman, who had looked after an invalid wife for many years, found himself bereaved and living alone in an assisted-living facility. His comment was, "The days are long, but the nights are longer."

A 90-year-old, good-humored woman combated loneliness by reaching out to help others as she discovered a new world of opportunities to serve. She wrote, "I seldom get out. I get so lonesome I could die, but I just keep hanging on. I try to keep cheerful and help all I can with people that are worse off than me."

Being alone, though sometimes challenging, does not mean you must be lonely. One friend summed it up this way: "Keep busy doing the things that make your life happy. Reach out for something new— really new and novel. Find humor when you can; cry when you need to. Keep your expectations of health, wealth and happiness within reasonable reach."

Maintain a close relationship with the Lord, nurture friendships, and find opportunities to serve and grow.

FINDING OPPORTUNITIES FOR GROWTH AND SERVICE

One key to happiness in the LDS Church is involvement rather than isolation. Latter-day Saints, by the very nature of our gospel participation, interact with others. Seclusion, on the other hand, preempts service, thwarts rich interpersonal relationships, and limits learning from others. As we retire from gainful employment and are no longer obliged to interact with work colleagues on a daily basis, we must seek opportunities for regular, meaningful involvement with others.

In addition to church callings, local community service opportunities abound for singles, such as mentoring underprivileged children, reading books for the blind, and being politically involved (see the chapter on service). Volunteering as a tutor in an elementary school takes little time but can result in benefits for generations to come. I admire the generosity of two women associated with the medical profession. They spend three weeks each year in a village in Africa, at their own expense, giving not only professional help, but also large doses of love and compassion.

While not always true, it is often assumed that singles, in the absence of family responsibilities, have unique opportunities for service and growth. Although the opportunities may not be unique, singles need to be open to giving service. One of my gregarious friends responded: "I found that I have a lot to offer a family ward, stake, and community. I think the second verse of the song 'Have I Done Any Good?'[6] was written for the single members of this church. 'There are chances for work all around just now, Opportunities right in our way,' and the chorus that says, 'Wake up and do something more Than dream of your mansion above.' There are so many opportunities in this church to love, to serve, and to have a great influence in lives of others. We as singles do need to wake up and not worry about our mansion. Give that worry to the Lord and discover the pleasure and the joy of serving. Also, enjoy the pleasure of naps; married friends may not get a Sunday nap when they need one."

In addition to serving others, there is no better preparation for the future than experiencing the joy and fulfillment that comes from continual learning. No matter how old we grow, we can add life to our years by obtaining knowledge of new things and applying that knowledge in our relationships and our service.

Elder David A. Bednar explains, "The overarching purpose of Heavenly Father's great plan of happiness is to provide His spirit children with opportunities to learn."[7] Continual learning can bring great happiness and feelings of success.

I enjoyed the mature insight of a single mother of adult children who found a way to combine formal education with her God-given talents: "I have been blessed with an open mind that is always trying to discover the truth, figure out the error of my ways, and strike out on a new adventure. This quest has led me to my career as a teacher of students with disabilities. This career has given me a forum to combine my calling (a teacher) with my craft (an organizer). The drudgery of this earth life has truly passed me by. My love of early-morning exercise and good food has kept me just above the sinking point. I have been able to comfort and strengthen others as I have so often needed to be comforted and strengthened. I don't make casseroles or cookies, but I share what I have to share."

Continual learning in formal and informal settings and in service brings growth and a greater ability to serve. In turn, this growth fosters relationships and greater satisfaction.

MAINTAINING FAMILY CONNECTIONS, FRIENDS, AND ASSOCIATES

Beyond the references above to the importance of relationships and connections for single people, this topic merits special mention of its own. Knowing we are loved and cared for by God adds perspective, purpose, and comfort to our lives, particularly as we age. A sense of family and community can be gained through those around us.

As stated by one friend, "I cherish the time I have with my aging parents. In addition, my friends have been the biggest blessing in my life. They are truly a lifeline for me."

In this same regard, a retired university professor proclaimed: "Family connections are my mainstay. Some give me support with spiritual grounding, others outside of the spiritual, but also most-needed. I try to make myself available when needed, try not to impose when I'm not. I want above all to keep the connections open so that I can laugh, cry, pray, and play with my family at all ages."

Another friend refers to close friends as "family by affection." There is a dilemma, however, when parents who have always been a mainstay in life are aged or dying and neighbors who have become family by affection move away. It is difficult for a middle-aged person to establish a new network of friends and family—difficult, but possible.

PREPARING FOR THE FUTURE BY HAVING A HAPPY LIFE TODAY

Varied thoughts come to mind when preparing for the future. One friend commented: "Planning for the future. Well, I have a 401K [retirement savings account], does that count? And I'm working for an employer that has a wonderful retirement plan. What does a full and happy life mean? How do you measure it? I used to think it was based on the number of people who attend a funeral. If the chairs went back into the gym, you knew that person had a full and happy life. But it's hard to base everything on something that happens at the *end* of a life."

Even the terms "preparing" and "planning" suggest doing something now. As suggested in the title of this chapter, "Choose Life," it is important to have a happy and full life now. The Lord will strengthen us in time of need when we own what we have control over and leave the rest to Him. The Atonement allows the Lord to take away burdens, leaving us free to focus on what we can control. Let's consider some of those things that are in our control.

We can choose the way we spend our time. We can choose to be positive. We can choose to be faithful. We can choose to serve. We can choose to enrich our minds, strengthen our bodies, and nourish our spirits to stimulate growth and happiness. And it is reaffirming to know we are not left alone in our decisions.

"Praying for the future really helps," one friend wisely stated. "I didn't think that was a good thing to ask for; I thought it was just something you were supposed to have. But, why not? Why not pray for extra help to keep going and help bring hope for the future? That's what I need the most—help to keep going and to have as much joy along the way as I can."

Reality is facing each day with a positive outlook, even if circumstances may not be as you anticipated. "Once, my dad, the wisest man I know, comforted me for the fact I was not yet married, saying, 'I'd rather have you happy, active in the Church, doing good things and single, than married for the wrong reason and to the wrong man.' Who is more blessed than I am?"

A recently widowed woman wrote of actively pursuing life in the present. She shared:

> There is a metamorphosis that happens when your spouse dies. I feel like I've been pushed out into the ocean all alone. I know how to sail, I know where I'm going, but I'm on a raft! I remember how sails feel, having a captain and a boat, skimming across the waves under me and being full of joy. I would add that I also know how to swim, and that is what seems to be needed now. And I can see the shore!
>
> My earth life didn't end with my husband's. It felt like it did for some days, but then I began understanding that *my* mission was not finished. It is not as well-defined as it was at the side of my amazing husband, but it is ongoing.
>
> My life is full, really full, and happy. I learned early on that the same people who needed me before my husband's death still need me. The gospel is still true. God lives. I am connected in real ways to heaven.

Those who are waiting their time out on earth by merely being busy are missing the measure of their creation—to have joy, to be filled with light and love, and to rejoice all our days. There is much in this world to celebrate. We are living. We have the truth. We have been born in these days of the restored gospel. We have the right to choose. The recurring messages from my friends on how to prepare for a happy life entail being the best you can be, seeking for growth and personal excellence, contributing in meaningful ways, and being unwavering in our faith in Jesus Christ.

Notes

1. Deuteronomy 30:19.
2. Deuteronomy 30:20; emphasis added.
3. See James E. Faust, "Welcoming Every Single One," *Ensign*, Aug. 2007, 5.
4. See Ephesians 2:19.
5. 2 Nephi 2:25.
6. *Hymns of The Church of Jesus Christ of Latter-day Saints* (Salt Lake City: The Church of Jesus Christ of Latter-day Saints, 1985), no. 223.
7. David A. Bednar, "Learning to Love Learning," *Ensign*, Feb. 2010, 26.

10

PREPARING FOR YOUR MISSION

Elder John H. Groberg

Nearly fifty years ago I served as mission president in Tonga. In those days, calls to local couple missionaries were issued by the mission president according to local needs. Since there were no stakes in Tonga then, the mission president held the keys to the work there. We had many small struggling branches, but also many large branches with couples who could help.

The social and economic circumstances in Tonga were very different than today. Relatively few people worked for wages, and nearly everyone was involved with subsistence farming. Most families built their own *fale* (home) from locally available trees and other plant material. Thus, a couple could build a home almost anywhere, including on the small island or in the remote branch they may be assigned to.

It still took great courage, faith and sacrifice for them to go on a mission, as they had to leave family, friends, and familiar surroundings, and live among strangers. With the help of local members, they built a *fale*, planted a garden, caught fish, and otherwise took care of

John H. Groberg, an Emeritus Seventy, served in the Presidency of the Quorum of Seventy and as president of the Idaho Falls Idaho Temple. He is the author of three books that recount his missionary experiences while he served in the Pacific, in South America, in Asia, and in areas in the United States. The movie *The Other Side of Heaven* is based on his first book.

themselves and their family. Their children attended local schools, and the family fit into the fabric of their new community.

The small amount of money needed was usually provided by family and friends. Calls lasted about two years, and in most cases the husband served in the branch presidency and the wife in the Relief Society presidency. They studied the gospel, taught investigators, fellowshipped less-active members, and generally kept the branch alive. Some couples stayed in one branch their whole mission, while others served in several different branches, depending on needs. When they finished their missions, they returned to their native villages full of the spirit of the Lord, deeply founded in the gospel, and better able to contribute to the building of the kingdom and to their community.

There was great need for couples (just as there is today, throughout the world), so we were always looking for any who could serve. Calling couples on missions was always a tender and inspirational experience, as the following example shows.

INSPIRATION FOR THE CALL

While attending a district conference in Ha'apai, my attention was drawn to a fairly young couple with two small children. They participated happily and enthusiastically in the conference, and I felt impressed to talk to them about serving a mission.

After the conference I called them in for an interview. They had received the same prompting of the spirit as I had, so they were prepared and eager to serve. They were expecting their third child in a few weeks, so I suggested that they report to the mission office in three months. They agreed.

I was surprised when, just a little over a month later, they came to my office. It was obvious that the wife had already had the baby. I told them I hadn't expected them for another two months and asked if everything was all right.

They said, "Everything is fine. Our baby came early, but only lived one day. We buried him under the big tree in our front yard. It was a beautiful service."

"I'm sorry to hear that," I replied. "Maybe under the circumstances, we should postpone your mission for a while."

They looked at me almost in shock. "Oh no, President. Naturally we are sad to lose our baby son, but are grateful we have this mission call to look forward to. We know our son is in the celestial kingdom, and we want to get on our mission as soon as possible so we can better prepare to be with him one day. Please let us start now."

Seldom have I felt such sincere faith. I asked that we kneel together in prayer. During the prayer, I felt impressed to set them apart right then. While doing so, I had the unmistakable impression that an additional spirit was present and participating.

As I concluded the setting apart, I knew exactly where they should be assigned. When everyone had wiped their tears and regained their composure, I said, "You are a special, faithful family. The Lord has blessed you and will continue to bless you. You do not go on this mission alone. I know where the Lord wants you to serve."

Before I could say any more, they both looked at me and said, "We are happy to go to Matuku and stay as long as you want."

I tried not to act surprised. Matuku was the very place that had come to my mind. It was clear that the inspiration for them to serve there had been given to them at the same time it had been given to me. As I looked at them, I had the same feelings of wonder I had when I first extended the call to them in Ha'apai.

"Yes, Matuku," I replied, "that is where the Lord wants you to serve, and where you will bless many people and will, in turn, be blessed. There you will move closer to your goal of being reunited with your son." I encouraged them to remain faithful and humble, to work hard and be obedient. Their faces glowed as they said they would.

When they left to make arrangements to sail to Matuku, I again knelt and thanked the Lord for such faith and for allowing me to participate in this miraculous process of calling and assigning missionaries.

For two years, they served wonderfully well. When they were released, they returned home with their two children, plus a new baby boy. I could tell from the glow in their countenances that their testimonies had grown greatly and they were closer to their goal of the celestial kingdom. How I wish we could all have such faith in and love for the Lord.

Times have changed, and young couples are no longer called under those circumstances. However, faith and love and work and goodness and progress towards the celestial kingdom have not changed—nor will they. God has always blessed missionaries and their families, and He always will.

As I think of this couple, I think of hundreds of other couples, as well as thousands of single missionaries and their families who have served, and continue to serve, in all parts of the world in all types of circumstances. They bless the lives of many, and, in turn, are blessed.

THE TRANSFORMING POWER OF LOVE

Another powerful experience occurred more recently in Salt Lake City, Utah, when I was serving as a General Authority. Even though the circumstances were very different, the same type of blessings came to pass.

I became casually acquainted with a gentleman who was a convert to the Church, but not very active at the time. Our paths crossed only occasionally, and our conversations at first were quite brief. I could tell he was struggling with something, so one day I asked him what was wrong. He said his wife had recently passed away and that he was having a hard time, especially in giving proper care to their three teenage children.

I expressed my sympathy and asked if there was anything I could do. He said he felt he needed greater faith and deeper understanding of God's plan for him and his family. I asked if he was attending church. He said he took the children most of the time and they seemed to enjoy it, but he felt alone and inadequate. I told him that if he would attend regularly and get acquainted with the bishop and other members, they would be a great help to him. He promised to try.

Over the next few months, he reported that the bishop was nice, the members were helpful, and the children had good friends. One day he had a worried look on his face and said that his oldest son had asked about serving a mission. He didn't want him to go, because he felt he needed his help with his younger brother and sister.

I told him that serving a mission would be a marvelous blessing to him, his son, and his family and that those blessings would more than compensate for his son's being gone for two years. I explained that to be a blessing, missions always require some sacrifice, for it is "sacrifice [that] brings forth the blessings of heaven."[1] He had not served a mission, so it was difficult for him to understand the principle.

When we next met he said he had visited more with his bishop, but still felt he needed his son's help at home. He also said that when he told the bishop we were somewhat acquainted, the bishop instructed him to seek my advice and follow it.

"Well," I said. "Since the bishop asked you to follow my advice, that is exactly what you should do. My advice is that you encourage your son to go on a mission."

He laughed a little and said he already knew that was what I would say. Then he added that even if he did want his son to go on a mission, he did not have the income to support him. (This was before the equalization program for missionary support.) I assured him that his bishop and stake president would work that part out.

He was still hesitant so I felt impressed to ask, "There's something else, isn't there?"

He sighed and replied, "I understand the Church has a mission in Japan. That means there is a possibility my son could get called there. I simply can't allow that. I fought in the Pacific during the war and have bitter feelings towards the Japanese people. I do not want my son to associate with them."

I was shocked at this attitude and replied, "These feelings come mostly from your lack of faith in God, not from your war experiences." He disagreed. Then I asked if he remembered the warm feelings he had when he was baptized and told him he should have those feelings of warmth and love for all people.

He shook his head and murmured, "I don't think I can." I assured him he could and encouraged him to continue attending church, visiting with his bishop, and trying to remember the feelings he had when he was baptized. I asked him to especially concentrate on those feelings during the sacrament.

Over the next few weeks, he said he was starting to lean towards letting his son go on a mission, but he still wanted me to assure him that his son would not go to Japan.

I smiled and said that since there were around 150 missions in the Church, the chances of his son getting called to Japan were very small. But then, an impression came to me. I looked him straight in the eye and said, "Your problem is not Japan. It is your lack of faith in and understanding of the Savior and His mission. He died for all people, including the Japanese people. You need to have the missionaries come to your home and give you the missionary discussions."

He was a little defensive and said that he knew the doctrines of the Church well enough, but was sure no one else understood the terrible things he went through during the war.

"The Savior understands," I replied. "He has been through much more. It's not the war; it's your faith in Him. Please invite the missionaries to dinner; ask them to give you a lesson. Try to remember the love and warmth you felt when you were baptized."

A week or so later, he reported that the full-time missionaries had come to dinner and taught a lesson. He felt a warm spirit and was impressed with their politeness, respect and enthusiasm.

"I believe a mission would be good for my son," he said. I told him to have his son work with his bishop and get his mission papers submitted immediately.

Again, he asked if I could promise that his son would not go to Japan. On a prompting, I said, "Because God loves you and knows you are being held back spiritually by your bad feelings for His children in Japan, that is probably where God will send him."

"I just can't take that chance," he blurted out.

"Not only can you, but you will. This is a test of your trust in God, and you need to pass it. When you develop sufficient faith to accept God's will, whatever it is, everything will be all right, and it won't matter where your son is called."

"Well, I guess I can risk it."

"It is not a risk," I said. "It is submitting to the Lord's will. That is the opposite of a risk. When you submit to His will, you are 100% certain that you are doing that which will bring you joy and salvation. Pray for faith in the Savior. Pray for willingness to do His will. Pray to remember all He has done for you. He loves you and will do nothing that will not be a blessing for you."

He became a little teary-eyed and asked if we could have a prayer together. He promised to pray more fervently and ask for more trust in God.

A few weeks went by. Then one day he rushed in and whispered, "It's Japan! I don't know if I can take it."

"You can and you will, and this call will prove to be one of the greatest blessings in your life," I said.

"This is hard. I am working with the bishop so I can go to the temple with my son, but I am worried." I assured him that many people on both sides of the veil were praying for him and his family and that everything would be all right.

During our occasional visits over the next two years, I noticed steady movement from the tentativeness of: "He's doing okay," to, "He's loving his work," to, "He loves the Japanese people."

One day he excitedly reported that his son had baptized a family and that the father was a former soldier in the Pacific war. A few weeks later, he showed me a letter from this former Japanese soldier thanking him for sending his son to bring the gospel to his family.

I sensed a softness in his voice, pride in his son and the beginning of love for the people among whom his son was working. During the mission, his hard feelings fell away and were replaced by love and tenderness.

Two years passed quickly, and when his son returned, he was met at the airport by a throng of people led by his father driving a new Toyota! His son had grown majestically in the gospel, loved the Japanese people, and was a marvelous help to his father and their family.

His second son served a mission in Guatemala. His daughter and both sons were married in the temple. Everything about the family seemed to improve, except the father's health. At about the same time we received an assignment to serve overseas, he was diagnosed with a rather fast-moving cancer. On our last visit before we moved, he thanked me and said he constantly thanked the Lord for loving him enough to help him get over his hard feelings. He tenderly said that he felt he was now ready to meet his wife, his Savior, and many faithful Japanese people.

A few months into our overseas assignment, his children informed me of his passing. I thanked them for their good lives and expressed my confidence that they would continue faithful, reminding them that the Lord's work continues on both sides of the veil.

WHY SERVE MISSIONS?

We should serve missions to show our love for our Lord and Savior Jesus Christ and to express our gratitude for all He has done and continues to do for us. When our hearts are filled with this love and gratitude, we naturally ask: What can I do to show that love and gratitude?

He gives us the answer: "If ye love me, keep my commandments,"[2] "A new commandment I give unto you, That ye love one another," and explains how to do this: "As I have loved you . . . love one another."[3]

How did He love us? By sacrificing, teaching, providing ordinances, and showing us the way to eternal life and everlasting joy. To love one another as He loves us, we do the same things—sacrifice, teach, provide ordinances, and show the way to eternal life and everlasting joy. This is called missionary work.

There are many types of missions and ways to serve, all of which are meaningful and helpful. If our health, family or financial circumstances preclude us from one type of mission, other types are available. For example, serving in the temple is an important type of missionary work. So is family history, and so are numerous other areas of service. The key ingredient to serving any mission is to have a true desire and deep faith in God, for *with God all things are possible.*"[4]

We can all serve in some way, at some time, and in some place. Desire, faith, patience, love—in other words, spiritual preparation—is what we need most. When we express our desires and let our leaders know about any health issues, financial constraints, family concerns, etc., we can then put ourselves into the hands of God and watch great miracles occur.

Every mission call, regardless of type, comes through inspiration from those who hold the proper authority. Since the Lord knows our needs as well as the needs of others, He matches our strengths and needs with the strengths and needs of others. Thus, while we serve, we are also served.

Each call is customized for us and for those among whom we serve

and contains within itself the seeds of its own blessings. When we accept a call with a humble heart, regardless of when or where, everything is in place for those seeds to germinate. As they come to fruition,
they will bring great joy and increased strength to us, to those we serve,
and to the kingdom of God.

While there are thousands of examples of how missions have
blessed and continue to bless the lives of countless people, to me, the
two examples given here embody the main elements we need to work
on as we prepare to serve missions. The basic principles of inspiration,
faith, diligence and blessings from God shine through both. Remember
that those same eternal principles are equally in force today and will
bring great blessings to you and to all who serve.

Life is a gift from God. Understanding our purpose in life is a gift
from God. The opportunity to help others understand their purpose in
life is a gift from God. The opportunity to serve a mission is a gift from
God. In fact, the opportunity to help anyone in any eternally meaningful way is a gift from God.

As long as we have the gift of life, we can serve in some way. It does
not matter *when* or *where* we serve but *how* we serve. We are to serve
with all our "heart, might, mind and strength."[5] President Spencer W.
Kimball once said, "I suppose if I have learned anything in life, it is
that we are to keep moving, keep trying—as long as we breathe! If we
do, we will be surprised at how much more can still be done."[6]

CONCERNS

Some are concerned about family, especially leaving children and
grandchildren. When we are away on a mission, we may physically
miss a few births or blessings, baptisms or marriages, but the spiritual
impact of what we are doing will always be present and will make the
most powerful and lasting impression we can imagine. I wonder how
Heavenly Father keeps track of falling sparrows, but some way, He

does. I wonder how He is present at each marriage or birth or baptism, but some way, He is. As we represent Him, He represents us!

Some may not be sure what to do with their house or business, or other such matters. As they counsel with the Lord and their local leaders, they will find the right answers and be at peace. When we serve any type of mission with firm faith, deep desire and true love, we pull away from the cares and limitations of this world and put ourselves into the everlasting love and unlimited hands of God.

This is the Lord's work. We serve Him because we love Him. He has sacrificed for us and for all people. He has asked us to help bring souls unto Him through teaching eternal truths. As we do, we and others can be forgiven and partake of the fruit of eternal life made available to everyone through the Savior's Atonement and His great plan of happiness.

What blessings missions are! I know they bring about miracles. When we trust the Lord and put our lives fully into His hands, we are assured that the very best will happen to us, our families, and to those we love and serve.

I hope faithful members everywhere will serve missions, both in their youth and in their later years. To help with your questions about and plans and preparations for missionary service, see the following information below.

GETTING READY

The missionary department of the Church posts wonderful material online at lds.org to help seniors prepare for missions. The Full-Time Senior and Church-Service Mission Opportunities website has exciting videos and links to provide accurate information and answers to nearly every conceivable question about seniors serving missions.[7] Referring to the Church website is the best way to proceed to stay abreast of frequent updates about opportunities to serve. Bishops and stake presidents—and, in missions, branch, district and mission presidents—receive regular mailings of current information, and they can provide you with information.

Senior couples and sisters[8] serve in many countries and in a variety of capacities, in proselytizing, in secretarial work and administrative support, in Church education, in public affairs, in family history, in temples, in medical roles, in humanitarian service, in technical support, and a host of other assignments geared to individuals' unique strengths, professional skills, talents and capabilities.

Full-Time Senior Mission Opportunities on the website spells out the terms of service for senior missionaries. "No calls will be issued that are inconsistent with the health, safety or financial capability of the missionary."[9] Recommendations for senior couples may be submitted up to six months in advance of their availability date.

The services of senior couples are particularly sought after in small, struggling branches or as the bulwark to fledgling programs where their experience and maturity in the gospel are stabilizing influences. In third-world countries, their technical expertise and know-how help provide the path to a brighter future. Seniors couples will be pleased to know that they do not have to follow the rigorous schedule of young missionaries.

Church-service missions, which provide for service at home, both part-time and full-time, have also provided "a growing and varied number of opportunities to serve" since 1979. The variety of service missions, often in administrative support, is almost limitless, ranging from family history to church education, welfare services, physical facilities, church-owned farms, and many others. Church-service missionaries serve at least eight hours per week. They normally serve for six to twenty-four months.

"All Church-service missionaries must be worthy to hold a temple recommend. They must be physically, mentally, and emotionally able to fulfill the specific call and its related duties. . . . Church-service missionaries are responsible for their own medical and dental needs, including eye-care and prescription-drug expenses."[10]

Senior couples and single members should consider, in consultation with their priesthood leaders, what kinds of missionary service best meets their particular needs. Bishops and branch presidents interview prospective candidates and make recommendations. "The health requirement for service missionaries is a simple health history and inventory."[11] Missionaries are called by their stake president, and don't usually serve under a mission president.

For seniors planning to serve full-time missions, in addition to an interview with their bishop or branch president, there are health requirements, which require a variety of tests and a physician's appraisal. Once ward or branch leaders have interviewed the prospective missionaries and completed the application, stake or mission presidents conduct interviews and forward the application to the Missionary Department in Salt Lake City. Missions and other service agencies may also request the services of specific senior couples or individuals. Then comes the glorious day of receiving your mission call, an event to be celebrated with children and grandchildren. "Grandpa and Grandma are going on a mission!"

Do Not Delay

If you are approaching retirement or have already retired, you should consider missionary service as soon as possible, before the onset of unexpected health or other issues that delay or hinder a mission. In the words of President Thomas S. Monson, "It is in *doing*—not just *dreaming*—that lives are blessed, others are guided, and souls are saved."[12] The great rewards that attend missionary service, both to others and to ourselves, should never be lost from sight.

"Therefore, if ye have desires to serve God ye are called to the work; For behold the field is white already to harvest; and lo, he that thrusteth in his sickle with his might, the same layeth up in store that he perisheth not, but bringeth salvation to his soul."[13] To the returning Seventy, Christ declared, "rejoice not, that the spirits are subject unto you; but rather rejoice, because your names are written in heaven."[14] Nothing can compare with the exhilaration of being in the service of the Lord. Missionary service is an opportunity not to be missed. Do not procrastinate. "Do it" now!

Notes

1. *Hymns of The Church of Jesus Christ of Latter-day Saints* (Salt Lake City: The Church of Jesus Christ of Latter-day Saints, 1985), no. 27.
2. John 14:15.
3. John 13:34.
4. Matthew 19:26; emphasis added.
5. D&C 4:2.
6. Spencer W. Kimball, "Do Not Weary by the Way," *Ensign*, Nov. 1980.
7. See http://lds.org/csm/index.html (consulted Nov. 5, 2010).
8. Senior Single Brothers Are Not Recommended for Full-Time Missionary Service.
9. "Senior Missionary Opportunities Bulletin, Oct. 29, 2010," http://lds.org/csm/pdfs/MissOpp.pdf (consulted Nov. 5, 2010).
10. "Church-Service Mission Opportunities" and follow links "Current Opportunities," and "Frequently Asked Questions," http://lds.org/csm/csm.html (consulted Nov. 5, 2010).
11. Donald B. Doty, Chairman Missionary Department Health Services, Salt Lake City, e-mail message to Roy A. Prete, Nov. 7, 2010.
12. Thomas S. Monson, "Do Your Duty—That Is Best," *Ensign*, Nov. 2005, 59.
13. D&C 4:3–4.
14. Luke 10:20.

11

It's Not a Term Paper: Compiling a Personal History

Elder Dennis B. Neuenschwander

Well, congratulations, you made it! At long last and after a lifetime of work, you have reached that wonderful season of life when you promised yourself that you would finally have the time to get into your family history. As you do so, you become part of a great legion, both within and without the Church, for which family research and the preservation of family and personal histories are a personal passion and mission. This chapter contains a few suggestions that will help you begin and enjoy the wonderful journey that lies ahead of you.

Family history is a sacred endeavor, especially among the Latter-day Saints. The Atonement of Jesus Christ and the plan of salvation are the very backbone of family history research and the writing of personal and family histories. The Atonement, including the Resurrection, opens the door for each of God's children to accept the gospel and be rescued from death and saved from sin. The blessings of the Atonement are extended to all, regardless of when or where they

Dennis B. Neuenschwander was president of the Austria Vienna East mission from 1987–1991. Called as a Seventy in 1991, he was granted emeritus status in 2009. During his service he served in the Presidency of the Seventy and as editor of Church magazines. He holds a Ph.D. in Russian literature from Syracuse University.

lived. The performance of both live and proxy priesthood ordinances are an essential part of the return journey into the presence of God.

In 1836, Elijah, in fulfillment of Malachi's ancient prophecy,[1] returned to earth and committed the keys relating to the sealing power of priesthood ordinances in both time and eternity to Joseph Smith and Oliver Cowdery.[2] From that moment research on one's family lines and the preservation of personal and family histories have steadily grown in importance and significance across the world. This extraordinary sealing power has the ability to turn hearts toward ancestors and posterity alike and bind them together.

The Prophet Joseph Smith wrote: "What is this office and work of Elijah? It is one of the greatest and most important subjects that God has revealed. He should send Elijah to seal the children to the fathers, and the fathers to the children."[3]

Certainly we look with gratitude on the promises extended to Abraham that through his posterity: "all the families of the earth [shall] be blessed, even with the blessings of the Gospel, which are the blessings of salvation, even of life eternal."[4] In a very personal manner, this work of Elijah turns our hearts both to our fathers—our ancestors, and to our children—our posterity.

In contrast to the marvelous promise of eternal blessing and connection, Malachi also speaks of a spiritual obscurity in which one stands alone, disconnected from ancestors and posterity alike.[5] Can there be a more frightening prospect for those whom we love? We are all under a spiritual obligation to ensure that this does not occur in our own families. Yet unless we do something to prevent it, by the second or third generation, our ancestors will live in obscurity. Likewise, by the second or third generation of our posterity, we are the ones who will slip away from the knowledge of our own descendants. Family history research, coupled with the performance of proxy ordinances and the preservation of family and personal histories, not only rescues our ancestors from their spiritual obscurity, but it rescues us as well.

Family history is a broad topic with many facets. The focus of this chapter will be on the writing of personal histories. However, the compilation of ancestral data to extend the generations of your family remains an equally sacred obligation. The Family History Library, your local family history center, and local genealogical societies and libraries have resources and interested staff who can help you with your research. In addition, the Family Search website can provide you with numerous links to both Church and commercial sites where help and instruction are readily available.

WRITING YOUR PERSONAL HISTORY

Writing a personal history may seem like an insurmountable task. The more you think about it, the more complex it can become. If you aren't careful, you'll be tempted to postpone it to a more convenient time. Unfortunately, such a time does not exist. Keep in mind that as far as your life history is concerned, there is no better time to begin than the present. It might help you to remember that some things, such as writing your life story, can only be done at this stage of your life. Your posterity will thank you eternally for every word you record about yourself.

Knowledge of your own ancestors has influenced the quality of your life. This knowledge has given you a sense of identity and personal responsibility that you could not have received in any other way. As you came to know them and became familiar with the strength and courage of their lives, you began to emulate them and to speak of them. Even if you had scoundrels in your family, you learned from them and might even have enjoyed reading about them. If it is true that your ancestors have influenced your life, then it is equally true that you can influence the lives of your posterity. Sadly, without knowledge of your life, your posterity can become disconnected from their roots and the nourishment those roots provide. Do not let this happen.

The following are a few principles that will help you write your personal and family history. They are simple, even familiar, principles. Hopefully, they will remove some of the apprehension you may feel. When it comes right down to it, you just have to get started.

JUST GET STARTED

The best way to begin any project is to identify your goal and write it down. Throughout your life, you have worked with goals and deadlines and know how important they are in the accomplishment of anything worthwhile. Writing your personal history is no different. The first step is to record on paper your commitment to write your history. Then put the paper where you can see it every day. If you will do this one simple thing, you will neither forget your goal nor postpone it. The setting of goals is of particular importance now that you have a little more discretionary time at your disposal. You have probably already discovered how quickly a day can fill up with busy errands and little projects. Make your discretionary time count toward the writing of your personal history with clearly defined goals.

You don't have to do everything at once. If you sit down with the intent of writing a book, the task will seem overwhelming, and you will become discouraged very quickly. Rather, divide your history into smaller steps. Consider writing a little about one experience, a special event in your life, or of something that has particular meaning for you. Start with familiar topics that can be written independently of each other. If you can, set a deadline for completing each of them. This provides a continual sense of accomplishment and gives you courage to complete your main goal. Your personal history will begin to take shape through these smaller steps.

Identify a starting date, and then get going. It is not that bad once you begin. In fact you will find writing your personal history to be most enjoyable. It is important to devote part of every day to your project. Share your writing with family members. You'll be surprised at their excitement and their anticipation of your final product. They will be at once your best critics and greatest fan club. Their encouragement will be tremendously helpful to you.

GATHER YOUR MATERIALS

Most of us have valuable historical material (photographs, letters, travel documents, etc.) stored away in a variety of places such as filing cabinets, boxes—in the garage, closets, basement or attic—and in albums, journals, and diaries. Find these sources and gather them into one place where you can organize them. Speaking of place, it's helpful to dedicate a secure place in your home where you can spread your materials out, shuffle them around, and keep them immediately available to you, at least until you're finished with them. You may wish to organize your materials by time period, person, event, or some other way. This whole process may look messy and unorganized to others, but to you it will be a sacred mess.

As you review and organize your materials, ideas and memories will flood your mind. Keep a notebook and pen handy. Take time to write your thoughts and feelings down. Don't fall victim to the idea that you will remember everything or that something that seems unforgettable to you in one moment will be so in another ten minutes. You will find these little moments to be inspirational and full of insight. Don't lose them. It will surprise you how fast you can forget important details if you don't record them for later use. You may also find it helpful to list significant events of your life on a word processor, where you can cut and paste them into a document as they come to you.

Reviewing your materials will also identify periods of your life for which you may have surprisingly little material and/or no memory. This is also important to find out. There may still be time for you to approach relatives and friends for information that will help you fill the gaps.

OVERCOME YOUR FEARS

Those struggling to write their personal history seem to share a number of questions, including: "What is a history?" "What should I write?" "I don't know how to write; how can I overcome that?" "Do I really have to write?" and, "Who can help me?"

Do any of those sound familiar? Let's take them one at a time.

What is a personal history? The simplest answer to this question is that your history is what you choose to record. There is no set pattern to writing a personal history and no required length or number of words to write. Writing a personal history is a labor of love, not one of academic excellence. You aren't writing it to satisfy a course requirement. Your history won't be graded, and no one will read it only to hand it back for rewriting.

Your history is not a term paper!

Certainly you would wish to include significant dates such as your birth, baptism, marriage, and the birth of your children. You should also identify important relationships such as spouse, parents, grandparents, as well as brothers and sisters, aunts, uncles, and cousins. You may also include the addresses where you lived and the schools you attended. Recording these things puts you into a unique historical setting and will provide important and accurate information for your posterity.

What should I write? A good way of defining what you should write is to think of what you wish your ancestors would have written about themselves. Use that as a guideline, and you will not go wrong.

You may choose to take a simple, chronological approach in the writing of your history, recording the experiences of childhood, school years, mission, dating, higher education, marriage, etc. As interesting as these are, however, your posterity will certainly be more interested in the human side of your life. They'll want to know what your experiences meant to you, what you learned from the experiences, and how they shaped and made you who you are. As difficult as it may be, don't eliminate the difficult—and often embarrassing—experiences that taught you life's greatest lessons. If you define what you wish your posterity to learn from you, your lessons will become their best teachers.

You may say to yourself that your life has been so ordinary that nothing of interest to others has happened. Nothing could be further from the truth. After a generation or two, there is nothing about you that *wouldn't* be of interest to those who will know you only through your history. Don't hesitate to include the daily details of life: a typical daily schedule, how laundry was done when you were growing up, what life on a farm was like when you were young, or what your favorite Church activities were. Your reflections, descriptions, and observations of the world in which you grew up and lived, both secular and spiritual, will be a true window into the past for those who will read your words.

Photographs are an excellent stimulant to memory. If you have pictures of events in your life—even informal snapshots—pick them up and just tell about the event the picture captures. Where was the picture taken? When? Who is in it? What were the circumstances around the event?

If you can't think of anything you consider of interest, talk to your children or grandchildren. They'll tell you in a moment what they want to know. You can also write of particular experiences and feelings you wish to share with each child and grandchild.

I don't know how to write. How can I overcome that? You may take some comfort in knowing that many people feel incapable of writing. It may feel difficult, but many things will help you along the way.

Remember that no one knows your history like you do. Once you identify the events, memories, and experiences you wish to record, the intensity of your passion will shine through your words. Words become the means by which you record what you know better than anyone else. When you have something to say, you'll find the words to express it.

Keep your audience in mind—those who love you and who are interested in every word you write. Perfection is not nearly as important to them, as it may be to you. Indeed, after a few generations, your imperfections may be the most enduring and endearing aspect of your written history.

Practice makes perfect. Devote part of every day to your writing. You will be pleased and surprised at how ideas and memories longforgotten will come to your mind and connect themselves to the ideas you are recording at the moment.

When possible, write in a place conducive to the experience you are trying to describe. If you are writing about your parents, it may be helpful to write in the kitchen, where familiar smells and aromas can be a quick catalyst to memory. You may also wish to find a quiet spot outside, where the sounds of nature can stir the mind. Thoughtful repose in a cemetery can call forth memories close to the surface in such a sacred place. Some have found it helpful to identify just one place where they devote time to reflection and writing.

Think of some event in your life that was especially meaningful to you. Envision yourself just telling the story of that event, and write it down. When you have completed that experience, choose another one. They do not even need to be connected at this point. After you have written about several such experiences, write a connecting bridge between the events. Your personal history will begin to take shape.

Do I really have to write? The written word is not the only means of recording your personal history. If writing is just not your thing, or you are a better speaker than a writer, you can choose from among a wonderful variety of electronic devices to record your history. If you decide on this method, have another person in the room to work the recording device and to be an audience.

You will greatly enhance the recording of your history if, in advance, you compose an outline of what you wish to say. You could also write down a number of experiences you plan to share or a set of questions to which you could respond. Ask your children or grandchildren what they would most like to hear from you and invite them to compose a list of questions. This list will be an excellent guide in the preparation of your recording. You may also consider having someone you trust interview you. That person can write down or otherwise record your thoughts and feelings as you speak. Recording your personal history electronically has the added advantage of preserving your voice, your manner of speaking, and the feelings you have for the events you are describing.

There is certainly more than one way of achieving your goal of preserving your personal history.

Who can help me? Children and grandchildren are also excellent resources in helping to navigate the computer. They can assist you with scanning pictures or other documents to include in your history. Their participation will increase their anticipation for your history, which can increase your motivation.

Within the LDS community, the local family history centers and ward consultants can be good resources. Remember those among your family or acquaintances who have already written a personal or family history. Speak with them and look at what they have done. One good example is worth more than a dozen explanations.

In almost every community, you'll find local historical societies and family history organizations that promote personal histories. Members of these organizations are knowledgeable about resources and are willing to assist you. They can also inform you of local seminars or classes on various aspects of writing, recording, and compiling a personal history.

Many online resources relating to the writing of personal and family histories can give you good direction and help. Two particularly helpful sites were brought to my attention by Mr. Curt B. Witcher, manager of the Genealogy Center and Special Collections at the Allen County Public Library in Fort Wayne, Indiana. The first is <ancestry.com/learn/library /article.aspx?article=8270>. This link brings you to *Ancestry Magazine* for July/August 2003, which has excellent articles on writing a family history. The second site is personalhistorians.org. Among other helps, this site provides a link to a comprehensive list of interview questions. There is also an excellent page that suggests ideas for writing a personal history found on the research wiki entitled "Write a Personal History" at https://wiki.familysearch.org/en/Write_a_Personal_History.

YOU ARE UNIQUE

Your personal history is unique. Not another person has experienced life in quite the same way you have. Enjoy your memories; enjoy recalling them, thinking about them, and making them available to your beloved posterity. It's worth the effort, work, and time it will take. Your history will be interesting and sacred to all who have the privilege of reading it.

Notes

1. See Malachi 4:5–6.
2. See D&C 110.
3. Joseph Smith, *Teachings of the Prophet Joseph Smith*, comp. Joseph Fielding Smith (Salt Lake City: Deseret Book Co., 1976), 337.
4. Abraham 2:11.
5. See Malachi 4:1.

12

Now Let Us Rejoice!
The Temple and Family History
Helen K. Warner

Even though it was a busy day at the temple, I had noticed her several times throughout the day. Now she was sitting alone on a couch in the main foyer. As I walked by, I had the impression that I should go and hug her.

My immediate thought was, *What if she is one of those people who doesn't like being hugged?*

Still, the feeling persisted, so I walked over to her and said, "I am the matron of the temple, and I feel that you need a hug today. Would you allow me to hug you?"

"Of course," she replied, and moved over to make room for me to sit beside her.

As I put my arms around her, she began sobbing. I comforted her as I would one of my children and asked, "Is there anything I can do to help?"

Helen K. Warner served as matron of the Toronto Ontario Temple and is currently public affairs director for Ontario, Quebec, and the Atlantic Provinces. She has published in *Regional Studies in Latter-day Saint Church History, Ohio and Upper Canada* and is a contributor to the *Brampton Heritage Times;* she is formerly a researcher and docent for the Museum of Church History and Art, and is currently a researcher for the Brampton Heritage Board.

She told me, "My mother is dying in El Salvador, and I don't have the money to go to her, so I came to spend the day in the temple."

I said, "The Lord has heard your prayers. 'Matron' means 'mother,' and He has sent the mother of the temple to comfort you."

Over and over during my three years as matron of the Toronto Ontario Temple and years as an ordinance worker, I have seen saints come to the temple as a place of refuge. I learned, too, that the temple is a place of joy, of love, and of learning.

PRAYERS FROM BEYOND THE VEIL

As a new matron, I opened my desk and found the notes and files of the matrons who preceded me. A page of quotes by General Authorities on temple work provided words of inspiration. One of the notes read:

> Melvin J. Ballard asked the question: "Why is it that some-times only one of a city or household receives the gospel?" In response to his question, he then shared his revealed insight: "It was made known to me that it is because the righteous dead who have received the gospel in the spirit world are exercising themselves, and in answer to their prayers, elders in the Church are sent to the homes of their posterity so that the gospel might be taught to them, and that descendant is then privileged to do the work for his kindred dead." He also added, "It is with greater intensity that the hearts of the fathers and mothers in the spirit world are turned to their children now in the flesh than that our hearts are turned to them."[1]

The words seared into my soul, and in the years that followed, I often heard stories from patrons and temple workers whose experiences testified of the veracity of Elder Ballard's words. Let me share a few.

Dennis and Olga Cantlon were living in Burlington, Ontario, with their young family when Dennis found it necessary to find a new job as a chartered accountant. The only job available was in Wingham, almost three hours from their home, and they decided that Dennis would take the job, stay there during the week, and come home on weekends. One day at work, a police officer came into the office and asked Dennis if he could speak to one of the employees.

A clerk spoke up and said, "Mr. Cantlon. I know who he is. I'll get him."

The police officer asked in surprise, "Did he say your name was Cantlon?"

Dennis assured him he had heard correctly. The officer explained that he had purchased a house in the area in an estate sale. While cleaning out the basement, he'd found a thick, typewritten manuscript. The inscription inside the cover read, "To save these historic family records for future generations of Cantlons, please bequeath this manuscript copy to a member of the family with the 'Cantlon' surname."

The officer looked in the phone book and asked people in the town, but there were no Cantlons to be found. Today we could find all the Cantlons in North America in minutes on the Internet, but the officer didn't have that option, so he kept the book in case some member of the family showed up.

Dennis arranged to see it, and discovered it was the history of his family back to A.D. 1000. The book was given to him in fulfillment of the wishes of the author, a distant cousin. Soon after, Dennis was offered a job back in Burlington, and he returned to his family, with his family history in tow. It was there that two young Latter-day Saint missionaries knocked on the door and taught the family the gospel with its glorious principles of temple work in which we have the opportunity of binding the generations of our family together.

I thrilled to think that the prayers of generations of the Cantlon family had precipitated a heavenly set of circumstances that took a member of the family to the place where the records were kept, then sent missionaries to a place where the gospel would be accepted and the temple work would be done.

When I shared Elder Melvin J. Ballard's words with Velvet Rollin of the Owen Sound Ward, she told me she could attest that his words were true, for after she was baptized, she asked her relatives if anyone in the family did genealogy. She was directed to e-mail a relative in Holland. This relative and another member of the family had spent their lives researching the history of the family. They sent her forty-one generations of research going back to A.D. 700. The Spirit witnessed that her family was waiting for their work to be done.

Not all families are handed their family history in such dramatic fashion. Some of us have our family histories bequeathed to us by ancestors who have faithfully done the research and temple work for generations in the Church.

One such couple is Meg and Kent Broadbent, originally from Logan, Utah. Their genealogy was done, they were told, so they decided to verify all that had been completed using the vast resources for research now available to us.

As they rechecked each name, they were surprised to discover over two hundred family members who had not been included in the family history. Their ancestors had done their best with the records they had, but records are available now that weren't then. Can you imagine what it would be like to have all your children sealed to you except one? I have always loved reading family histories in the scriptures, because they demonstrate to me that each one of us is important to the Lord. How grateful their ancestors must be that this couple found their forgotten children.

Some of us have the opposite situation, where we simply cannot locate any records for our family. What about those for whom no earthly records exist? President Brigham Young said that "during the millennium, those on the other side will work hand in hand with those in mortality and will furnish the names of the dead which we are unable to obtain through our research, and thus every soul that is entitled to these blessings shall be ferreted out and his work done for him. I fully believe that *many among the dead* . . . are even now engaged in *compiling* records and *arranging information,* if it has not already been done, for this very purpose."[2] Those who have not yet found their own records have the opportunity and blessing of going to the temple and performing the saving ordinances for others.

Even though we sometimes feel we are busier in retirement than we ever were when we were employed, we do have more options for how we will spend our time. There is great joy in devoting time to family research and temple work. Elder Boyd K. Packer has said, "There is no work that I know of that is so immersed in the spirit as this sacred work of preparing names for the temple and the subsequent ordinances. . . . It takes the spirit and the heart."[3]

MOVING FORWARD FROM WHERE YOU ARE

Whether we are new members of the Church or found life too hectic when we were younger to get started, we often feel nudges from the Spirit to begin our family history research. Now is the time to start.

The question is, "How?"

First, identify what you already know about your family. Some experts suggest that you start with a pedigree chart. Put your name on the first line, and enter the names of your parents and grandparents, if possible. Do you know any dates and places where these people were born, married and died? If so, write them down. Do you have any documents (birth, marriage and death certificates, diaries, wills, etc.) that could provide more information? Search for them to find missing data. Do you have living relatives who might have more information? Contact them to see what they know. Record additional information they give you. Now look at your pedigree chart. It will contain some information, but there will likely be areas where information is missing. Once you can see what you know and what you don't know, pray for guidance. Then select one name on your pedigree that you are drawn to.

Now you are ready to begin researching records. The Church has an excellent family history class normally taught during Sunday School. Sign up for the next one or ask that one be started. The Family Search web site offers free lessons for both beginners and experienced researchers. To access them, click on "Free Online Classes." Ward or branch family history consultants can provide help and encouragement. Talk to friends and family members who already have the genealogy bug and let their knowledge and enthusiasm rub off on you.

Acquaint yourself with what has already been done. Get maps to see where your family lived. Learn the names, stories, the details of the lives of your ancestors. This will give you a firmer foundation on which to begin your own research.

Make a plan about where to search for more information about the ancestor you have selected. The staff at your local Family History Center will be helpful to you at this stage. They may have records containing information that you need, or they may help you identify records in the Family History Library in Salt Lake City that can be ordered on microfilm or microfiche. They may introduce you to the wealth of data available on the internet, if you haven't discovered it already. You may also find needed information at local libraries. Government archives can provide official documents of birth, marriage and death. Census records also provide useful information, including names of brothers, sisters and sometimes even extended family members of the person you are researching.

Fill out family group records for each family unit, grouping parents and children together. Search the records you have identified, and record relevant information, taking care to meticulously record the sources of all your information.

Once you have found basic information about the ancestor you were focusing on, select another ancestor whose information is incomplete and repeat the process. Family history research can seem overwhelming and daunting, but when you break it down into doable tasks, you can make significant progress. Remember that family history research is a form of detective work! Sometimes an obscure clue can lead to the desired information. Hone your sleuthing skills and be prepared for amazing breakthroughs, for those on the other side are praying for your success.

I have found that even though we weren't born in the computer generation, and we may not be as quick as our grandchildren, we *can* learn. The Church has made it a priority for research on the Church websites to be user-friendly and accessible to all. With a computer, we can now clear names for temple work from home, but even without computer skills and internet access, we can still do family history by gathering information. Our ward or branch family history consultant can help us prepare the names we have gathered for temple ordinance work. Taking our own names to the temple to perform ordinances for our kindred dead is the sweetest reward of all.

In the past, hundreds or even thousands of descendants of a common ancestor were working on the same line, and the result was duplication of research and ordinances. A solution has been found with new.familysearch.org, a compilation of several previous Church programs. That such a research tool exists is the fulfillment of prophecy.

A Remarkable Prophecy

Almost a hundred years ago, Nephi Anderson, one of the founders of the Genealogical Society of Utah, made a remarkable prediction:

> I see the records of the dead and their histories gathered from every nation under the heaven to one great central library in Zion—the largest and best equipped for its particular work in the world. Branch libraries may be established in the nations, but in Zion will be the records of last resort and final

authority. . . . Then, as temples multiply, and the work enlarges to its ultimate proportions, this Society, or some organization growing out of this Society, will have in its care some elaborate, but perfect system of exact registration and checking, so that the work in the temples may be conducted without confusion or duplication. And so throughout the years, reaching into the Millennium of peace, this work of salvation will go on.[4]

We who have reached retirement age have seen this prophecy fulfilled in our lifetimes. Many of us have seen, or ourselves used, the oversized handwritten or typed family group sheets once sent by mail to Salt Lake City to be processed. Then we moved to 8½ x 11" pages that could be processed for temple work in our local family history centers. We have seen the records of the world microfilmed and stored in the Granite Mountain Records Vault in Salt Lake City, which now holds millions of names and billions of images in 170 languages.

In the 1970s, with the family extraction program, it became possible for members to convert family history information from older temple records, census documents, and other vital records to automated computer files in the FamilySearch computer system.

When the family extraction program started, Boyd and Wanda Christensen, of Layton, Utah, set up two computers in their study and became volunteers. They worked well into their eighties, extracting names at home. Even when the only Church meeting they could physically attend was weekly sacrament meeting, they could each sit for twenty or thirty minutes at a time at their computers, carefully adding to the vast network of names.

Moving forward with Nephi Anderson's prediction: in the last few years, databases created by volunteer indexers have become available to us online in our homes. This is a process where records from around the world are converted into digital images and then stored online. Volunteers can download the images onto their computers, transcribe them, and send them to a searchable, online index which has free access at the FamilySearch web site. With thousands of new names added daily, it's a modern miracle.

We can register to begin and to download the program at http://indexing.familysearch.org. Toronto Temple District Family History Advisors Joe and Monika Brooks suggest that before trying to index, we click on the Help tab and take the tutorial with the lesson on indexing. They stress that it is important to read the instructions for each separate project started and to read "Field Helps" for the first couple of entries.

Another indexer somewhere in the world indexes the same record, and the results are compared. If there is a difference between the two reports, a third person, serving as an arbitrator, determines the correct indexing. The result is a very accurate record.

To address another part of Nephi Anderson's prediction—that there would be a system so temple ordinances would not be duplicated—new.familysearch.org, fills this need. It can be accessed at home on our own computers or at the closest Family History Center. If you don't already have an LDS account, you'll create one to register for the site. For that you'll need your membership number and date of birth. You'll be asked to create a user ID and password. Once you are in the system, you can add ancestors to your family tree and immediately see if temple ordinances have been completed for them and as well as what still needs to be done.

From that site, we can clear names directly for temple work. It's as easy as printing out a Family Ordinance Request form and taking it to the temple, where ordinance cards are printed. If you knew my computer skills, when I say it's easy, it must be!

FAMILIES FOR ETERNITY—TIES THAT BIND

I believe temple work saves the present generation as well as the dead. It draws family members closer together. One of our sweetest experiences in the temple was when Bryan Espenschied, the missionary who had taught my husband's parents the gospel in Ottawa, Ontario, in the 1940s, and who was then in his eighties, acted as the sealer in the Bountiful Temple as two of our married sons and their wives, and a niece and her fiancé, gathered in a sealing room with us to seal Warner family names. Generations of our family were represented, and we were being bound together with each other, with our ancestors, and with the dear sealer who had so blessed our family.

Some families have formed research organizations and rejoice together when each new link in the family chain is found. Others have family temple nights and set aside a certain day each month to meet together in the temple. The joy of one twelve-year-old girl spilled over when she told me that her mother was making a family tree, and she was going to be baptized for every female name on it. Robert and Claudette Labelle travelled from Alberta to the Toronto Temple with family names and invited their children and grandchildren from Ontario to join them at the temple for a family day in the baptistry. We could feel the excitement of the youth and their love for their grandparents as they spent the day together in the House of the Lord.

Another couple found solace and hope by attending the temple weekly when their sixteen-year-old son announced, "You have taught me all my life that we have agency. Now is the time to test whether you really believe it, because I am using my agency to choose not to be part of the Church anymore." No amount of reasoning could convince him otherwise, so they decided to accept his decision and surround him with their love. They attended every function he was involved in, and they took their sorrow and prayers faithfully to the temple each week, where they added his name to the prayer roll and sat, holding hands in the celestial room, silently pleading with the Lord for their son. On his nineteenth birthday, they travelled to his university and took him out to dinner.

He said later, "Even though I knew your hearts were breaking, you allowed me to make my own choice." They saw their son choose a different path a few years later when he came back to full participation in the Church, went on a mission, and had a temple marriage.

One couple was told by their returned missionary son and daughter-in-law, who had been sealed in the temple, that they had decided to leave the Church. Heart-broken, their mother called a friend who had a child who made a similar choice.

She asked her friend, "How do you keep from crying?"

Her friend told her, "I believe the promises."

Calmness came into her soul as she affirmed, "I believe the promises too."

What are the promises? President Brigham Young taught:

> Let the father and mother, who are members of this Church and kingdom, take a righteous course, and strive with all their might never to do a wrong, but to do good all their lives; if they have one child or one hundred children, if they conduct themselves towards them as they should, binding them to the Lord by their faith and prayers, I care not where those children go, they are bound up to their parents by an everlasting tie, and no power of earth or hell can separate them from their parents in eternity; they will return again to the fountain from whence they sprang.[5]

She remembered the words of Orson F. Whitney who said:

> The Prophet Joseph Smith declared—and he never taught more comforting doctrine—that the eternal sealings of faithful parents and the divine promises made to them for valiant service in the Cause of Truth, would save not only themselves, but likewise their posterity. Though some of the sheep may wander, the eye of the Shepherd is upon them, and sooner or later they will feel . . . Divine Providence reaching out after them and

drawing them back to the fold. Either in this life or the life to
come . . . they will suffer for their sins; and may tread a thorny
path; but if it leads them at last, like the penitent Prodigal, to
a loving and forgiving father's heart and home, the painful experience will not have been in vain. Pray for your careless and
disobedient children; hold on to them with your faith. Hope
on, trust on, till you see the salvation of God.

Who are these straying sheep—these wayward sons and
daughters? They are children of the Covenant, heirs to the
promises, and have received, if baptized, the gift of the Holy
Ghost, which makes manifest the things of God. Could all that
go for naught?[6]

With the promise of the binding of temple covenants, we can do as
Heavenly Father does. He loves His children, blesses them, and reaches
out to them even though they, and we ourselves, don't do all we should.

TEMPLE COVENANTS BRING PROTECTION

President Ezra Taft Benson told us that the covenants we make
in the temple bring protection and power. He said, "There is a
power associated with the ordinances of heaven—even the power of
godliness—which can and will thwart the forces of evil if we will be
worthy of those sacred blessings [made in the temple of the Lord]. Our
families will be protected, our children will be safeguarded, as we live
the gospel, visit the temple, and live close to the Lord."[7]

We who live in an increasingly evil world can protect our families
by being in the temple. My sister June and I were both matrons of the
Toronto Ontario Temple, and we feel that our mother, who recently
died just before her 100th birthday, was cared for and loved by the staff
of her nursing home for seventeen years, even when we were far away
on missions, because of our daily service in the temple.

Finding out Who We Really Are

Just as the temple becomes a bridge between those on the other side of the veil and ourselves, we become a bridge between our ancestors and the generations to come. Our children may be able to find the names and dates on the internet, but we know the stories that can bring our families strength and power. Let me illustrate.

My maternal grandparents emigrated from Poland in 1913 because my grandfather knew there was going to be a war in Europe and wanted to protect his family. They came with six children, and three more were born in Canada. When I was young, my grandfather, Daniel Snider, lived upstairs in our home. Often as a child I would sit at his knee and ask him to tell me stories about his youth in Poland.

He told me one story about walking home in the snow when it was bitterly cold. He could hear wolves howling and was so sleepy he wanted to lie down in the snow, but he didn't because his father had warned him that no matter how sleepy he got in the cold, he must keep going and never give up. This and other stories influenced me. When things got hard for me, I remembered to keep going and never give up, just like my grandfather.

Long after my grandfather died, a dear niece called to tell me that she and her husband had just had a baby they were naming Daniel. "How wonderful," I told her. "You've named him after your great-grandfather." She astonished me by telling me she never knew his name was Daniel. In only a few generations, his descendants didn't know his name.

I realized I was the only one in the family who knew the stories, because no one else had asked about them, and it was my job to pass them on. I bought a small photograph album and called it *A Book for Daniel*. On each page I told one of my grandfather's stories. Across from each story, I drew a picture. Even though I'm no artist, I knew that baby Daniel wouldn't be offended by my drawings. I drew a picture of a young boy walking through the snow with wolves on the hillside and his house in the distance with a light in the window. I told him that his great-great grandfather never gave up. On page after page I chronicled the stories and the lessons of faith, sacrifice and love.

The last words in the book are, "I think that Grandfather Daniel would be very happy to know that in 1994, a new great-great grandson was born, and his name is Daniel."

What happened next was a gift to me. Little Daniel's parents read the book to him, and he slept with it under his pillow. Even though we didn't see each other often, there is a special bond between Daniel and me. He is now a teenager, and last year at school, he was asked to bring the three things he valued most to share with his class. I was touched to learn that one of the treasures he brought was *A Book for Daniel*.

If we know stories, we must pass them on to our family. Meg and Kent Broadbent, who found the two hundred family names, are now writing their family histories, which will be given to their posterity for Christmas.

Alex Haley, author of the popular book *Roots*, talked about our need to be connected with our ancestors. He said, "In all of us there is a hunger, marrow-deep, to know our heritage—to know who we are and where we came from."[8] His search took him to Gambia, Africa, where he was able to verify the stories that family members had passed on to him.

As a first-generation Canadian on both sides of my family, I always felt the need to know where I came from in England and Poland, my parents' ancestral homelands. Travelling there, I learned unexpected lessons. In the English village where my father's mother was born, I felt an incredible kinship to the land itself. It seemed that if I stood still, my feet would take root in the ground; if I picked up a piece of earth and held it to my skin, it would become part of my flesh. Our sons had the same experience as we took them to the farmhouse of a pioneer ances-tor of their father's family in Ontario. They didn't talk there; it was a sacred place. If you can, take your children to your family's birthplace and let them feel the connection with their ancestors.

When my husband and I returned to Poland with our teenaged son, we met a distant cousin who was in her late eighties. We had written our family telling them our plans. I had never seen a photograph of my relatives, nor did I expect any to be waiting for us at the hotel in Czestochowa when our tour bus arrived, yet when we walked into the crowded lobby, I saw an elderly woman across the room, and our eyes met. I started to cry, and so did she. We ran into each other's arms.

I told my husband, "I don't know who she is, but I know she's mine."

We discovered that her name was Honorata, and that she was my mother's first cousin. She brought her granddaughter, who knew a little English, to act as our interpreter. As we talked, we learned she had a garden plot in the country that she travelled to by bus. I told her I loved to garden too, and that we would return after the bus tour in a rented car, and I would work in her garden with her. A few weeks later, when we drove to Honorata's garden, I was astonished to discover that it could have been my garden—the same vegetables were laid out in the same way. I planted what my mother, aunts and grandmother planted. Of course. We had the same maternal ancestors. I thought the garden was mine. I learned it was an inheritance from ancestors who had passed their love on to me.

Will it be like that when we cross the veil? Will we be drawn to our ancestors, to that family who has been praying for us? Will we discover that many of our talents and passions were an inheritance we received from them? President Ezra Taft Benson said, "If we only knew it, heavenly hosts are pulling for us—friends in heaven that we cannot now remember who yearn for our victory."[9]

I was once asked, by someone who loves me, how I could spend my time in the temple performing acts they felt were meaningless for people who were dead. I told him, "You are not there, so you can't know what goes on there. I am, and I can tell you that miracles happen in the temple every day." The greatest miracles are the ordinances and the covenants made there and the assurances we have that they are accepted. But there are other tiny miracles that confirm the Lord's connection with this work. Perhaps we're short an ordinance worker, and one shows up from another shift and says, "Do you need me today?"

Recently, one Saturday afternoon, the coordinator asked me to greet a young woman who was coming to be married. As I stood behind the recommend desk waiting for her to arrive, I thought about the years that had passed since I had been matron and often had this privilege. When the young woman entered the temple, her mother was familiar to me. I realized it was the same woman I had hugged years before when her mother was dying in El Salvador. We embraced again and realized it was no coincidence that I was there on that day to remind her that her family on the other side of the veil was rejoicing that another of their descendants had chosen to be sealed in the temple, adding to the long line of faithful family members.

Often husbands and wives, or stake and ward leaders, come to the temple together seeking to learn the Lord's will, and for them the silence in our temples is a singular blessing. When even supermarkets and elevators today are piped with music and we see people with gadgets in their ears as they walk down the street, it is a gift to go to a place where no phones ring, and the Lord can speak to us without interruption. That is one reason we are asked to be quiet in the temple. We don't know why patrons have come, what burdens they are carrying or what answers they are seeking. We would not want to interfere with revelation they are receiving from the Lord. Revelation sought can be for the challenges of our lives and also for understanding the ordinances themselves. I learned that endowment sessions are not passive exercises and that a whole new world opens when we ask ourselves, "What principles am I being taught?" As we seek to understand and ask—

actually being analytical in our spiritual quest—the Lord promises He will make the answers known unto us.[10]

Conclusion

In the dedicatory prayer of the Toronto Ontario Temple, President Gordon B. Hinckley described the importance of temple work and why we do it. "In this Thy house will be administered those ordinances which are eternal, even as thou, our God, art eternal. These ordinances bear witness of the immortality of the human soul. Through them we are made certain that life continues beyond the veil of death. Within this sacred house a great and marvelous work of vicarious service will be performed in behalf of the dead."

As the rooms were dedicated, their purposes were explained: "We dedicate the rooms where other ordinances will be administered, including those in which thy worthy saints will be endowed and given understanding of man's eternal journey and of the reality of life in Thy celestial kingdom. We dedicate the sealing rooms with their sacred altars where 'the fullness of the priesthood' will be exercised to bind in the heavens that which is bound upon the earth."[11] When we understand the purpose of temples, can we doubt that Heavenly Father loves his children?

Temples are places of love and learning. In the temple we feel the love of the Lord and receive instruction from Him. One young man told me he had returned to the temple after several years of inactivity. I asked him why he had left and what brought him back. He thought for a minute and said, "I think I forgot who I was, and what I could become." It is in the temple we are taught those lessons. The temple marks the path to exaltation.

Temple workers reach out with love as representatives of the Lord. As we serve there, we are refined, and our capacity for love is increased. Often as I stood greeting and welcoming patrons, I would pray to feel the love the Lord has for them, and I would be overwhelmed with His love for all who entered. Sealer Bryan Espenschied, now 92 years old, says that he never goes into a sealing room without first seeking the counsel of the Lord. He prays before every live sealing, that he might impart to the young couple what they need to hear, for the Lord knows them better than he does. He says that when you serve as an instrument in the Lord's hands, His Spirit passes through you and enlarges you.

Of all the things we do in retirement, temple work, and the family history that is associated with it, protects us, refines us and brings us closer to our Heavenly home.

Notes

1. Melvin J. Ballard, *Three Degrees of Glory, A Discourse* (Salt Lake City: Magazine Printing Company, 1955), 27.
2. Joseph Fielding Smith, *Doctrines of Salvation*, compiled by Bruce R. McConkie (Salt Lake City: Bookcraft Inc., 1955) 2:120.
3. Boyd K. Packer, Family History Broadcast, Nov. 18, 1999.
4. Nephi Anderson, "Genealogy's Place in the Plan of Salvation," read at the Quarterly Meeting of the Genealogical Society of Utah, Assembly Hall, Salt Lake City, Oct. 6, 1911, *The Utah Genealogical and Historical Magazine*, Jan. 1912, 21–22.
5. John A. Widtsoe, comp., *Discourses of Brigham Young* (Salt Lake City: Deseret Book Co., 1954), 208.
6. Orson F. Whitney, Conference Report, Apr. 1929, 110.
7. Ezra Taft Benson, *Teachings of Ezra Taft Benson* (Salt Lake City: Bookcraft, 1988), 256.
8. Alex Haley, quoted in the 30th anniversary edition of *Roots* (Cambridge, MA: Vanguard Press, 2007), back cover.
9. Ezra Taft Benson, *Ensign*, Dec. 1988, 6.
10. See Matthew 7:7–8.
11. "Dedicatory Prayer, Toronto Ontario Temple," *Church News*, Sept. 1, 1990.

13

THE JOY OF INTIMACY
Douglas E. Brinley

One advantage older couples have over their younger counterparts is time, including time for intimacy. Once past the child-bearing years, retired or semi-retired, older couples have the freedom to enjoy intimate moments together to a greater extent than at any time since they married. The downside of this stage of life, on the other hand, is that half of all sexual problems mature couples face are related to complications associated with age: physical limitations, loss of libido, loss of estrogen/testosterone, arthritis/joint issues, and medications that hamper enjoyable sexual relations.

Nonetheless, older healthy couples continue to report that sexual intimacy is an important element of marital happiness. This union allows both spouses to express emotional and spiritual passion for one another in a way that conveys appreciation, affection, respect, worth, and an ongoing commitment to the marital enterprise. The ability to function as sexual partners is something most couples want to continue as long as health and desire allow.

It is generally believed by the younger set that as individuals age,

BYU professor emeritus Douglas E. Brinley is author or co-author of nine books on marriage, including *Between Husband and Wife: Gospel Perspectives on Marital Intimacy*, *Living a Covenant Marriage*, and *First Comes Love, Then Comes Marriage*. He served as mission president in Texas, Dallas, 1987–1990 and is currently on a CES Mission to BYU Hawaii.

sexual interest wanes. Young people are sure that their parents and grandparents are living celibate lives after the milestone decades of 50, 60, 70, and beyond. While it's true that the frequency of sexual relations tends to drop off as couples age, many of the United States' more than thirty million people sixty and older are sexually active. Like their younger counterparts, mature couples find sexual activity an important cog that keeps their marital gears well-oiled. Intimate episodes help sweethearts maintain feelings of self-worth and self-confidence. The assumption that sexual *interest* automatically declines with age is simply untrue.

This relationship allows older couples to maintain feelings of companionship rather than simply being "roommates." Though health issues may limit the extent and quality of conjugal relations, the sexual attraction husbands and wives feel for each other is an integral part of being married. Interest in each other's physical and emotional wellbeing will always be a high priority for happily married couples.

Of course it is possible to live a meaningful life without sexual relations, as many widows, widowers, and divorcees can attest. But in visiting with older singles, one thing they miss most is the comfort and warmth of another body snuggled up next to their own. Going to bed alone is a sober reminder of the days when marriage and marital intimacy were important elements of their married life.

PURPOSES OF MARITAL INTIMACY

Beyond the fundamental purpose of having children in their early years, marital intimacy has at least four major purposes:

1. A profound expression of mature love
2. Strengthening emotional bonds
3. Enriching spiritual bonds
4. Marital therapy

Expressing Mature Love. Latter-day Saints view sexual relations within marriage as a way by which couples express their love and appreciation for each other while at the same time pledging fidelity and reassuring mutual trust. President Spencer W. Kimball observed: "There is nothing unholy or degrading about sexuality in itself, for by that means men and women join . . . in an expression of love."[1] Parley P. Pratt, an early apostle of the Restoration, stated: "There is not a more pure and holy principle in existence than the affection which glows in the bosom of a virtuous man for his companion."[2]

Strengthening emotional bonds. Happily married couples develop deep and lasting emotional attachments that we label "love." Their years together provide abundant and varied experiences, wherein they establish foundations of mutual trust and confidence in each other. Over the life cycle, husbands and wives learn to cherish each other through experiences such as childbirth and parenting opportunities, home management, children leaving home for missions and marriages, sustaining each other in a variety of church callings, and finally, aging gracefully together as empty nesters.

A temple marriage adds assurances that regardless of what the future brings, this union stands for time and all eternity; death is merely a temporary separation. They understand that intimacy resumes in a spirit-world reunion and a later resurrection restores procreative powers. The Prophet Joseph Smith explained: "Except a man and his wife enter into an everlasting covenant and be married for eternity, while in this probation, by the power and authority of the Holy Priesthood, they will cease to increase when they die; that is they will not have any children after the resurrection. But those who are married by the power and authority of the priesthood in this life [and continue faithful] will continue to increase and have children in the celestial glory."[3]

Enriching spiritual bonds. President Joseph F. Smith declared: "Sexual union is lawful in wedlock, and if participated in with right intent, is honorable and sanctifying."[4] What could be more enriching to a marriage than for both spouses to know that despite living, at the moment, in a telestial world, a spouse's love is a spiritual anchor in a world of uncertainty? This yoking together raises both companions to a greater level of spirituality. Elder Jeffrey R. Holland observed:

> Sexual intimacy is not only a symbolic union between a man and a woman—the uniting of their very souls—but it is also symbolic of a union between mortals and deity, between otherwise ordinary and fallible humans uniting for a rare and special moment. . . . In this latter sense, human intimacy is a sacrament, a very special kind of symbol. I know of virtually *no* other divine privilege so routinely given to us all—women or men, ordained or unordained, Latter-day Saint or non-Latter-day Saint—than the miraculous and majestic power of transmitting life, the unspeakable, unfathomable, unbroken power of procreation.[5]

Marital therapy. Again from Elder Pratt: "The object of the Union of the sexes is . . . mutual comfort and assistance in this world of toil and sorrow."[6]

Elder Boyd K. Packer expressed this thought: "In marriage all of the worthy yearnings of the human soul, all that is physical and emotional and spiritual, can be fulfilled."[7] In this modern era, as couples are separated during the day because of different responsibilities, the physical and emotional reunion at day's end renews their companionship and commitment to each other. It offers a therapeutic time to re-knit hearts together in an unbreakable bond that increases the desire of each to be a more effective spouse.

REMARRIAGE

It is not uncommon when, following death or divorce for one or both partners, a spouse in a new marriage has feelings that he or she is being unfaithful to their former spouse, even committing adultery or having an affair, or breaking a divine covenant. Such feelings of concern typically diminish and disappear in time as the newly formed couple develops their own strengths and unique relationship.

FEMALE CONCERNS

A great fear women have as they age is the possibility of spending their later years alone as a widow. Because women in the United States typically live seven years longer than men, they face a growing lack of potential available husbands.

Menopause and other health issues bring more concerns. Typically as women age, they experience a cessation of menstruation, with an accompanying drop in estrogen blood levels. This drop brings unwanted effects, such as vaginal atrophy, with an accompanying loss of lubrication. Unless attended to, vaginal tissues tend to thin and crack. Bleeding may occur during intercourse, creating a painful experience for the wife. The good news is that women in relatively good health can function sexually—including reaching orgasm—into their later decades.

Even though other bodily changes may occur during aging— shrinking clitoris, flaccid vaginal lips, loss of fatty tissue in the pubic area, a loss of lubrication—these changes should not prevent women from enjoying sexual relations.[8] Actually, wives have a greater capacity for sexual relations than husbands because anatomically, they do not need an erection. Therefore, where pregnancy and childbirth are no longer issues, mature women may enjoy the physical side of intimacy more than they did in earlier years.

Sometimes a hysterectomy—surgical removal of the uterus—is necessary. Historically it was assumed that this procedure brought an end to a woman's enjoyment of sex, but recent studies show such is not always the case. In fact, many women report that their sex life is enhanced, or at least remains unaffected. Perhaps the general rule is that those who enjoyed sexual relations prior to a hysterectomy will still find this relationship satisfying.

Male Concerns

A major fear that men face as they grow older is the fear of impotence, the inability to achieve or maintain an erection sufficient to enjoy sexual intercourse. This worry is especially true where sexual relations have been an ongoing and satisfying part of a husband's marital history. When men hear of the possible effects of impotence, their concern is that they, too, will face a sexless, loveless marriage.

The medical term for impotence is *erectile dysfunction*, usually shortened to ED. The advent of medications such as Viagra, Levitra, and Cialis has brought this topic to light because of their ability to help men overcome erectile dysfunction.

Experiencing ED for the first time can be a setback to a husband's sense of manhood. Out of nowhere, it seems, the first episode takes place. At first, a husband hopes the experience is simply due to overeating, job-related stress, or the lateness of the hour, but as it continues, ED may take on a psychological dimension that becomes self-fulfilling. When a husband worries about his ability to have or sustain an erection, this new stress in his life may cause a continued problem in attempting sexual relations. Unfortunately this onset causes some men to avoid sexual encounters with their wives.[9]

Pharmaceutical aids. In the past, there was little in the way of help for men with serious erectile dysfunction unless they ventured into the arena of vacuum devices, intra-cavernosal injections, penile implants, testosterone injections, or herbal remedies. The good news for men in recent years has been the advent of ED medications that are quite effective for a high percentage of men.[10] These drugs require ingestion about an hour before sexual arousal and intercourse. Viagra and Levitra are usually effective for 4–6 hours, though individual effects may vary. Cialis advertises a thirty-six hour window of effectiveness.[11] With chemical assistance, men are able to retain sexual functioning well into the later decades. A husband's penis does not lose its erectile capacity with age.

A wife related this experience: "In the early years of marriage, my husband was after me all the time. In these later years, however, things have changed, because he has trouble with an erection. At first it was embarrassing for him, but with Viagra, he now has no problem other than spontaneity, as we typically must wait up to an hour or more. But that's easy enough. Now our sex life has resumed, and I think that even though our frequency has dropped off in our later years, I feel like the quality of our relationship is better than ever for me, and I think he agrees."

Premature ejaculation. A second problem affecting men of all ages is premature ejaculation—a climax during the early stages of sexual excitement or soon after the insertion of the penis into the vagina. This frustration is often attached to the excitement phase of sexual arousal, when sexual relations are new or there have been extended periods of abstinence. The excitement of resuming sexual activity for a widower or divorcee may present the same problem in a new marriage. The good news is that this problem generally subsides after a brief period.[12]

OTHER HEALTH ISSUES

Other health factors impinge on sexual activity. Following a heart attack, for example, doctors suggest forgoing sexual relations for six to eight weeks. After an adequate period of recovery, the resumption of sex is recommended when a husband's health reaches a safe level of fitness. This resumption of intimate activity is good for a husband's mental and physical health and wellbeing, while the chance of another heart attack during sexual relations is quite remote.[13]

Strokes, diabetes, joint pain, stress, chronic prostatitis (inflammation of the prostate gland), Peyronie's disease, arthritis, anemia, skeletal issues, back pain, hernias, and even depression, are health issues that may hamper sexual relations.[14] Maintaining a schedule of consistent exercise and nutrition helps husbands maintain sufficient health to allow them to enjoy intimacy far into the golden years.

Prostate Issues. Prostate enlargement seemingly is an inevitable result of aging. The present generation lives longer than earlier counterparts, and a substantial number of men experience this non-cancerous enlargement of the prostate, known as Benign Prostatic Hyperplasia, or BPH. It's detected by urological digital exam, ultra-sound, or an alert triggered by an elevation in PSA test results.[15] A tell-tale sign of BPH is a restriction in the flow of urine. Prescriptions and herbal formulations exist to help shrink the prostate gland, but inasmuch as prostate cancer is always a concern for older men, periodic urological screenings are wise.

Medications that hamper male arousal. Although sickness stifles sexual activity for both genders, a number of medications hamper a man's ability to achieve an erection. Culprits include nonprescription medicines such as cold and/or allergy formulations. Blood-pressure medications are notorious for causing episodes of impotence. Anti-depressive medications also have a negative impact. The general rule is that when ED surfaces, the first step is to examine current medications.[16]

SUGGESTIONS FOR IMPROVING MARITAL INTIMACY IN THE LATER YEARS

The first principle of enjoyable sexual relations remains the same regardless of age: the quality of the marriage. Happily married people enjoy intimate exchanges; unhappily married people find intimacy problematic. Unfortunately some older couples become critical or sarcastic with each other, and such negativism dampens desire for intimate contact. Harping on each other's faults or bringing up negative topics also results in a loss of the Spirit of the Lord and a lessening interest in intimate contact. Retirement seems to be an especially dangerous time, as spouses spend more time together. Intimacy enriches a marriage only when marital satisfaction is high.

It is important for couples to maintain a regimen of gospel practices: prayer together morning and night, attending the temple frequently, dating, relaxing, reading good gospel literature, attending church meetings, fulfilling callings, regular exercise, and taking time for enjoyable talks.

Consistent sexual *and* non-sexual contact is an essential element of happy marriages. If spiritual activities drop off, couples often become critical of each other and can thereby undo years of earlier compatibility. Don't let that happen to your marriage!

ENRICHING MARITAL INTIMACY

Here are six fundamental principles that will assist older couples in enjoying their intimate lives together.

First, sexual fulfillment for both spouses depends on the quality of life in the non-sexual areas of marriage. What happens *outside* the bedroom greatly impacts the quality of marital intimacy. It is difficult for either spouse to give freely and fully to the other without fear of being hurt when the companion is upset, angry, moody, or temperamental.

Sexual activity is a fairly reliable indicator of the quality of a marriage, and its regularity is an important component of marital satisfaction. Dating and courting within marriage should remain life-long activities, where romantic feelings are created and sustained, and which consequently set the stage for heightened sexual interest, pleasure, and "mutual therapy."

Second, no matter how many years a couple has been married, this intimate exchange requires patience, understanding, and a willingness to communicate. Amorous feelings require frequent monitoring by each spouse, especially in the later years, because desires, health issues, energy, and libido are never static. It is important for couples to share personal feelings and preferences and provide feedback on what is pleasurable and enjoyable. Sweethearts must cooperate, assist, and provide gentle, clear instruction to each other concerning what is stimulating and arousing.

As couples age, the complexities of life increase, along with accompanying physical changes that affect individual sexual responses. Sexual interest, or libido, is impacted by hormonal levels and overall health. The good news again is that healthy couples should be able to enjoy sexual intimacy their entire lives.

Third, men typically find sexual activity exciting and pleasurable because their sexual response is generally more predictable than for wives. If a husband has an erection, there is a good probability he will have an ejaculation, a climax. An orgasm for most wives is not as predictable. Still, in some marriages, the wife would like more sexual activity than her husband. (My best guess is that this occurs in about twenty percent of marriages.) The point is that each couple is unique in the way they view intimate contact, and couples must feel free to discuss feelings and preferences so as to arrive at a comfortable schedule and enjoyable methods of arousal.

Charity must always be the ruling virtue in sexual behavior. Older husbands may find it necessary to exercise self-control, restraint, and personal preferences when their wife's stress levels, physical and emotional needs, interests, and state of health demand. On the other hand, husbands feel a greater sense of love and acceptance when wives show an interest in intimate contact. Both spouses have a need to know they are loved. Both spouses should have a sincere desire to please the other, and charity allows either spouse to be comfortable initiating or declining intimacy as health and other situations limit desire or contact.

As husbands age, *andropause* brings a drop in libido. This natural hormonal change (often a loss of testosterone) makes it easier for husbands to adapt to less sexual activity and cope with a spouse's health issues. Here is a typical response from a husband as he reflected on his life's sexual cycle:

> I think when I was first married I thought we would spend most of our lives in bed "making love!" However, that expectation turned out to be pretty lame. At first I thought my wife

didn't love me because she didn't care to be intimate with me as much as I wanted. However, some maturity on my part and a growing concern for her welfare and happiness helped me realize that I needed to be considerate of her, her feelings, and her needs. I have learned how to control my desires while she recognizes intimacy is enjoyable and therapeutic to me—so she is my "therapist," and hopefully, I am hers. There are times when intimacy is not good for her, and I see the need to "bridle my passions." But now as we have both advanced in years, we still find love in each other's embrace. I think sex is the frosting on the cake of our relationship. We love each other now with a love born of experiences together that makes growing old enjoyable. And let me tell you that despite the effects of aging—aching joints, sagging bodies, wrinkled faces and torsos—physical intimacy is still an important part of our relationship in these later years.

Fourth, knowing that husbands and wives are aroused differently is an important reminder for both partners. Kisses, hugs, and gentle, stimulating touches accompanied by genuine verbal and nonverbal expressions of love and tenderness, constitute important elements of sexual arousal for both companions. Most men require less time for sexual arousal, while a wife's interest may be affected by a variety of events that take place during the day. Also, if either spouse is grumpy and irritable, the other is not likely to be an enthusiastic partner.

Fifth, both spouses should be aware of factors that hinder sexual pleasure. For example, if either spouse is unsympathetic to the pressures, worries, or health of the other, or if physical factors such as weight, halitosis, hygiene, or technique interfere, sexual responses are blunted. There will be times when neither spouse feels very sexy. There are no performance standards to be met, no one to please except each other. Both companions can help the other to an arousal of sexual passion that enriches the relationship.

Sixth, the best source of help in learning how to be a lover at any age is the spouse. He or she can best provide feedback and instruction on what constitutes enjoyable and therapeutic sexual stimulation. Sometimes couples are hesitant to share their arousal preferences, because they do not want to appear selfish or offend their partner. Hopefully mature couples, after years of intimate exchanges, have learned enjoyable and therapeutic ways to bless each other. Of course, a sense of humor is always appreciated—neither one embarrassing the other—as physical limitations make sexual activities more difficult. Spouses help each other to an expression of sexual passion that expresses the most tender and charitable feelings.

Just as a good marriage strengthens marital intimacy, satisfactory sexual relations contribute soul-binding emotional strength to the marriage relationship. Emotional and spiritual exchanges of feelings, where admiration and appreciation for each other are ongoing and genuine, make marriage enjoyable.

Couples escape worldly pressures through this unique coupling. Increased feelings of love and a willingness to cooperate and share in the joys and challenges of mortality are powerful blessings that stem from this union.

More specifically, here are three simple reminders to improve marital intimacy:

1. Acquire/use a vocabulary that allows both of you to discuss intimacy comfortably. Though married for decades, some couples fail to talk together about ways to enrich the sexual aspect of marriage. I recall one couple where the husband liked to be intimate in the backyard, the basement, near the fireplace—locations other than the bedroom—while the wife preferred to be in bed with the covers up to her neck. Differences in sexual preferences can be resolved in most cases.

2. Over the years you two have learned what pleases you, what

sensations and stimulation are preferable. It is important that you communicate this information to your companion for your spouse to know how to be a better lover. Many unhappy wives have never taught their husbands how to be their lovers, nor have they communicated what kinds of sexual arousal are pleasurable and preferable. Wives, don't assume your husband is a good mind-reader. Be a kind and gentle instructor as you help him learn how to assist you in reaching a state of arousal that meets your needs. Mutual feedback about sexual responses is important. A husband might ask his wife, "What can I do to make this part of our marriage more comfortable and enjoyable for you? Are you comfortable with our frequency? How about my efforts to meet your needs? What could I do that would make this a better experience for you?"

A wife might ask her husband, "What are your feelings about our intimate relations? Are you comfortable with our frequency? What could I do to make our relationship a better experience for you?"

3. Don't skip the preliminary steps of sexual arousal even though you have been there many times in the past. Important aspects of arousal exist between the first physical touch and the most passionate embrace.

WHAT IF SEXUAL RELATIONS ARE NO LONGER POSSIBLE OR DESIRABLE?

With aging come inevitable accidents, injuries, diseases, pain, and/or other health issues that prevent or hamper conjugal relations. What then? Though health issues may impact the ability to participate in intimate relations as couples age, the need for contact comfort remains. Both verbal and nonverbal expressions of endearment, love, and appreciation are almost always available to spouses, regardless of health issues. Such couples find enjoyment in simple intimate physical touches.

The onset of sexual health issues may be particularly distressing, because so much of self-identity, sense of worth and wholeness is associated with satisfactory sexual relations. The sense of failure, loss of self-esteem, and the realization that one is growing older, generally accompany the onset of these health issues. It is important to remember that this issue is inevitable with age, and for husbands, often a treatable matter. Frequent communication and a compassionate consideration of each other's needs may help lessen the sense of loss until a mutually acceptable accommodation is achieved.

It is important that in instances where one spouse is incapable of sexual functioning that the other is accepting of such limitations. Doctrinally, Latter-day Saints understand that death and resurrection restore sexual function. That knowledge helps couples learn to deal with the physical limitations in their later years. For one spouse to make disparaging comments to the other, who suffers from physical limitations or an inability to be a sexual partner, however, is unkind and insensitive.

Even in the most difficult of health situations, couples can communicate passion, love, loyalty, appreciation, and an understanding of what causes a cessation of sexual relations. Perhaps there is no greater manifestation of true love—or pure love—than when one spouse must be a caregiver for their eternal companion, their sweetheart, the parent of their children. This may preclude sexual activity. Inasmuch as both spouses have sacrificed for each other over their years together, their mature love makes it easier to deal with any limitations. If caretaking becomes too difficult or physically demanding—Alzheimer's, elimination functions, mental faculties, etc.—it may be necessary for other family members to become involved to provide some type of assisted-living situation.

In summary, there is no reason why couples cannot continue to convey love and appreciation verbally and physically through embraces, strokes, massages, kisses, manual stimulation, cuddling, holding hands, etc., depending on spousal desire and preference. Such caring for each other in the twilight years will be forever appreciated by the spouse.[17]

Conclusion

President Howard W. Hunter, in a masterful address to the priesthood brethren of the Church, counseled husbands, "Be faithful in your marriage covenants in thought, word, and deed. Pornography, flirtations, and unwholesome fantasies erode one's character and strike at the foundation of a happy marriage. Unity and trust within a marriage are thereby destroyed. . . . Tenderness and respect—never selfishness—must be the guiding principles in the intimate relationship between husband and wife. Each partner must be considerate and sensitive to the other's needs and desires. Any domineering, indecent, or uncontrolled behavior in the intimate relationship between husband and wife is condemned by the Lord."[18]

Marital relations were designed by the Lord to be an enriching element of marriage, not a chore, duty or a pressured performance. It *is* a way whereby two covenant people express their love and appreciation for each other in a sacred, profound, and marriage-enhancing way. Marriage is enriched when couples take time to enjoy each other spiritually, emotionally, and physically. This sacred union then becomes a sanctifying experience for both, regardless of age or health issues.

Notes

1. *The Teachings of Spencer W. Kimball,* ed. Edward L. Kimball (Salt Lake City: Bookcraft, 1982), 311.
2. Parker P. Robinson, *The Writings of Parley Parker Pratt* (Salt Lake City: Deseret News Press, 1952), 52.
3. Joseph Smith, *History of the Church* (Salt Lake City: Deseret Book Co., 1991), 5:391.
4. Bruce R. McConkie, *Mormon Doctrine,* 2nd ed. (Salt Lake City: Bookcraft, 1966), 309.
5. "Of Souls, Symbols, and Sacraments," BYU 1987–88 Devotional and Fireside Speeches (Brigham Young University Press, 1988), 82–83.
6. Parley P. Pratt, *Key to the Science of Theology/A Voice of Warning* (Salt Lake City: Deseret Book Co., 1965), 164.
7. Boyd K. Packer, "Marriage," *Ensign,* May 1981, 15.

8. There have been mixed findings in recent years concerning hormone replacement therapy. Because of its ever-changing state, it is suggested that women consult regularly with a gynecologist on the most recent research findings.

9. Though the initial episode of impotence may be temporary, continued difficulty may indicate the need for a physical exam to determine if there are underlying causes (i.e. diabetes, stress, low testosterone, marital unhappiness, restricted blood flow, or offending medications). Also, wives may not understand their husband's avoidance behavior and could wonder if their husbands no longer love them. This can lead to trips to hairdressers and surgeons in an effort to enhance their beauty when the real problem is a husband who is embarrassed by his inability to engage in sexual relations.

10. With the new century came drugs to help men deal with impotence. Viagra, Levitra, and Cialis—three ED medications—are readily available by prescription. They belong to a family of drugs called phosphodiesterase-5 inhibitors, which inhibit the action of a PDE-5 enzyme, which leads to a relaxation of the smooth muscles in the penis itself. This relaxation allows blood to engorge the penis. The value of these medications is that they treat impotence, whether psychologically or physically based. These medications must not be used by men who require nitrates (especially nitroglycerin) for heart issues, because of a lowering of blood pressure that could cause serious heart issues.

11. Cialis has developed a smaller dosage to be taken daily.

12. With access to the internet, it is easy to obtain information on the "squeeze technique," a method of resolving premature ejaculation.

13. If heart abnormalities require the use of nitrates, specifically nitroglycerin, men are not to use ED medications because of the possibility of a lowering of blood pressure to unsafe levels.

14. Peyronie's disease affects the curvature of the penis due to a thickening of the walls of the blood vessels within the penis itself to such an extent that it can be difficult to have sexual intercourse.

15. The Prostate-Specific Antigen test is administered periodically. Generally, a safe level is anywhere under four. If the number is greater than four, and the test results indicate a rise each time the test is taken, check with a urologist.

16. For a list of drugs that negatively impact a man's or woman's libido, see Douglas E. Brinley, *Between Husband & Wife: Gospel Perspectives on Marital Intimacy,* Appendix A (American Fork, UT: Covenant Communications, 2008).

17. Masturbation is self-stimulation. Husbands and wives may stimulate and caress each other in a variety of ways that are appropriate and acceptable to each other without offending the Spirit of the Lord.

18. "Being a Righteous Husband and Father," *Ensign,* Nov. 1994, 51.

14

COPING WITH ILLNESS

Dr. James O. Mason and Joseph E. Davis

AGING IS PART OF LIFE'S ADVENTURE

Today, in greater numbers than ever before, older people enjoy good health and live longer, with positive expectations, achieving the goal of successful aging. Most seniors are able to live happily and independently while gradually declining at an individual pace. A reasonably healthy older person has a robust, durable physical body and a mind quite capable of coping with life's challenges well into very old age. The senior years, for many, are truly golden years.

What is aging? Old stereotypes of aging must be replaced with more up-to-date information that is rapidly changing. People are living longer. They retire later, and then many launch new businesses or contribute significantly through fulfilling church and community service projects. Today's seniors remain productive and active. The best evidence available today suggests that most seniors have surprisingly

---

A former member of the Seventy, Dr. James O. Mason was formerly US Assistant Secretary for Health (including Head of US Public Health Services and Acting Surgeon General), has served as president and CEO of Avalon HealthCare, and is the author or associate editor of two books. A four-star admiral, he is an expert in public health and the control of communicable disease

Joseph E. Davis is chief financial officer of Rideaucrest Home, a municipal seniors' residence, in Kingston, Ontario, has published in environmental reclamation of brownfields, and is president of the Kingston Ontario District.

little "inevitable decline" in function with age. Many seniors maintain excellent function into their eighties and nineties.[1] Critical organ activity, such as cardiac output, muscle strength, kidney function, brain metabolism and mental performance, is maintained (or regained) in persons eighty or more years of age.[2] Indeed, only a relatively few changes associated with aging may be considered inevitable.

In addition to the gradual changes that affect everyone, a person may have a genetically determined predisposition to certain diseases that manifest themselves in the course of aging, such as rheumatoid arthritis, Alzheimer's disease, or an increased risk of osteoporosis after menopause. Most of the changes associated with aging, however, are better called *extrinsic*, in that they are the result of lifestyle choices. The lifestyle-related decline may well be avoidable or at least modifiable.[3]

SLOWING DECLINE AND PROLONGING LIFE IN OLD AGE

Our attitude and activities during our senior years should be centered upon living life to the fullest. Healthy aging consists of doing what we can do and enjoying what we are doing—not in counting days, but in making each remaining day count. The future is now. The goal is to live healthy and well, compressing serious disease and disability into the smallest possible period at the end of life.

The number of years allotted to a person is not too important in the eternal scheme of things. Quality of life is more important than duration. Extensive scientific literature indicates that behavioral factors are strongly associated with the risk of disability and death in old age. Smoking, too little physical activity, and obesity are associated with increased risk of earlier disability and death. All kinds of fad diets and nostrums are aggressively promoted with claims to check the current epidemic of obesity and chronic disease. However, the Lord's practical rules tell it all: eat abundantly of fruits, vegetables and whole grains. The "flesh also of beasts and of the fowl of the air, I, the Lord, have ordained for the use of man with thanksgiving; nevertheless they are to be used sparingly."[4] Older persons who follow those simple instructions don't need expensive supplements or fad diets.

Look carefully at claims made for a wide range of untested and often expensive products that supposedly cure disease, prevent cancer, and help us lose weight or cleanse our colon. Aging is often looked upon as a disease to be avoided or cured like cancer. If we have that perspective, as soon as we reach some magical age, whether it is fifty or seventy-five years, the goal becomes to reverse aging. The internet provides an enormous number of sites that deal with aging, including more than 67,000 that focus on reversing the aging process.[5] Mankind seeks after some magic elixir or potent cream to remove wrinkles, or a fountain of youth that will keep us from growing old. Too many seniors die with a medicine cabinet full of prescriptions and over-the-counter nostrums. Every prescribed or over-the-counter medication or supplement has potentially adverse reactions associated with it. Keep the number of substances you use to a minimum. However, when a specific medicine is prescribed to treat a diagnosed disease or problem such as hypertension, thyroid deficiency or diabetes, it is very important that we take it exactly as directed.

COMMON DISABLING CONDITIONS DURING OLD AGE

What are the most common disabling chronic conditions in older persons? The table below summarizes the results of United States survey data reported to the National Center for Health Statistics for older individuals. Senior citizens living in other developed countries have similar disabling conditions.

Percentage of People Age 65 and Over
Who Reported Having Selected
Chronic Conditions, 2005–2006[6]

Condition	Percent Reporting
Hypertension	Men, 52; Women, 54
Arthritis	Men, 43; Women, 54
Heart Disease	Men, 37; Women, 26
Any Cancer	Men, 24; Women, 19
Diabetes	Men, 19; Women, 17
Chronic Bronchitis & Emphysema	Men, 11; Women, 10
Asthma	Men, 10; Women, 12
Stroke	Men, 10; Women, 8

Other chronic conditions mentioned in the survey include visual and hearing impairment, dementia, varicose veins, and orthopedic problems, including hip fracture. Almost none of these common conditions, with the exception of heart disease, is immediately life-threatening. Most persons over sixty-five experience at least one chronic illness. Six percent of seniors over the age of sixty-five, and forty percent over the age of eighty-five, need some help with activities of daily living.[7]

What are the most common causes of death in older persons? The table below summarizes data on causes of death reported to the National Center for Health Statistics by individuals age sixty-five and older living in the United States.

Leading Cause of Death for Persons
Ages 65 and Older by Age, 2005[8]

Condition	Percent
Heart Disease	29.7
Cancer	21.7
Stroke	6.9
Chronic Respiratory Disease	6.3
Alzheimer's Disease	4.0
Diabetes	3.1
Influenza and Pneumonia	3.1
Unintentional Injury	2.0
All Other	23.3

The percent of deaths for persons over age 65 caused by heart disease and stroke are declining as a result of early diagnosis and treatment of hypertension and reduced use of tobacco. Cancer as a cause of death has declined because fewer people smoke and more are being screened for breast, colon and cervical cancers. Alzheimer's disease and diabetes are contributing to a higher percentage of deaths in older people today.

AGING IN PLACE

Aging in place, or maintaining independence by remaining in one's home as long as possible, is the lifestyle most individuals prefer as they get older. A great variety of support systems are helpful in assisting older people experiencing normal aging to remain at home longer instead of shifting to an institutional setting.

The extended family is the first and most important pillar to aging in place. Community and private support systems also can aid the elderly to live independently in their own homes for as long as they confidently and comfortably can. Electronic monitors and other assistive technologies are being developed to enhance safety by monitoring the wellbeing of elderly people in their homes. Even a person taking their prescription medications can be remotely monitored through devices no more intrusive than a wristwatch. Home renovation can replace outdoor steps with ramps and modify bathrooms and kitchens, which may be necessary to support aging in place.[9]

These options, although available to all of us, are often considered too late. As we age, we often fail to acknowledge our declining physical and mental capacities. As a result, we overestimate our ability to continue on our own. Couples, working together, may try to compensate for each other's disabilities, which may put them at increased risk of staying in their home longer than is safe.

Nearly all of us have had direct experience or know of instances of major family disruption over the issue of institutional care for a reluctant ailing elderly person, when homecare is no longer feasible. Be sure your family knows your wishes before the onset of a disability. When there are no other options, a plan will already be in place. But be warned—this may not make it easier for our loved ones to direct us to a safer environment when the critical moment comes. At the very least, however, they will know that our decisions were made when we were more capable of making them.

CARE AT HOME

The following are examples of community support services available to assist the elderly to remain in their homes:

Meals on Wheels. This organization delivers meals to individuals at home who are unable to purchase or prepare their own. Many programs deliver a nutritionally balanced hot meal at lunch and/or dinnertime. Many of the meal recipients are the elderly who, without meal help, would need to be placed in an assisted-living facility or nursing home. The volunteers preparing and delivering the meals frequently are able-bodied elderly.

Homecare. This is help provided in the older person's home by family, friends and/or professional caregivers. The term "homecare" is used to distinguish non-medical care or services provided by those who are not nurses, doctors, or other licensed medical personnel. These services include help with daily tasks such as meal preparation, medication reminders, laundry, light housekeeping, errands, shopping and transportation. Estimates based on interviews with non-institutionalized elderly indicate that about seven percent of adults age 65 or older need help for activities of daily living, such as bathing, dressing, using the toilet, eating, and walking. Those 85 or older are at least six times more likely to need assistance.

Home Healthcare. This term refers to care provided in the home by licensed personnel, such as doctor and nurse visits, psychological assessment, wound care, medication counseling, pain management, disease education, and management and rehabilitation (therapy).

Rehabilitative Services. These help disabled and handicapped older persons regain and maintain as much independence and function as possible. Success in rehabilitation depends upon the disabled individual's desire for an improved quality of life. A number of professional disciplines may be called upon to help in the home with rehabilitation. These include physical, speech, and occupational therapy, and social work and psychology. A team approach that includes key family members works best.

INSTITUTIONAL CARE

Assisted-living Facilities. Homes or institutions provide assistance with activities of daily living. Many seniors in an assisted-living facility are unable to manage at home even with the help of home health services. Assisted living helps maintain independence and dignity by using trained staff to assist residents by supervising the taking of medications and by providing personal care services. Trained staff is onsite around the clock to provide needed help. Registered nurses (RNs) and licensed practical nurses (LPNs) are available by phone or e-mail 24 hours a day. Assisted-living facilities usually do not have special medical monitoring equipment.

Staff perform household chores, change sheets, do laundry, and cook and serve food. Some homes even have a beauty parlor on site. Grocery service is also often available. People who live in assisted-living facilities often have a self-contained private apartment with a bedroom, bathroom and small kitchen. Individual living spaces in some facilities may resemble a dormitory or hotel with private or semi-private sleeping areas and a shared bathroom. The typical assisted-living resident is an older man, woman, or married couple who do not require the intensive care of a nursing home.

Skilled Nursing Facilities (SNF). In the United States, a nursing home is a place of residence for people who require constant nursing care and need help with activities of daily living. Nursing-home residents include the elderly and younger adults with physical or mental disabilities. Most skilled nursing facilities in the United States are certified to participate in government Medicare and Medicaid programs. Medicare is a federal program primarily for seniors who contributed to Social Security and Medicare while they were employed. Medicare patients may remain in a skilled nursing facility for up to 100 days. Skilled Nursing Facilities also accept patients who have long-term care insurance or who pay using their own funds. Medicaid is a federal program that provides healthcare and related services to those who are financially needy. Those eligible for Medicaid may be aged or disabled. Each state defines "poverty" and, therefore, Medicaid eligibility.

Skilled Nursing Facilities that participate in Medicare and/or Medicaid are required to have registered nurses or licensed practical nurses and certified nurse assistants on duty 24 hours a day. Special medical monitoring equipment is available. Services provided in nursing homes include administration of medications, nursing care, mental-health counseling and physical, occupational and speech therapy. Many patients in Skilled Nursing Facilities have been discharged from an acute care hospital after a stroke or hip or knee replacement surgery. These patients return to their homes after receiving needed physical, occupational or speech therapy. In 2005, there were 16,094 licensed nursing homes in the U.S.[10]

Long-term Care Facilities. In Canada, these facilities provide 24-hour care by professional staff to perform daily tasks for their residents. The range of care is dependent upon the need of the resident. Long-term care facilities are licensed by the provinces and are governed to ensure that at least a minimum standard of care is provided to residents. For example, in Ontario, the Long Term Care Act, 2007, places its emphasis on restorative care, not just providing basic care. *Restorative care* means that staff works with and encourages residents to become as independent as possible, given their individual state and desire to do so. Each care plan is individually developed with the resident and family members to achieve as much independence as possible. This can provide a more meaningful life experience during a time that will likely be the last days before death.

A common question asked is, "When will I know that I need long-term care verses home care, or some form of assisted living?" Often a single health incident will prompt this type of question, or our family may find us in a compromised state in our home. It becomes a question of whether we are able, even with the help of our families and community services, to care for ourselves in our homes. Most healthcare agencies have some form of an assessment tool that would be used to determine this. The assessment tool will look at questions such as the following:

1. Are you able to administer your medications correctly?
2. Are you able to manage your hygiene appropriately?
3. Are you managing your finances competently?

4.   Are there incidents of falls or other mishaps that put you at risk?

5.   Does your diet give you the proper nutrition?

An actual assessment is much longer and more detailed than this brief list.

LOVE CAN TURN TO PERCEIVED HATE

Be aware of extreme conditions that may come with age. This applies to both the persons aging and their family/care providers. As a result of diminished capacity, our relationships may become strained with our spouse, our children and other family members. As our health declines, we may become insecure, worried, frightened and uncertain of ourselves. We may feel we are in less control of our lives and more dependent on those around us. Our reactions to these situations may be as varied as the individuals involved.

For example, some parents become so nasty and hateful towards their children that when they are critically ill, the children feel guilty about some of the feelings they may have harbored toward a parent or parents. The children may also feel that Mom or Dad does not or did not love them. Of course, this is not true, but these are often the feelings that are felt upon a parent's death.

It is thus important to live life to the fullest and let our family know of our love for them. Build strong family ties now by creating family moments and events that can be remembered when needed most—when health issues become difficult. Build up spiritual and emotional reserves and a cheerful positive attitude so that, when faced with new challenges, we don't become embittered seniors. Remember, the purpose of this book is to help us prepare for our golden years. The earlier we deal with later-life health issues, the more likely we will get the kind of care we want at a time when we may not be able to give appropriate directions ourselves. This will make the process much easier for those who will need to give directions on our behalf.

SPECIAL PROBLEMS OF OLDER AGE

Urinary Incontinence

Urinary incontinence, the inability to control urination, is often associated with aging. It can also happen to persons of any age. Urinary incontinence may be due to:

- Weak or overactive bladder muscles.
- Damage to nerves that control the bladder in diseases like multiple sclerosis or Parkinson's disease.
- Loss of bladder control due to stroke, seizure or unconsciousness.
- Inability to get to the bathroom on time because of arthritis or other impairment.
- Blockage in men from an enlarged prostate gland.

During urination, muscles at the bladder outlet relax, and bladder muscles constrict to allow urine to pass out through the urethra. Incontinence results when these muscles tighten or relax without warning. Seeing a doctor about incontinence is the first step in treatment.

There are several types of urinary incontinence:

- *Stress incontinence* occurs when urine leaks as pressure is put on the bladder, such as during coughing, sneezing or laughing.
- *Urge incontinence* occurs when a person has a sudden urge to urinate and can't wait long enough to get to a toilet. This may occur in a person with diabetes, Alzheimer's disease, stroke or multiple sclerosis.
- *Overflow incontinence* occurs when small amounts of urine leak from a full bladder. A man may have trouble emptying his bladder if an enlarged prostate gland is blocking the urethra. Diabetes and spinal cord injury may also cause this problem.
- *Functional incontinence* occurs in older persons who have normal control, but have difficulty getting to the bathroom at all because of arthritis or other disorders that make it hard to move.

Several approaches have been developed to help people suffering with urinary incontinence. The choice depends on the diagnosis and the individual's circumstances. Bladder control training, behavioral management, and medications and medical devices are the most common treatments. Incontinence can often be cured, and when a treatment is not fully successful, behavioral management will help the individual feel more comfortable and confident. For more information consult:

NIH SeniorHealth (www.nihseniorhealth.gov), a senior-friendly website from the National Institute on Aging and the National Medical Library of Medicine.

> National Association for Continence:
> P.O. Box 1019
> Charleston, SC 29402–1019
> 800-252-5390 (toll-free)
> www.nafc.org

COPING WITH ALZHEIMER'S DISEASE

Forgetting where you put things happens with younger as well as older persons. When we're tired or distracted, everyone experiences episodes of forgetfulness. The aging brain, however, does undergo structural and biochemical changes. It shrinks by as much as 5–10 percent as the years pass.[11] Older people, however, don't become less intelligent as a result of these changes. Abundant intellectual capacity remains even though there is less gray matter. As one cell dies, another that has been relatively dormant or unused steps up to take its place. Mental abilities, such as adding to one's vocabulary, continue in many people into their eighties.[12] Memory loss occurs at different rates for different people, since both genetic and environmental factors affect our minds as we age.

Dementia is a term applied to a number of conditions that affect nearly ten percent of the over 65 population. Dementia is usually a progressive condition that affects memory and ability to reason. It begins insidiously and often progresses until it severely affects a person's ability to complete routine daily tasks or remember recent conversations and experiences. Expressing ideas and opinions becomes troublesome, and patients with dementia often struggle to find the right word. Tasks involving several steps become increasingly difficult. Persons suffering with dementia may become passive or irritable.

Alzheimer's disease is the most common form of dementia, and is not a component of normal aging. The disease is named after the German physician Dr. Alois Alzheimer, who, in 1906, first noticed the telltale plaques and tangles that strangle neurons in areas of the brain that control thought, memory and language. Mental decline in Alzheimer's disease appears to be largely related to altered connections among brain cells. It is estimated that 5.1 million Americans are living with Alzheimer's disease.[13] It affects about 13 percent of people over age 65, and nearly half of those over age 85 have symptoms. Today, while other age-related deaths are decreasing, the number of deaths attributed directly to Alzheimer's disease is steadily rising. Alzheimer's disease attacks memory and the very core of one's identity. It ushers in a sad pattern of regression that mirrors child development in reverse. Nancy Reagan described Alzheimer's disease as "the long goodbye." There is no cure for Alzheimer's disease, and the underlying cause is, unfortunately, still unknown.

The Alzheimer's Association recommends that, to prevent or delay onset of the disease, we keep our brains active every day. Some activities they recommend we do include:

- Stay curious and involved—commit to lifetime learning.
- Keep informed about current events.
- Read books, newspapers, and magazines. Watching television or listening to the radio does not provide the brain stimulation that reading does.

- Work crosswords, brain teasers and other puzzles.
- Tinker with cars, computers or small appliances.
- Play board and card games.
- Design and plant a garden or container arrangement.
- Write letters and emails.

Medicines for Alzheimer's disease patients are intended to help sufferers maintain mental function and slow the disease's progression. They appear to work by regulating neurotransmitters (chemicals that transmit messages between neurons). They may help maintain thinking, memory and speaking skills, and they help with certain behavioral problems. These medicines all have underlying adverse side effects, they don't change the underlying disease, and they may help for only a few months.[14]

Caring for a person with Alzheimer's disease has physical, emotional, and financial costs. Developing a strong support network of family and friends is an important way caregivers can help themselves handle the stresses of caring for a loved one with Alzheimer's disease. Some Alzheimer's caregivers have found that participating in a support group is helpful. Support networks can be especially valuable when caregivers face the difficult decision of whether and when to place a loved one in an assisted-living facility or nursing home.[15] For more information about at-home caregiving, see "Caring for a Person with Alzheimer's Disease: Your Easy-to-Use Guide from the National Institute on Aging" at www.nia.nih.gov/Alzheimers/Publications/CaringAD.

To learn about support groups, services, research centers, research studies, and publications about Alzheimer's disease, contact:

Alzheimer's Disease Education and Referral (ADEAR) Center
P.O. Box 8250
Silver Spring, MD 20907–8250
1-800-438-4380 (toll-free)
www.nia.nih.gov/Alzheimers

Coping with Terminal Illness

The late Elder Neal A. Maxwell, who was intimately familiar with terminal illness, observed, "One's life . . . is brevity compared to eternity—like being dropped off by a parent for a day at school. But what a day!"[16]

We are all going to die. We are often reluctant, however, to acknowledge our vulnerability. We fret about not being in total control. Intellectually, as a result of our faith in revealed religion, we recognize that it is just as important to die as it is to be born. Both are necessary experiences. We know that through the Savior's Atonement, death is the passageway to immortality and eternal life. The Lord has promised, "And it shall come to pass that those that die in me shall not taste of death, for it shall be sweet unto them."[17]

Terminal illness is a medical term used to describe an active disease that cannot be cured and is reasonably expected to result in death. A person is considered to be terminally ill when life expectancy is estimated to be six months or less, assuming that the disease runs its normal course. The six-month standard is arbitrary, and estimates of longevity are inexact. Consequently, though a given person may properly be considered terminal, it is not a guarantee that he or she will die within six months.

Most individuals with a terminal illness prefer to think of themselves as a person living with a life-threatening condition, rather than as a dying patient. Some are frightened when they learn that mortality will soon end for them. Fear is a natural and common reaction. Others become angry when they learn that they are not going to recover. In the past, grief and grieving were thought to be best when the outcome was acceptance. Today, the most desirable outcome is thought to be accommodation. You do not need to accept that you're going to die before you thought you would. Accommodation includes living as fully as possible while adapting and accommodating to the illness that will soon end life.

Denial is a common coping mechanism. The thought of impending death for some is too overwhelming. Denial allows a person to let reality in a little at a time. Fears of pain, becoming a burden to others, and losing control of bodily functions are more than many initially can cope with. Talk to family or caregivers about these concerns. Sometimes the dying person may wish to spare a spouse or children from these concerns. Family members should let their terminally ill loved one know that they are prepared to talk about these matters. Some terminally ill persons are more comfortable expressing their fears to a doctor, nurse or bishop.

More and more older persons are finding their terminal illness to be a pleasant, meaningful period of their lives. This is especially true when there is close family support. Dying at home, surrounded by loved ones, is the ideal situation. Loved ones let the terminally ill person know they are willing to listen as they sit at the patient's bedside. Then, it's time to talk about feelings and listen to concerns. Family and friends should understand that just being there is comforting and supportive, even though they feel they are not doing anything. A terminal illness should not be a time of severe or uncontrollable pain. The possibility of addiction to pain medication is of no concern during a terminal illness.

The question often comes up about how far we should go in holding on to a dying loved one. Modern medicine can maintain life almost indefinitely by using various artificial support systems such as a ventilator and intravenous feeding. Obviously one would never consider taking life.

Faith in eternal life after physical death assists a person and his/her loved ones in making wise decisions about the use of artificial life-support systems to prolong life when usual means of treating disease and restoring function are exhausted. The Church Handbook of Instructions contains this advice about prolonging life: "When severe illness strikes, Church members should exercise faith in the Lord and

seek competent medical assistance. However, when dying becomes inevitable, death should be looked upon as a blessing and a purposeful
part of an eternal existence. Members should not feel obligated to extend mortal life by means that are unreasonable. These judgments are
best made by family members after receiving wise and competent medical advice and seeking divine guidance through fasting and prayer."[18]

Hospice Care

Hospice care—palliative care for the terminally ill—focuses on
assisting and supporting the terminally ill person and his or her family.
Hospice care has rapidly expanded throughout the United Kingdom,
Canada and the United States, becoming a significant part of the
modern healthcare system. In 2008, 1.45 million individuals and their
families in the United States received hospice care. Hospice includes
pharmaceuticals, medical equipment and twenty-four hour/seven
days a week access to care for the terminally ill patient. It also includes
support for family members following a death. Medicare, Medicaid and
many private insurance plans in the United States cover hospice care.
Most hospice care is delivered at home; however, it is also available to
people in home-like hospice residences, nursing homes, assisted-living
facilities, veterans' facilities, hospitals, and prisons. More than one-third
of dying Americans currently utilize hospice service.[19]

For more information contact:

National Hospice and Palliative Care Organization
1731 King Street, Suite 100
Alexandria, Virginia 22314
703/837-1500 (phone)
703/837-1233 (fax)
http://www.nhpco.org/templates/1/homepage.cfm

International Association Hospice and Palliative Care
5535 Memorial Dr. Suite F - PMB 509
Houston, TX 77007 USA
Ph +1 (936) 321-9846
Toll Free +1 (866) 374-2472
Fax +1 (713) 880-2948
http://www.hospicecare.com/contact.htm

CONCLUSION

Aging is a process that begins with birth and continues as long as
we live. Our genes and the environment influence how we age. We
control our environment to some extent through the choices we make
daily. Avoiding harmful behaviors and substances, eating wisely, and
getting sufficient physical activity enhance quality of life and longevity.
Healthy aging consists of doing what we can do and enjoying what we
are doing. Most old people prefer to age in place by remaining at home
as long as possible. But preparation needs to be made for a time when
that may no longer be feasible, and some form of institutional care may
be required. Gathering information on available options, and frank discussions with family members before the onset of debilitating illness,
paves the way for a better transition. Alzheimer's disease, incontinence
and terminal illness are conditions that may occur in old age. Family
and church support and community services exist to assist the elderly
and their loved ones in coping with these conditions.

Notes

1. See R. P. Abeles, H. C. Gift & M. G. Ory Eds., *Aging and Quality of Life* (New
   York: Springer Publishing Co., 1994), ix–xi.
2. See H. Creary, & S. I. Rapoport, "The Aging Human Brain," *Annals of
   Neurology* (1985), 17:2–10.
3. See T. F. Williams, "Rehabilitation in Old Age," in R. P. Abeles, H. G. Gift
   & M. G. Ory Eds., *Aging and Quality of Life* (New York: Springer Publishing
   Co., 1994), 121–30.

4. D&C 89:12.
5. See "All About Life Challenges," http://www.allaboutlifechallenges.org/reverse-aging.htm (consulted May 17, 2010).
6. See Centers for Disease Control and Prevention, National Center for Health Statistics, National Health Interview Survey, http://www.silverbook.org/browse.php?id=21# (consulted May 17, 2010).
7. See Karen Henderson, http://www.fpajournal.org/BetweentheIssues/LastMonth/Articles/FacingtheTruthAboutLossofIndependenceHowAdvisorsCa/ (consulted May 17, 2010).
8. See Y. Gorina, D. Hoyert, H. Lentzner, and M. Goulding, "Trends in Causes of Death Among Older Persons in the United States," *Aging Trends,* No 6. (Hyattsville, Maryland: National Center for Health Statistics, 2006).
9. See "AIP Remodeling," http://aginginplace.com/home-modification (consulted May 17, 2010).
10. See "Nursing Home," http://en.wikopedia.org/wiki/Nursing (consulted May 17, 2010).
11. See "The Aging Brain," *The USC Health Magazine,* http://www.usc.edu/hsc/info/pr/hmm/01spring/brain.html (consulted May 17, 2010).
12. See "Writers at Eighty and Ninety," http://www.squidoo.com/writers_80_90 (consulted May 17, 2010).
13. See "What Is Alzheimer's," http://www.alz.org/alzheimers_disease_what_is_alzheimers.asp (consulted May 17, 2010).
14. See "Alzheimer's Disease Fact Sheet," National Institute on Aging, http://www.nia.nih.gov/Alzheimers/Publications/adfact.htm (consulted May 17, 2010).
15. See "Caring for a Person with Alzheimer's Disease: Your Easy to Use Guide from the National Institute on Aging," 75, http://www.nia.nih.gov/NR/rdonlyres/6A0E9F3C-E429-4F03-818E-D1B60235D5F8/0/100711_LoRes2.pdf (consulted May 17, 2010).
16. Neal A. Maxwell, "Premortality, a Glorious Reality," *Ensign,* Nov. 1985, 17.
17. D&C 42:46.
18. *General Handbook of Instructions,* The Church of Jesus Christ of Latter-day Saints, 11–6 (Salt Lake City, 1959).
19. "While Hospice Care Is Growing, Not All Have Access," *Forbes* (Apr. 10, 2008).

15

Dealing with Disabilities
Dr. Richard O. Cowan

We are surrounded by remarkable technologies that make our lives more comfortable, convenient, and fulfilling. Computers make mathematical calculations or locate items in volumes of data much more rapidly and accurately than we can. Various mechanical devices can exert much more physical force than we can muster unaided. Still, our physical bodies are more wonderful than all these manmade creations. Scientists have yet to develop a single mechanism that can reproduce all the varied functions of the human body. Unfortunately, like these machines, our bodies have parts that will eventually wear out.

We often hear that the so-called golden years are lined with lead, and that "aging is not for sissies." Yet we must separate in our thinking the eternal spirit, which does not age, from our mortal tabernacle, which does.

We can empathize with Elder LeGrand Richards, who lived to be one of the oldest Apostles in our dispensation. When asked how he was, he would respond, "I'm just fine if you don't want the details. This eye doesn't see [pointing to his right eye], this ear doesn't hear

Richard O. Cowan, author or co-author of eight books, has taught in the BYU Religion faculty since 1961. While earning his doctorate at Stanford University, he was one of four visually impaired students to be honored by President Dwight D. Eisenhower at the White House in 1959. He is a patriarch in his Provo stake. He and his wife, Dawn, are the parents of six children and twenty-two grandchildren.

[pointing to his left ear], and I've lost all my hair [pointing to his head]. LeGrand Richards is doing fine, but this house which I inhabit is a little decrepit."[1] Doctors had to remove one of his big toes due to gangrene. Later he lost more of his lower leg as the condition worsened. At age 96, he expressed gratitude for his new artificial foot, saying, "It doesn't have a sore on it, and it doesn't hurt."[2]

"Since the Lord decided to take me a part at a time," he quipped, "I'm glad He didn't start at the other end."[3]

The onset of disabilities poses its particular challenges. During most of our adult lives, we feel completely in charge. We assume that we can accomplish just about anything if we are only willing to put forth sufficient effort. When a part of our physical body begins to fail, however, the bubble of our unbridled optimism is burst; we may feel a great sense of loss, the erosion of our self-esteem, and a decline in our sense of usefulness and therefore of value to others. We may also feel discouragement, despondency and despair; we may even feel betrayed.

These responses to our changing physical condition certainly are not the most productive. At the April 2010 general conference, Elder Donald L. Hallstrom of the Presidency of the Seventy declared, "No matter the size of the issue, how we respond can reset the course of our life."[4]

Speaking later in the same conference, Elder James B. Martino, also of the Seventy, expressed a similar thought: "Each of us will face trials and tests, and . . . it is how we react to those difficulties that will determine our success and happiness."[5]

As disabilities come, we must accept them as a normal aspect of life and perhaps even as blessings. Denying that they exist will not help. We must be determined to meet them and to live successfully despite them.

My own life has taught me this lesson. Since birth, I have lived with the challenge of vision loss. In my younger years, I had enough sight to recognize landmarks and therefore get around on my own. I never could see well enough to read print without effort or be able to recognize people visually. Of course I could never drive a car. Still, I developed means to cope and have enjoyed a long and successful career as a professor of religion at Brigham Young University.

In more recent years, my eyesight declined to the point that all remaining vision was gone. Furthermore, my hearing has become worse, and yet other disabilities have arisen. Attitudes developed over the years, and strategies I have learned more recently, are now helping me meet these new challenges.

A Variety of Challenges

Not all disabilities present the same kind of challenges. For example, one of the main byproducts of blindness is the inability to access the vast reservoirs of information available through the printed word. Deafness, on the other hand, disrupts interpersonal relationships because of the inability to hear the spoken word. The weakening of our muscles may impair our mobility and our ability to perform a variety of daily tasks. The inability to remember names or to think of a needed term may cause frustration. Still, there are proven means to cope with all these challenges.

Help is available. For example, the Church publishes the scriptures in Braille and makes the *Ensign* and selected lesson materials available in recorded form for those with visual disabilities. (To obtain these materials, call Church headquarters at 1-800-453-3860 and ask for extension 22477.) The Church also convened a conference of hard of hearing and deaf members and those who work with them to develop a standardized set of signs to stand for uniquely Latter-day Saint terms or concepts. The scriptures and selected other items are available in American Sign Language (ASL) on DVD. (For information about these materials and services, as well as practical suggestions for dealing with a wide variety of disabilities, go to Disabilities.LDS.org.) The Church also designs new buildings and, where possible, retrofits older structures to be wheelchair accessible. With such help, we can move forward, but the ultimate responsibility for coping rests with each one of us individually.

THE RIGHT ATTITUDE

A positive attitude is crucial. Not the disabilities themselves, but our response to them determines what lasting impact they will have in our lives. As a common poem states:

> One ship sails East,
> And another West,
> By the self-same winds that blow,
> 'Tis the set of the sails
> And not the gales,
> That tells the way we go.[6]

Let me use an experience of my own to illustrate. A few years ago, I had to walk across the Brigham Young University campus at night. I had always suffered from night blindness—being able to see lights but not what they were illuminating. I decided to regard this potentially difficult experience as an adventure. I imagined what it might have been like in the early days of aviation, when night flying was still a challenge. Just as those early pilots flew from one mountain-top beacon to another, I walked from one landmark to another—a fan I could hear on the side of the science building, a prominent overhead light, a rough spot in the pavement, etc., until I reached my destination.

Giving support to our positive attitude is faith in the Lord Jesus Christ. I have several favorite scriptures that show what He can do to provide the help we need. Through the ancient prophet Moroni, the Lord declared: "I give unto men weakness that they may be humble; and my grace is sufficient for all men that humble themselves before me; for if they humble themselves before me, and have faith in me, then will I make weak things become strong unto them."[7] Humbling oneself is not an acknowledgement of inferiority, but rather it is recognition of one's true relationship to others. In this case it is an acknowledgement of our dependence on the Savior.

Through His Atonement, Jesus suffered for more than just the sins of mankind. Decades before the Savior's mortal ministry, Alma taught: "He will take upon him death, that he may loose the bands of death which bind his people; and he will take upon him their infirmities, that his bowels may be filled with mercy, according to the flesh, that he may know according to the flesh how to succor his people according to their infirmities."[8]

A sinner does all he can through repentance to overcome his sins; he then turns to the Lord to blot out the stains caused by the sins and ultimately to become holy through sanctification by the baptism of fire. In like manner, we should do all we can to face our disabilities, recognizing that we do need help from the Master, and then allowing Him to fulfill His promise to transform weaknesses into strengths.

Our faith in an ultimate, glorious resurrection assures us that disabilities are only temporary. Alma declared: "Every limb and joint shall be restored to its body; yea, even a hair of the head shall not be lost; but all things shall be restored to their proper and perfect frame."[9]

In latter-day revelation, the Lord counseled: "Be thou humble; and the Lord thy God shall lead thee by the hand, and give thee answer to thy prayers."[10] In another revelation, the Lord described the intimate relationship He would like to have with each of us: "I will go before your face. I will be on your right hand and on your left, and my Spirit shall be in your hearts, and mine angels round about you, to bear you up."[11]

DEVELOPING NEEDED SKILLS

With a positive attitude in place, the next step is to acknowledge that the disability exists and then move forward to confront its challenges head-on. If the problem is impaired hearing, don't be embarrassed to use a hearing aid if it will help. Likewise, confidently use a cane or a walker if stability is the issue. One can develop specific skills to deal with particular disabilities. Most localities have a government department of vocational rehabilitation with trained personnel who can help you learn these skills and who can recommend devices that might help.

I learned this lesson slowly. Through junior high, I was in a program called Sight-Saving. The emphasis was on learning to use whatever useful vision we had. By the time I entered high school, my vision had deteriorated to the point that I was transferred out of this program and was assigned to learn Braille. I resented this, as I associated Braille with a helpless blind man on the street with a tin cup begging for alms. I learned Braille, but didn't use it.

During the early months of my Spanish-speaking mission in Texas and New Mexico, however, I had a change of attitude. I realized that I had been stupid to not take advantage of a skill that could be very helpful. I bought a small three-ring binder and began listing scriptural references in Braille on separate pages according to topics we missionaries frequently used. One day, as we went to an appointment with an investigator, we found his minister waiting for us. A vigorous discussion followed. I had my hand inconspicuously inside my notebook on my lap. When the minister demanded some scriptural references to support the point we were making, I gave him quite a few.

He was impressed. "My, Elder Cowan, you know the scriptures well."

"Yes, reverend," I responded with a touch of humor, "I have them at my fingertips." Afterwards, I decided to make even more use of Braille, so I studied a more advanced system, something like shorthand. Over the years, this has been extremely useful, as I have taught classes, given "Know Your Religion" talks, or just made notes for myself.

I had a similar experience a number of years later as my vision continued to decline. I had resisted using a white cane. Once again, I reached the point that I concluded a cane really could provide help.

I decided I'd rather the cane hit an obstacle instead of my running into it with my nose. With training from a rehabilitation counselor, I learned how to use the cane as a means to detect the boundaries of sidewalks or hallways, to locate stairs, and to be aware of my surroundings in other ways. Furthermore, I came to appreciate that the cane immediately signaled to others that I might need help or simply to a clear path ahead.

We can develop necessary abilities to compensate for our particular disability. A common belief is that blind people are always blessed with superior hearing. This is not true. I have learned that I need to pay more attention to what I hear. As a student, this meant listening to teachers or to what someone was reading to me. This undoubtedly helped me develop my memory. I also used my hearing to develop even subtle clues for getting around. For example, you can "hear" when you pass by an object such as an automobile parked next to a sidewalk. Similarly, after walking down a hallway, you can "hear" when you emerge into a large room. As an experiment, you can drop silverware onto a hard surface and notice the distinctive sounds made by knives, forks, and spoons.

As a university professor, I needed to be innovative in the classroom. I have used humor in telling students about my disability: "Using Braille has an advantage; I never have to look down at my notes." I instruct them not to raise their hands, but just speak up when they wish to make a comment or ask a question. To compensate for my inability to write on the board, I have developed numerous visual aids; as technology has developed, these have gone from large posters to overhead transparencies to PowerPoint. I have felt the need to be more thoroughly prepared than most teachers so students would think of me as a good teacher rather than just as the one with a disability.

GENERAL WELLBEING

Along with learning specific skills, it is important to maintain general wellbeing. Dealing with a disability is easier if one is generally well.

Therefore, exercise, eat nutritious foods, and get enough sleep. There is no sense in adding more problems we have the power to avoid. Also, a generally healthy body will have the additional strength and specific capacities we need to respond to our particular challenges.

Emotional wellbeing is also important. Studies have shown that those with wholesome relationships with family or friends are in a better position to cope.

Spiritual strength is especially important. Even as we take steps to provide a balanced diet for our physical bodies, we should also provide food for our spirit. This can include regularly searching the scriptures, studying and heeding the teachings of living prophets, providing quiet times when we can be responsive to the still, small voice of the Spirit, singing hymns and memorizing those that have special meaning for us, participating in worship and other church activities, pondering one's patriarchal blessing, and attending the temple.

Balancing Independence and Dependence

As we deal with our disabilities, we should realize that we don't have to do everything alone. A popular song has affirmed that "no man is an island." While I have wanted to be as independent as possible despite my blindness, there are tasks I just cannot do. I can't drive a car, for example. There are other tasks that I can do, but can be accomplished much more easily with the help of others. I recruit students in class to help hand back completed assignments. This chapter is being written on a talking computer, using Braille notes I have made with research assistants helping me review source materials. I have learned that there needs to be a healthy balance between independence and appropriate dependence.

At home, I have also worked out strategies to accomplish daily tasks. If I will be wearing a particular suit coat or pair of slacks again right away, I hang them at the left end of the closet. Putting things away in the right place so they can be found again is important to everybody, but essential for me. I am grateful for a loving wife who continues to play a major role in what I am able to accomplish. I therefore like to take on extra tasks, such as washing dishes, to show my appreciation for the many things she does for me.

No matter how well-organized we may think we are, and despite our best efforts, there are occasions when we do not experience success. But we should not give up. President Thomas S. Monson, then a member of the Quorum of the Twelve Apostles, encouraged: "Our task is to become our best selves. One of God's greatest gifts to us is the joy of trying again, for no failure ever need be final."[12]

As Winston Churchill counseled his countrymen during Britain's darkest hour at the outbreak of World War II, "Never, never, never, never give up!"

FRUITS OF PERSEVERING

So, what can we learn from this experience? Even disabilities can be opportunities. Just as a man may develop his arm muscles by lifting weights, overcoming the pull of gravity, we can strengthen our character by overcoming difficulties. After Joseph Smith had languished in Liberty Jail for over three months, he pleaded with the Lord to understand the reason for, and meaning of, his suffering.

In response, the Master gave this assurance: "Thine adversity and thine afflictions shall be but a small moment; and then, if thou endure it well, God shall exalt thee on high."[13] Later, the Lord reviewed many of the trials Joseph and his family had experienced and then affirmed: "Know thou, my son, that all these things shall give thee experience, and shall be for thy good."[14]

Yes, even our disabilities can be for our good. The key is how we respond to them. Another latter-day revelation counsels, "Search diligently, pray always, and be believing, and all things shall work together for your good, if ye walk uprightly and remember [your covenants]."[15] Moroni was right. Weaknesses can be opportunities, and if humbly we turn in faith to the Lord for help, He will transform our weaknesses into strengths.[16]

"There is a divine purpose in the adversities we encounter every day," testified President James E. Faust. "They prepare, they purge, they purify, and thus they bless."[17]

Furthermore, there is a feeling of satisfaction and joy that comes from accomplishment. This is heightened when we realize that the accomplishment has been achieved by overcoming challenges, despite our disabilities.

Elder Neal A. Maxwell affirmed, "Men's and nations' finest hour consists of those moments when extraordinary challenge is met by extraordinary response."[18] Still, we must not forget those who have helped us along the way. Particularly we owe a debt of gratitude to the Savior, who has given us our very lives and whose power sustains and blesses us day after day. We have been commanded to "thank the Lord thy God"[19] for everything, being warned that we offend Him when we "confess not his hand in all things."[20]

As we face our disabilities, we can rejoice in the assurance expressed by the Angel Gabriel to Mary, "For with God nothing shall be impossible."[21]

Notes

 1. Conversation with LeGrand Richards (grandson of Elder LeGrand Richards), June 12, 2010.
 2. "Elder Richards' Artificial Foot 'Doesn't Have Sores, Doesn't Hurt,'" *Church News,* June 26, 1982, 10.
 3. Richards' interview.
 4. Donald L. Hallstrom, "Turn to the Lord," *Ensign,* May 2010, 80.
 5. James B. Martino, "All Things Work Together for Good," *Ensign,* May 2010, 101.
 6. Ella Wheeler Wilcox, "'Tis the Set of the Sail."
 7. Ether 12:27.
 8. Alma 7:12; compare D&C 62:1.
 9. Alma 40:23.
10. D&C 112:10.

11. D&C 84:88.
12. Thomas S. Monson, "Pres. Monson: 'No Failure Ever Need Be Final,'" *Church News*, July 17, 1999, 14.
13. D&C 121:7–8.
14. D&C 122:7.
15. D&C 90:24.
16. Ether 12:27.
17. James E. Faust, "The Refiner's Fire," *Ensign*, May 1979, 53.
18. Neal A. Maxwell, *"Behold, I Say Unto You, I Cannot Say the Smallest Part Which I Feel"* (Salt Lake City: Deseret Book Co., 1973), 75.
19. D&C 59:7.
20. D&C 59:21.
21. Luke 1:37.

16

Coping with Bereavement
Barbara R. Wheeler

If we live long enough, we'll experience grief and sorrow. And we don't have to live long at all to find out what we know about helping others through their bereavement. Sorrow and grief are impossible to escape in life, and the longer the life, the greater the number of sorrows as well as joys. In our later years, we are typically faced with several losses, many of which trigger a multi-faceted grief response. These losses may include income, family moving away, and loss of health caused by illness, or the natural aging process. At some point, we'll lose our parents and some friends. Some of us will lose our children, siblings, spouses and even pets. Loss can also come in the form of regrets memorialized in Robert Frost's "The Road Not Taken."

These life events are like photographs—moments preserved in time. We cannot change them even if we wished to. When they are experienced, they may present mild challenges and temporary sadness or devastating chaos in our personal world. Any and all reactions are normal and necessary to experience so that we can move on with our lives. Just like shaping and, perhaps, adjusting our response to the

Barbara R. Wheeler holds masters and doctorate degrees in social work. She is currently a professor emeritus of Brigham Young University, where she served on the faculty and was the director of the School of Social Work. Dr. Wheeler has authored many publications and has practiced social work in various settings, including independent clinical practice for over twenty-five years.

snapshots we revisit, the events of our lives take on the meanings we assign and re-assign to them. Whether or not our later years are fulfilling will depend on the significance we ultimately find in these crucial life experiences.

Grief is a common and normal reaction for all of us, yet each person will respond in his or her own way. Normalcy, with the recognition of differences among people, is a paradox: *we are all uniquely the same.*

KNOWING OF — AND KNOWING

"You don't have to be a cow to know what milk is."

I always used this example to assure my graduate students that you can help people with all kinds of problems, even though you may not have experienced them yourself. They were preparing to become clinical social workers, and they wondered how much the cow knew about milk that they didn't know.

Was I telling them the truth? Could they lead clients through territory they had never known firsthand? Looking back, I question my instruction; I wonder about the effectiveness of my therapeutic interventions with people struggling with grief. While there is wisdom in the cow and milk illustration, the cow does have a significant inside perspective that we as consumers, or even farmers, cannot quite have.

The uncertainty about my past approach to directly helping clients, as well as students and friends, came when I was faced with the traumatic loss of my husband four years ago. That's when I realized my inside perspective had been missing. I now have a deeper understanding of bereavement and am better able to help others understand and cope with loss.

What would I do differently as a social worker, teacher or friend when, metaphorically, I don't know what the cow knows? I would tell those I work with that there are ways to compensate for incomplete life experience, but that it demands a lot of them. They must learn to go to the depths of empathy, using their partial understanding of loss to grasp a profound loss. I would tell them they must go to the far distances of knowledge about loss and the grieving process. This applies to both sides of the equation—those bereaved and those extending guidance or comfort to the bereaved. And perhaps this applies to you, the reader, who has turned to this chapter possibly because the time is right.

COMMON REACTIONS TO GRIEF

Understanding ourselves and others who are grieving is the most important step in coping with bereavement. Grief can be on a continuum. Current psychological literature differentiates between grief that is *normal, complicated* and *traumatic.*

Complicated grief includes the normal mourning process that leads to chronic or ongoing mourning.

Traumatic grief overlaps with Post-traumatic Stress Disorder (PTSD) and involves reactions to traumatic aspects of the actual death. Both *complicated* and *traumatic* grief are rare and may require professional help.

Grief is not depression. Although some of the symptoms are similar, depression is something quite different. Depression can involve chemical and physical changes and is ongoing, without periods of relief. There is a feeling of pervasive heaviness and worthlessness without a focused cause and may be accompanied by suicidal thoughts. Daily tasks seem insurmountable. These characteristics are not common in grief, where a deep, poignant sadness—most often focused on loss—prevails.

Along with grief, loss typically creates enormous stress. On the life-stress scale, for example, death of a spouse has been rated as the most stressful of life experiences. Death of a close family member is fifth out of twenty-one studied variables.[1] Is it any wonder that typical stress reactions such as shock, anxiety, overwhelming sadness, guilt, anger, and loss of control are often the same as our responses to the death of a loved one?

It is not uncommon for fear to coexist with stress and loss. The same fear-related response can be present in grief. When C.S. Lewis wrote of his wife's death, he began by saying, "No one ever told me that grief felt so like fear. I am not afraid, but the sensation is like being afraid."[2] Lewis also told of a feeling similar to being mildly drunk and a sort of invisible blanket between the world and him—finding it hard to take in what anyone says. Similarly, others report "brain fog," describing an inability to think well or focus their attention for any significant length of time. One woman reported feeling "like something was broken inside of me."

The list of possible grief reactions is not all-inclusive, and some people may not be affected by many of the common grief responses but find their pain carving different paths. The feelings of grief do not necessarily occur in stages, as we originally thought. They are messy, complicated, and complex.[3] They ebb and flow just as do waves from the ocean.

People with whom I have talked after losing a loved one consistently report the phenomenon of the waves. They agree that there will be times when they are able to feel somewhat in control of their thoughts, feelings, and behaviors as they go about daily activities. Then, without any warning, a wave of emotion crashes over them. Suddenly they are out of control.

"It's as though grief has a life of its own," one widow observed. I didn't know about grief waves until I experienced them myself. Unexpected tears would appear—at the least convenient times, of course. One such time was when I ventured to the bank to change our account into my name. As the teller asked if she could help me, I felt my lip quiver and the tears distort my vision. I'm not sure if I was more caught off-guard or embarrassed. Grief was in charge. I was not.

A close friend of mine told me that after losing her husband, the reality of suddenly being single seemed like a bad dream. The nightmare kept rolling along without her consent. She had no idea how to manage her life as a single. She had only been aware of society's need to categorize and stereotype single people and did not know what it was like to be on the inside—to be one of "them."

Gordon B. Hinckley voiced his displeasure at the term, calling the *single* label a *badge* we pin on people. "I wish we would not do that," he said. "You are individuals, men and women, sons and daughters of God, not a mass of 'look-alikes' or 'do-alikes.'"[4]

It will be weeks, months and possibly years before my friend reinvents herself as she attempts to find her way in this new, unchosen life. Holding on to her individuality, while circumventing the *single* label, may help.

Reactions of friends, acquaintances, and yes, even family members of the bereaved, can be a bit of an enigma. Many seem to not know how to react, what to say or how to help. People are well-meaning and want to make it better. Their efforts come out of love and caring for their loved one's pain.

They think that the sooner the grieved one can get over it and move on, the better. As a result, the subject of grief and loss is sidestepped, along with other attempts to keep the grief-stricken friend or relative from thinking about or feeling the pain or its source. The problem is, there is no way others will have the power to obliterate or divert heartbreaking thoughts or feelings. Grief is a road through a tunnel that one must personally travel, and, in keeping with the common formula, the only way to get over it is to go *through* it. It seems society gives the grief-stricken only a few weeks or months to get back to normal—to their old self. That will never happen. Rather, a new normal, a new reality, a new life is waiting . . . in time. But "new" is not quite accurate; it is unmistakably "different."

The result of our culture's responses to those grieving often shuts down any chance for the bereaved to express themselves—a serious consequence. Not allowing or inviting talk about their grief and loss actually interferes with healing.

COPING STRATEGIES

Just as there are many different ways to react while mourning, there are many and varied ways of coping. As days and weeks pass, each person will stock their own "cope chest" with strategies that seem to work. It is essential that each of us accepts our own way of coping. There is no one correct or best way. One size does not fit all.

I have found in my personal and professional experience that people who accept their own way of filling their *cope chests* still find solace in talking with others who know sorrow firsthand. It helps to not feel so alone, or as one woman said, "not crazy." There is solace in sharing coping methods. The benefits are two-fold. Sharing allows the release of thoughts and feelings, while also discovering what others find helpful in their journeys through the sorrow.

After talking with a number of people and comparing their experiences with mine, I've discovered similarities in answer to "What do I do now?" We all draw on any strength we have to reach for self-preserving lifelines to help us survive from hour to hour, day to day. Some appear to us without our reaching. When that happens, survival becomes overwhelmingly poignant.

Lifelines take different forms. Those reported most often, not in any special order, are: talking, religious faith, family, and friends.

Most people experiencing bereavement need to express their thoughts and feelings. This is an integral part of moving forward. Within a few days after my mother suffered a stroke and could not speak, my father suddenly died. After sufficient time for my mother's healing, my sister and I went to the hospital to explain why her husband was no longer visiting her. Upon hearing the news, she began to cry, but because she was aphasic, she couldn't express her grief in words.

So many questions unasked—so many feelings and thoughts unspoken. The tears told the story of her internal torment. I said a silent prayer, asking for comfort and peace for my mother. I opened my eyes in time to see her gasp a deep, staccato breath then close her eyes in sleep. This is a story of expressing grief, but also of reaffirming the power of prayer.

The blessings of prayer are known to all who seek and use it. It is in times of the deepest emotional pain, like these, that communication with God takes on an even more significant meaning. The Lord, of course, knows our pain and sorrow. We do not even need to explain it in our conversations with Him. He has promised: "I will not leave you comfortless: I will come to you."[5] I was profoundly moved by His care, love, understanding and His ever-presence—comforting and guiding me. It deepened and strengthened my relationship with Him. That intimate relationship still exists four years after losing my husband, Jim. Others have reported a similar tender mercy in their lives after losing their loved one.

Is there more than prayer and one's deeper relationship with the Lord that makes the difference in healing from loss and grief? There certainly does not need to be more. Many studies have explored the relationship between spiritual beliefs and the resolution of bereavement. The findings seem to be consistent: the strength of spiritual belief is an important predictor to the healing process. People who profess stronger spiritual beliefs seem to resolve their grief more rapidly and completely after the death of a close person than do people with no spiritual beliefs.[6] Surprising? Probably not to those who have testimonies of the gospel of Jesus Christ directing their lives.

One study found that people who were more religious were more likely to be satisfied with their lives and to have made positive changes, such as rethinking the way they wanted to live their lives as a result of a death. One's faith seems to serve as a meaningful system within which the bereaved can reframe their loss, find coping resources, and discover areas of personal growth.[7]

People have talked of their beliefs in eternal life—that they will be reunited with their loved one—as "sustaining" them through their bereavement. Death ends a mortal life—not a relationship. To know that your spouse or child does live—that death is not the end of existence— brings unimaginable peace.

President Gordon B. Hinckley, speaking at the funeral of Elder Joseph B. Wirthlin's wife, Elisa, promised those who lose the ones they love "that in the quiet of the night a still, unheard voice whispers peace to our soul: 'All is well.'"[8]

Although some family members and friends may seem unsure of how to respond, they most often encircle those who are trying to cope with the loss of a loved one. The impulse to reach out with love, caring, and support is strong. One widower admitted that "without my family, neighbors, and friends, I'm not sure I would have survived. I really did not want to go on living after my wife died. Others were a life force that pulled me toward wanting to live." Perhaps an attempt to help, even though unsure of the "how," is better than no attempt at all.

In our later years, some are fortunate enough to have adult children. Several people have been pleasantly surprised by the reactions of their children to death. I confess, I was not quite sure how my children, as wonderful as they are, would react in the days following the loss of their father. None of us had ever experienced anything like this before. Their dad's death was as over-powering for them as it was for me. They were magnificent in their grief, reaching out to support me and helping me carry out all the details needing attention. Others have reported a similar experience. Whether or not this would be the same in all cases, I don't know, but the point is that children can be powerful lifelines in coping with grief.

Looking into the *cope chests* of those attempting to survive their losses, I found several additional strategies that are commonly used.

These attempts represent a reach for life-affirming support, such as physical exercise. When the mind and spirit are strained with sorrow or emotional pain, experts advise exercising the body. Brisk walking is an excellent way to increase endorphins in our system, helping to re-establish a sense of wellbeing. Endorphins are the body's natural feel-good chemicals, and when they are released through exercise, our mood is boosted naturally.

"Keeping busy" is another reported helpful coping method, as is music. I found that if I turned to music, it had to be uplifting. It was way too soon for sentimental love songs. It still is. I am hopeful that will change in time.

These are only examples of lifelines that have worked for me and others. It is worth repeating that each person must discover what works for him or her while coping with the death of a loved one. The thing to remember is *there is no one best way*. Others may help, but the emphasis here is on our personal responsibility to manage our pain. Each of us is ultimately in charge of our own healing (as much as I don't especially like to accept that).

There is hope. Things do change. Healing and progress are possible. Progress occurs at different rates for different people. Intense crying spells that come weeks and months after a death may confuse us. In fact, the sadness often gets worse before it gets better. It's ironic that "worse" can represent progress, but it can. Right after the loss, when we are frozen in time, survival is all we can expect of ourselves. Moving forward will later become the goal.

Elder Wirthlin reminds us of better days ahead: "It was a Friday filled with devastating, consuming sorrow that gnawed at the souls of those who loved and honored the Son of God . . . The despair did not linger because on Sunday, the resurrected Lord burst the bonds of death. . . . Each of us will have our Fridays. . . . No matter our desperation, no matter our grief, Sunday will come."[9]

No Sunday skips its turn, but our Sunday will not be the same as others we have known. We will recreate ourselves—our lives. Author Rachel Naomi Remen affirmed, "Every great loss demands that we choose life again."[10]

There is potential energy in pain. The source of our pain is the source of our power. The pain does not really go away, but we learn to live with it—to walk around it. The memories that were painful months and years ago will become the sweet soul food that sustains us for the rest of our lives. Our loved ones are in our heart, and, as the song goes, "[our] heart will go on."

We are in the process of looking back while moving forward. One day, we will realize that we, in fact, were changed by that extraordinarily painful loss. We may notice that we rely on the Lord more and trust Him more. Our faith has deepened. Our commitment to helping others has increased. We have learned we really are strong and can do hard things.

I learned the definition of a "problem." Being overscheduled or having a messy house, a broken light switch or arthritis—those are not problems. They are inconveniences. I now know what a problem is. Thank goodness there are few.

WIDOWHOOD AND SECOND MARRIAGES

Why do I feel so alone when currently, in the United States and other Western nations, one-third of the population sixty-five and over is widowed? It is estimated that in Western societies half of all marriages end with the death of the husband, and one-fifth will end with the wife's death.

Being a widow was not my plan. I did not sign on for this life. A widow, I felt, was someone who needed the local scout troop to cut her grass. I could not see myself as the poor widow down the street. Throughout our fifty-one years together, Jim and I envisioned the best scenario—we would go together. No one would be left to face loneliness and all the household chores. Neither of us would be left to orchestrate the family dynamics alone. Will this strange life ever feel like it fits? After four years, I'm still not there. It feels like I never will be, yet I know I am approaching some kind of "there."

Some seniors may be emphatic about never remarrying. Some may start out that way, but down the road, have a change of heart. Others may wish to remarry, especially when they feel they are ready. There is no best formula for either men or women.

Certainly, there is much to be said for companionship. We can love again, even in our later years. We can love again without diminishing our first love. Sharing a life together—traveling, family times, hobbies, interests and service—are meaningful, satisfying ways to live out our lives. We are never too old for new adventures.

Much could be, and has been, written about remarriage after a spouse's death. These few pages will not accommodate extensive discussion. However, some pertinent considerations are worth noting here.

How soon should a marriage take place after a spouse is deceased? That's not a question that needs to be asked—no magic number exists. There are mileposts for assessing readiness. For example, marrying out of loneliness is a red flag. Learning to accept and manage aloneness comes first. Readiness is also dependent upon moving past grief and possible guilt, which can be attached to different regrets or fears. Guilt often comes with the desire to remarry, yet fearing that doing so would feel like infidelity. Guilt can also exist when one regrets past conflicts and unkind words with the deceased.

Adversity introduces us to ourselves. Readiness depends on whether life's experience and gift of wisdom have given us self-knowledge and confidence. Knowing who we are gives us security as well as much-needed patience to accept others' quirks—both necessary ingredients in healthy relationships.

Choosing the right person to marry in later life is not much different than parents' advice to their eighteen-year-old, infatuated offspring. One difference is that seniors who are widowed often marry old friends, known for years. The advantage there is in knowing more about the person (although there is much more to learn). How do we learn more? Time spent together, of course, but also—to use an overworked cliché—communication. Even though life has taught us the importance of talking things through, we seem to still resist and pay the price later.

Among the crucial, relationship-saving topics for premarital discussions are finances, name change, friends of the former couple, relationships with former in-laws, recreational activities, future plans, daily living styles, and cemetery burial locations. Perhaps the most essential discussions would be those concerning living arrangements and children.

A widow who remarried a widower and moved into the deceased spouse's home was surprised to find that it was like "three of us were living there." Numerous personal belongings, mementos and pictures were just as the deceased spouse had left them. Most disturbing, the new, widowed husband resisted moving them.

"Putting them away would be like dishonoring my first wife," he insisted. Counselors of second marriages most often advise people in this situation to pick a new residence together, one that can be theirs. Besides alleviating the obvious third wheel feelings, a new place is symbolic of a new life together. Remember what a grown-up thrill that was when you first married—the two of you—choosing your first apartment? It was yours!

When I asked my friend, who was recently widowed, how his new marriage was going, he summed it up by saying, "I'm happy, but it's complicated." I asked him what he meant by that and he said, "Kids—hers and mine." He's a man of few words, but no more were needed. So often—although not always—adult children do not approve of their mother or father remarrying, or of the new step-parent, or of new step-siblings—they disapprove of the whole package.

"It's weird and unnecessary," they think. Part of the translation for that response is: "What will happen to my inheritance? What will happen to me?" Family traditions may be threatened, but need not be. They can be carried out, but with sensitivity and prudence.

The first caution when remarrying with adult children who have lived through the death of their parent, is to go slow. Turn off the pressure to blend families. Parents need to lower expectations of one big happy Brady Bunch. That may happen much later, but most likely, it will not. More commonly, and sometimes at best, the children's disapproval morphs into acceptance, but it may take a while.

HELPING THE BEREAVED

Most of us want to help others in emotional pain but feel inadequate. As a result, sadly, some of us do not respond at all, even though we'd like to. Caregiving is simply acting on one's concern for another. The job description certainly requires giving from the heart to those who mourn, but, as in all job descriptions, general guidelines may be helpful.

The guidelines are general, because everyone grieves differently. Being sensitive and accepting a person's individual way of grieving is still top priority. In choosing your approach, the Spirit can guide as to what would be helpful for this particular person.

Following are some universal guidelines:[11]

- Be available. Offer support in an unobtrusive but persistent manner.
- Listen without giving advice. Forcing people to share feelings if they do not want to, or are unable to, is not beneficial.
- Use caution in offering stories of your own. This can have the effect of dismissing the grieving person's pain. If you do tell of your experience, make sure the purpose is helpful to the bereaved.
- Allow the grieving person to express all and any feelings, including anger or bitterness. Refrain from saying, "Don't feel that way." Frequently, sharing feelings is a normal attempt to

find meaning in what has happened. "Meaning is a form of strength. . . . It strengthens the will to live in us."[12]

- Realize that no one can replace or undo the loss. To heal, people must endure the grief process. Allow them to feel the pain—as difficult as that might be for caregivers.

- Be patient, kind, and understanding without being patronizing. Don't claim to know what the other person is feeling. "I know exactly how you feel" is not helpful to hear. None of us will ever know exactly how another feels.

- Don't hesitate to use touch, such as a hug or handclasp, when appropriate. It can bring great comfort and sometimes is more powerful than words. A touch may be all that is needed.

- Be there later, when friends and family have all gone back to their routines.

- Remember holidays, birthdays, and anniversaries that have important meaning for those who mourn. Don't be afraid of reminding the person of the loss; he or she is already thinking about it . . . most likely, twenty-four/seven.

We are not cows. Yet we can know a lot about milk—enough to help ourselves and others. Pause and consider the cow with her soft eyes and docile manner. Consider what we can learn from her. Have you ever known any living creature more patient and tolerant than a cow? Healing would best be served if the bereaved, and those offering comfort, were patient and tolerant with themselves and with each other. We occasionally—unintentionally—say and do the wrong thing. We all need a little slack.

After all, are we not here in this mortal, latter-day learning laboratory to gain experience? As Neal A. Maxwell insightfully observed, "the Lord allows us to practice on each other, even with our imperfections"—as we travel the road of eternal progression.[13]

Notes

1. See Thomas Holmes and Richard Rahe, "The Social Readjustment Rating Scale," *Journal of Psychosomatic Research*, 213–18 (1967).
2. C.S. Lewis, *A Grief Observed* (New York: Seabury Press, 1963, circa 1961), 3.
3. See O'Rourke, Meghan, "Good Grief," *The New Yorker*, Feb. 2010, 66–72 (2002).
4 Gordon B. Hinckley, "To Single Adults," *Ensign*, June 1989, 72.
5. John 14:18.
6. Kiri Walsh, Michael King, Louise Jones, Adrian Tookman, and Robert Blizard, "Spiritual Beliefs May Affect Outcome of Bereavement: Prospective Study," Bmj.com, Dept. of Psychiatry and Behavioural Science, Royal Free Campus, Royal Free and University College Medical School, London, NW32PF, June 29, 2002, http://www.bmj.com/content/324/7353/1551.abridged (consulted July 2, 2010).
7. "People with Religious Beliefs Are More Affected by Grief, Research Shows," The Stress of Life (Apr. 25, 2003), http://thestressoflife.com/people_with_religious_beliefs_ar.htm (consulted June 5, 2010).
8. Joseph B. Wirthlin, "Sunday Will Come," *Ensign*, Oct. 2006, 29.
9. Ibid.
10. Rachel Naomi Remen, *My Grandfather's Blessings* (New York: Riverhead Books, 2000), 38.
11. Family Caregiver Alliance National Center on Caregiving, "Fact Sheet: Grief and Loss," http://www.caregiver.org/caregiver/jsp/content_node.jsp?nodeid=404 (consulted June 5, 2010).
12. Remen, *My Grandfather's Blessings*, 29, 170.
13. Neal A. Maxwell, "A Brother Offended," *Ensign*, May 1982, 38.

17

Prepare Every Needful Thing!
End-of-Life Planning

Roy A. Prete

Abraham, upon the death of Sarah, purchased a burial sepulcher in Machpelah before Mamre as a family burial place,[1] and succeeding generations were careful to make preparations that they, too, should be buried in the family gravesite. Abraham,[2] and later Isaac, Rebekah, and Leah were all buried there,[3] and Jacob's body was transported from Egypt for that purpose.[4] Joseph even made the Israelites promise that they would carry his bones to rest with his fathers, when they should flee from bondage in Egypt.[5] Joseph Smith, too, wanted to be buried near his father so that he could greet him in the resurrection.[6]

What arrangements have we made for the future day of our passing? End-of-life planning for things such as funeral services, burial and the disposition of property—including priceless heirlooms and mundane personal and household effects—may strengthen our legacy of faith and good works and foster harmony among our descendants.

Roy A. Prete served as bishop for five years, 1981–1986, during which time he attended several families confronted with the loss of a loved one. The funeral of a dear friend, C. Thomas Asplund, in 1990, was the occasion for his best sermon on the plan of salvation.

The author wishes to express his appreciation to LeRoy E. Whitehead for his contribution in preparing and editing this chapter.

FUNERALS AND FUNERAL PLANNING

The gospel brings comfort to those who mourn. In the Doctrine and Covenants we read, "Thou shalt live together in love, insomuch that thou shalt weep for the loss of them that die, and more especially for those that have not hope of a glorious resurrection. And it shall come to pass that those that die in me shall not taste of death, for it shall be sweet unto them."[7]

For Latter-day Saints, funerals, while often accompanied by grief and sorrow for the loss of a loved one, do not represent the final stage in our existence, nor the definitive separation from those we love. As the Apostle Paul said, "For as in Adam all die, even so in Christ shall all be made alive."[8]

In some cases, such as that of a severely handicapped or disabled forebear whose quality of life has diminished almost to zero, and who is in constant pain and suffering, death may be a welcome release, lightened by the hope of passage into a better world and a glorious reunion with family and friends.

Funerals are intended for the comfort and edification of the mourners and, in addition to a celebration of the life of the deceased, should provide a meaningful spiritual experience. They are meetings of the Church, and are conducted by the bishop (or branch president in branches) or, if he is unavailable, by a counselor. Funerals should be planned by the bishop or his counselor in consultation with the immediate family. The bishop "ensures that the funeral is simple and dignified, with music and brief addresses and sermons centered on the gospel, including the comfort afforded by the Savior's Atonement and Resurrection. Members of the family should not feel that they are required to speak or otherwise participate in the service," although many may wish to contribute. "It should be a spiritual occasion in addition to a family gathering."[9]

You may record your funeral wishes in advance, with the choice of special musical numbers and desired speakers. The best place to leave these plans is in a secure place with your immediate family, or with the bishop, the funeral director or your attorney. Be aware, however, that law offices may be closed during statutory holidays or when members of the firm are on vacation, leaving your wishes unavailable should you pass during those times. One friend I had known for many years had his funeral all worked out in advance, but his lawyer, with whom his funeral plan was on file with his will, was out of town when he died, and the information could not be accessed. His partially estranged wife—of another faith—and his daughter had to come up with a program on his behalf, without any knowledge of his wishes.

Be sure to determine in advance the location of your funeral service—whether in a church, at the funeral home, another public location or in your own home. This is particularly important when family members are of different religious persuasions.

Preplanning with the funeral home. Make at least tentative plans with an appropriate funeral home long before death takes place. It is possible, and even appropriate, to compare prices and services before selecting a funeral home. Many jurisdictions require funeral directors to itemize their fees and charges, rather than quoting a single package price.

Much pain and anguish can be avoided through appropriate preplanning of funeral arrangements.

I have poignant recollections from the time when I was a bishop of being with families in deep distress as they joined the funeral director in the basement of the funeral home to select a casket for the dearly departed. The $1500 "tin box" didn't seem quite adequate as a final way to honor the deceased, while the $8000 cherry casket, though not affordable, could well seem to be the final and best honor to bestow. This was clearly not a good environment for making economic decisions. The situation could have been avoided by adequate preparation.

I have been very impressed with the tradition in my wife's family of a family burial plot arranged in the local cemetery, with provision for succeeding generations to be buried in close proximity. Grandparents, their children and spouses, including my wife's parents, and an uncle and his wife, plus her father's twin brother who died in infancy, and her brother's wife, are all buried close by with matching headstones. These were purchased in advance and were already in place well before their demise, requiring only the engraving of the death date. This is planning at its best, alleviating all worry for survivors with regard to the choice, purchase and installation of a headstone.

The joining of families in burial, just as in Abraham's family, has always seemed to me to be symbolic of family closeness and faith in the eternal nature of the family. When I have accompanied my wife to this family burial plot, I have had the impression that I was standing on holy ground. Husbands and wives frequently wish to be buried side by side, even if their children have wandered so far from home that it is not feasible to have a collective resting place.

In some cemeteries, where the cost of two side-by-side burial plots would be prohibitive, it is possible to inter two caskets in the same grave, one atop the other, if the initial opening of the grave is made deep enough to accommodate both. Many cemeteries require the casket to be placed in a concrete or metal vault in the grave, which is an additional expense. A vault prevents the surface ground from sinking as the casket decays and collapses, and shields it from ground water and rodents. When purchasing a cemetery plot, you may also want to ask about regulations regarding displaying cut flowers and other items and about planting flowers, shrubs and trees at the grave site.

The more items that can be preplanned and pre-arranged, the less stress there will be for surviving family members. Most funeral homes offer a purchase-in-advance funeral plan on a pre-payment basis, which provides for all the details related to funerals and interment. Before purchasing a pre-paid plan, find out whether the plan is "inflation proof"—that is, whether the prepayment amount will be invested, with the interest being used to offset price increases due to inflation through the years before your demise. Provision also needs to be made to have funds readily available in a joint account or by other means to pay funeral expenses. Help the survivors by letting them know in advance about the likely costs and what arrangements have already been made.

What to expect. The death of a loved one raises many immediate issues related to funeral arrangements. By law, the deceased must be pronounced dead by an authorized medical practitioner or hospice nurse or attendant. In some jurisdictions, the funeral director can pronounce death in cases where death was expected—due to a terminal illness, for example. The funeral home will need to be instructed by the hospital— or by a survivor if the person dies at home—to pick up and prepare the body for burial. The surviving family member or members then consult with the funeral director and their church leaders on funeral arrangements.

The bishop (possibly accompanied by his counselors) is encouraged to visit the family to comfort them, assist them in making funeral arrangements and offer assistance from the ward.[10] My colleague LeRoy E. Whitehead, who served five years as a bishop, gives practical advice on how to manage immediate arrangements upon the decease of a family member.[11] While funeral directors may be very knowledgeable and helpful, LeRoy urges that the bishop (or his counselor, if he is unavailable) accompany the grieving survivor(s) to the funeral home to assist in making the necessary arrangements. This is a time of immense stress for the bereaved, who may still be in a state of shock. In this situation, priesthood leaders who know and love them can afford moral support and comfort, and provide helpful assistance in attending to the numerous and often confusing details needing attention.

Matters such as notification of family members and obituaries will need to be attended to. The issue of open or closed casket will have to be decided. The location, date and hours of visitation plus the location, date and time of the funeral will all have to be settled in accordance with the wishes and convenience of the family, some of whom may have to travel long distances. These items plus the location of the burial

will need to be decided in advance of releasing the obituary for publication. Opening of the grave, choice of casket, choice of pallbearers
and flowers will also need to be arranged.

As appropriate, the clothing of the body in temple clothing for endowed members of the Church will have to be arranged. While "the
Church does not normally encourage cremation," it is not forbid-
den and may be mandated in some jurisdictions. "If the body of an
endowed member is being cremated, it should be dressed in temple
clothing if possible"[12] If cremation is planned, the choice of urn or
receptacle, and of whether the ashes are to be buried, stored in a niche,
or scattered, are additional decisions to make.

The bishop will then make detailed arrangements for the funeral
service in consultation with family members, taking into account the
stated preferences of the deceased and the wishes of the family. Such
matters as an immediate pre-funeral viewing (if desired) and choosing
who is to give the family prayer before the casket is closed will need
to be decided. Arrangements for the funeral service normally include
who is to preside and conduct, the choice of speakers and their topics, hymns, special musical numbers, poems or special readings and
prayers. An organist and music director will need to assigned as well as
someone to make up the program, if one is desired. Arrangements will
need to be made for dedication of the grave. For former service men
and women, military ceremonies may be requested in conjunction with
the funeral service or at the gravesite.

"Others in the ward should also be called upon to provide comfort
and support. The bishop notifies the Melchizedek Priesthood leader
who is responsible for the family so he and other brethren, including
home teachers, can assist the bereaved family. Such assistance may include dressing the body of a deceased male for burial, safeguarding the
home during the funeral and providing other support. The bishop also
notifies the Relief Society president, so she and other sisters, including visiting teachers, can assist the family. Such assistance may include

dressing the body of a deceased female for burial, helping with flowers, tending small children, safeguarding the home during the funeral, and preparing meals."[13]

Those making funeral arrangements will also need to think ahead to the traditional reception after the funeral, its time, location and organization. Ward or branch Relief Societies have traditionally gone the extra mile in providing support in various ways to the bereaved, including providing food and service for receptions. In some places, the members of the Relief Society may wish to provide food for a reception and serve it, while in other places it may be customary only to serve food that is provided by the family.

At such a time as this, a spiritually-minded, thoughtful, and kind priesthood leader, assisted by loving ward members, can be of immeasurable comfort and consolation and render invaluable assistance, so that the simple mechanics of making funeral arrangements and organizing the funeral service will not be overwhelming. The burden of the grieving survivors will be immeasurably lightened by the pre-arrangement and preplanning of as many details as possible.

WILLS AND LIVING TRUSTS

Once the funeral is over, a new set of issues will arise relating to the distribution of property, household, and personal effects of the deceased, including heirlooms of sentimental value. Through careful planning well in advance, you can provide for a harmonious distribution of these among heirs.

A will is an important legal instrument for the disposition of our possessions when we die and should be prepared with the assistance of a qualified attorney. A will may be adequate for a straightforward distribution, but will normally require probate, i.e. determination by a judge that the will is valid and that its provisions have legal sanction. Probate can sometimes be a lengthy and costly process, depending on the complexity of the circumstances.

Although more expensive to set up, a living trust, which provides for administration of assets by a trustee before one dies, will not normally require probate. A living trust is a much more flexible instrument for the transmission of property than a will and is recommended for larger estates or where distributions are to be over time or varied among the heirs. It may be used in conjunction with a will. In the absence of a valid will or trust, your property will be disposed of according to law, not necessarily in accordance with your wishes. Good estate planning with a competent legal advisor can resolve most of the issues related to the distribution of major assets.

The next chapter by Layne T. Rushforth provides more detailed information on estate planning from a legal perspective. It also contains specifics on important matters relating to power of attorney for financial matters and power of attorney for healthcare for a time when you are unable to make decisions for yourself. It discusses living wills, which define the degree of terminal care you desire, and also your wishes relative to organ donation.

Choosing an executor or trustee. The choice of executor of the will is one of particular importance. The executor will have authority to manage the process for the distribution of all your assets, personal and household effects, and family heirlooms, excluding those assets for which other provision for their distribution has been made through joint tenancy or other joint property ownership arrangements. Life insurance payouts normally go to beneficiaries independent of a will or trust unless otherwise specified. The executor of a will is often a family member, though it may be anyone willing to take on the task, which is often unremunerated.

The choice of the trustee of a trust is also important, as that individual may perform all the duties of the executor of a will if so empowered, plus attend to the management of the estate both prior to and after the demise of the principal. A trustee's services, which may extend over a long period of time, are normally remunerated.

The sharing of inheritances has often been a thorny issue, which has led to long-standing ill will among family members, some of whom have not spoken to each other for years afterwards. The same problem was present in the Savior's time. Luke records that "one of the company said unto him, Master, speak to my brother, that he divide the inheritance with me."

The counsel Jesus gave has long-lasting value: "Beware of covetousness."[14] An executor or trustee needs to be recognized as someone who is capable, fair-minded and trustworthy, readily accessible, and who will not seek his own interests, but will put the harmony and general interests of the family ahead of any personal advantage.

DISTRIBUTION OF HEIRLOOMS AND PERSONAL AND HOUSEHOLD EFFECTS

We have all heard horror stories of children who have raided the family home the day of the funeral, or even before, and hauled off their choice of heirlooms—photos, china, jewelry or family keepsake items—before others had a chance to lay claim to them. The resultant hard feelings have poisoned family relations for a very long while.

How can such a scenario be prevented? Short of making a provision in your will or trust that the home be secured on the decease of the owner, and that access be denied—a measure that feels rigorous and untrusting—probably the surest way to assure the desired distribution of family heirlooms, household or personal affects (or particular properties), is to make distribution of them while you are yet alive. Failing that, specify distribution in a will or trust. A specified list of distributions may be appended to a will as a codicil, or addendum. This must be arranged through the attorney who prepared your will or through other counsel in the legal office in which it is located, so that it becomes part of the official document.

The original of a will should be kept in the lawyer's office for safekeeping, or in a safety deposit box, a fireproof safe, or some other secure place. It is generally not advisable to provide the executor with a copy of the will in order to avoid informal or unofficial changes, but it is desirable to summarize its terms. The most recent will has legal status. All previous wills should be destroyed to avoid confusion as to which one is valid. Take care to advise your executor where the original will is deposited.[15] Trust documents likewise need to be secured as advised by your attorney.

Assemble other important documents also and keep them in a safe place, with access for those who will need them. Such documents fall into two categories: those such as authorization of power of attorney and healthcare directives that will be required to administer your affairs in case of incapacity while you are yet alive, and those that will be needed after your passing to administer the many details of settling your estate. The latter, in addition to your will and trust agreements, include other important documents such as deeds, tax records, bank statements, insurance policies, annuities, retirement plans, mortgages, and credit card statements. They also include support obligations, unpaid bills and money others owe you, contracts, information on stocks and bonds—whatever may be required to manage your estate—even your marriage certificate.

In addition to a description of physical assets, you should provide your executor with information on bank accounts, annuities, insurance policies, retirement funds, stocks and bonds and other particulars that will later be needed in settling your estate. Billions of dollars in insurance payouts and bank accounts remain unclaimed each year because the beneficiaries or heirs are unaware of their location.[16]

What are the merits of disclosing the terms of a will (or trust arrangement) to potential inheritors? While doing so may take away something of the dramatic moment of reading the will as depicted in the movies, my wife and I have favored an open process. We have told our children what is in our will to prevent the speculation and second-guessing that often takes place. This has been our personal choice; others for a variety of reasons may decide to proceed otherwise.

Typically, the executor of a will, though not required by law, will gather heirs together to open the will, advisably in the office of the attorney who prepared it, and discuss the process for its execution. Many attorneys favor providing a copy of the will to heirs and beneficiaries after the principal's death while the will is being probated. Executors may draw on the experience of estate-management lawyers, accountants, and tax experts on how best to proceed. When no specific provision as to process has been made in the will, it falls to the executor of the will once probated (or if probate is not required) to arrange distribution of all assets covered in the document, including heirlooms and personal and household effects.

The normal process for the executor of the will is to pay all debts and outstanding taxes and to dispose of major assets—apart from personal or heirloom items of interest to the heirs—and to divide up the proceeds as instructed in the will. But note, heirlooms of significant value are also subject to tax requirements, and may need to have liens against them cleared, the same as other property.

The distribution of personal and household effects and family heirlooms of lesser value, plus smaller assets which may not be included in the above process, provide a particular challenge for the executor. Various creative systems have been devised to accomplish this end. The executor may draw on previous family experiences or the advice of professionals, or may find helpful suggestions on the internet.

The most logical process for the executor is to make a list of the more significant items and their approximate value. Unless a pre-arranged distribution has been provided, heirs could then indicate first, second and third choices, and so on, and hopefully, with some give-and-take, make a satisfactory distribution, with each receiving some treasured items.

One creative notion of which I am aware was for the executor to provide one or more personal keepsake item for each grandchild: a book, a tool, a piece of china, an item of jewelry or an ornament—then to have a family auction, with the heirs using apportioned future inheritance as scrip to make their purchases. Proceeds from the auction went back into the estate and were divided among the heirs. This worked quite well, although those who lived at a distance may have felt they were disadvantaged, as transporting items to their homes could become quite expensive.

Another approach that worked well was for heirs who were each designated an equal portion to assemble, and, as rooms were cleaned out in the familial home, each received one item of approximately equal value. Each item was added to his or her pile, whether a towel, a blanket, an appliance, books, videos, mechanical tools, garden tools or something else, with the understanding that trading could take place among the participants later. Large items of furniture, by common consent, often went to newlyweds or other grandchildren who had a specific need.

Heirlooms—items of personal or sentimental value—were identified and set aside for later distribution. Each person, starting from the youngest to the oldest, took a turn selecting the item each most desired for themselves or their family. This was deemed fair and worked without friction. In some cases, family members graciously yielded a desired item if they saw that another wanted it badly.

Leftover items were sold at a garage sale, and anything remaining after that went to a charity.

There are undoubtedly numerous approaches to dividing up such effects among heirs. A few principles may help make this a smooth and harmonious process. The first is good communication between the executor of the will and the heirs. This obviates suspicion and creates an atmosphere of trust. An open process to which all agree must be sought for: no one person should attempt to carry off or appropriate items without the knowledge and consent of all the principals. Finally, remember that "charity never faileth."[17] The Lord's counsel to "beware of covetousness" will stand us in good stead, as will the notion that family unity and strength are higher ideals than personal gain—that in effect, we should seek our brother's or sister's interest more than our own. Much personal satisfaction will come from knowing that items of great sentimental value ended up in the hands they should have—even if they weren't our own.

CONCLUSION

Gospel principles apply in every aspect of life. As we approach the end of our mortal existence, it behooves us, like the prophets of old, to "prepare every needful thing."[18] The better we plan for our funeral and burial, the less stress and distress will be felt by our survivors. Advance selection of an intended funeral home, place of burial, funeral arrangements, casket and headstone will greatly simplify the tasks for survivors, allowing them to focus on family and more meaningful reflections. The mourning and sense of loss associated with the death of a loved one can be eased by the loving support of family, friends and members of the Church and a reverent well-planned funeral service, which not only celebrates the life of the departed loved one, but builds faith in Jesus Christ and hope for the future in the life hereafter.

Provision needs to be made for the harmonious distribution of our worldly possessions through means such as wills, trusts, and careful estate planning. To the extent possible, provision should be made for the distribution of items that may have emotional significance to heirs, whether through prior distribution, spelling out of your desires in legal documents, or by appointing a trusted executor or trustee.

Truly the Lord has blessed us with many things over which we have served as stewards during our lifetimes. To be wise stewards over those resources after our passing, we need to make adequate preparation, in careful end-of-life planning. The instruction to "organize yourselves; prepare every needful thing"[19] applies as much in departing from this life as in living it. When the angelic visitants come to escort us to the next world, there will be considerable satisfaction in knowing that we have made adequate provision, both spiritually and temporally, for those cherished family members we have left behind.

Notes

1. Genesis 23.
2. Genesis 25:8.
3. Genesis 49:30–31.
4. Genesis 50:13.
5. Genesis 50:24–25.
6. Joseph Smith, *Teachings of the Prophet Joseph Smith* (Salt Lake City: Deseret Book Co., 1976), 295.
7. D&C 42:45–46.
8. 1 Corinthians 15:22.
9 Church Handbook of Instructions, *2, Administering the Church 2010*, 147.
10. Ibid.
11. Ibid, 148.
12. Ibid.
13. Ibid, 147.
14. See Luke 12:13, 15.
15. John Johnson, LL.D, "Executive Decisions: What You Need to Know About Being an Executor," *Fifty-Five Plus Magazine* (Sept. 2010), 19, 22.
16. Ibid; See Saabira Chaudhuri, "The 25 Documents You Need Before You Die," Designing Your Death Dossier—WSJ.com, at http://online.wsj.com/article_email/ SB10001424052702303627104576410234039258092- lMyQjAxMTAxMDAwNTEwNDUyWj.html (consulted July 6, 2011).
17. 1 Corinthians 13:8.
18. D&C 109:8.
19. D&C 88:119.

ESTATE PLANNING: LEAVING A LEGACY IN MORE WAYS THAN ONE

Layne T. Rushforth

We all have a natural yearning to make a difference. Those of us who are blessed with a loving family have an innate desire to leave a legacy for our family. Our primary focus should be to leave a legacy of faith, hope, and charity. In addition, some of us have the good fortune of having worldly possessions that will also be left behind, hopefully for the benefit of another generation. This chapter is intended to give practical ideas with respect to estate planning that is coordinated with (and not in opposition to) the greater legacy that we can leave.

A LEGACY OF FAITH, HOPE, AND CHARITY

When the Apostle Paul taught about spiritual gifts in his first epistle to the Corinthians,[1] he concluded by saying, "And now abideth faith, hope, charity, these three; but the greatest of these is charity."[2] Over the years, I have learned that:

Layne T. Rushforth is a practicing trust and estate attorney with his office in Las Vegas, Nevada. He is licensed in Nevada and Utah. Layne graduated from BYU in 1975 and from the J. Reuben Clark Law School at BYU in 1978. He has been a Fellow with the American College of Trust and Estate Counsel (ACTEC) since 1990 and served as the Nevada State Chair from 2005 to 2010. He lectures on estate planning and has published continuing education materials for estate-planning professionals.

Faith in something is knowing that *if* it is the will of the Lord, it will come to pass;[3]

Hope–which in the scriptural sense translates as "expectation"[4]–is knowing that something *is* the will of the Lord and expecting it to come to pass.

Charity, the pure love of Christ,[5] is knowing that something is the will of the Lord and, *doing* all we can to make it come to pass.

If our estate planning is motivated out of charity, we will leave a temporal legacy that will encourage a spiritual legacy of higher importance. If we have a true concern for our beneficiaries, our estate plan can continue to teach correct principles, even after we have left this mortal life, but it may have to contain provisions that might require "tough love."

ESTATE PLANNING INVOLVES MORE THAN JUST WORLDLY POSSESSIONS

We have been taught that the stewardship of life requires that we become self-reliant,[6] provide for our families,[7] and provide for the less fortunate.[8] At the end of one's life, if there are resources left over, we have to decide how we want to pass those resources on to others. When we account for our earthly stewardship, it is my belief that we will want to be able to say that we left our worldly wealth in a way that encouraged those who received it to be wise stewards. The assets that we leave behind should be accompanied with a legacy of gospel principles that will make sure that the worldly wealth does not become more important than spiritual goals.

The root of all evil is selfishness.[9] A poorly planned estate that does not take into consideration individual needs may encourage greed and selfishness. In contrast, a well-crafted estate plan involving a well-written will and/or one or more trusts can include provisions that discourage selfishness and encourage frugality, prudence, self-reliance, and even selflessness.

ESTATE-PLANNING BASICS

What is "estate planning"? Estate planning is the arrangements of one's financial affairs through asset ownership and legal documents to provide for one's goals related to the management and disposition of one's estate after death.[11] Your estate-planning goals might include the desire to assure the distribution of your estate to your intended beneficiaries, to reduce or eliminate taxes and other expenses, to coordinate business and retirement planning with other planning, to protect assets against lawsuits and other claims, to protect beneficiaries from mismanagement and from the claims of creditors and ex-spouses, and/or to discourage or encourage certain types of conduct for family members. Most people focus on having a will or trust that meets the minimum legal requirements, but for a truly effective estate plan, the minimum legal requirements are usually not enough. An effective estate plan is one that truly accomplishes *your* objectives and that balances competing objectives according to *your* priorities.

Asset transfers triggered by death. The methods for transferring assets at death fit into two categories: (1) nonprobate transfers and (2) testamentary transfers.

Nonprobate transfers generally fit into two subcategories: (a) assets for which ownership is transferred automatically by law (which includes forms of ownership with a right of survivorship, such as joint tenancy); and (b) transfers that occur under the terms of a contract (which includes contracts that allow the designation of one or more beneficiaries, such as life insurance and retirement plans). Nonprobate transfers include assets transferred under a living trust, which is a combination of law and contract.

Testamentary transfers require compliance with laws pertaining to probate proceedings. A probate proceeding involves filing of one or more petitions to get the court to accept a deceased person's will (if there is one) as being valid, to appoint a "personal representative" (an executor , if there is a will, or an administrator if there is not), to approve the personal representative's actions, to rule on the rights of creditors and beneficiaries, and to ultimately distribute the estate (assets) of the deceased person as required by law. The complexity and the formality of a probate proceeding varies greatly from one jurisdiction to the next, but except for very small estates, probate proceedings usually require the engagement of an attorney and can take months if not years to complete.

OVERVIEW OF ESTATE-PLANNING TOOLS

A good estate plan utilizes tools and techniques that fit into all of the asset-transfer categories.

Will. The most commonly recognized estate-planning device is the "last will and testament," which we now simply call a will. Each jurisdiction (state or province) establishes what is required to make a valid will, but a valid will must be in writing and signed by the person making the will (testator). Most jurisdictions require two or three witnesses who are not beneficiaries, but witnesses are not required for handwritten (holographic) wills in jurisdictions that recognize them. A person who dies with a valid will is said to die "testate," and a person who dies without a valid will is said to die "intestate." For a person who dies intestate, each state's "intestate succession laws" specify the "heirs" who will inherit that person's assets. A person's heirs are usually his or her spouse and/or closest blood relatives. A similar situation prevails in Canada; however, in most provinces, the wife receives an initial designated sum before other distributions are made.

In most jurisdictions, a will requires a probate proceeding to be effective. In some states, including Utah and Idaho, the terms of a will may be carried out without having to go through a probate process if

it is unlikely to be challenged. Generally this is done with the advice of
an attorney, where the estate is not extremely large and there are not
likely to be major complications. Assets owned in a nonprobate form
of ownership in which the transfer of ownership is automatic are not
usually subject to the will or subject to the probate process.

Trusts. A trust is an ownership arrangement by which a "trustee"
owns and controls one or more assets for the benefit of specified persons called "beneficiaries." If the trust is created under a will, the trust
is called a "testamentary trust," and the person creating the will is
referred to as the "testator." If the trust is created during one's lifetime,
the trust is considered an *"inter vivos* trust*"* or "living trust," and the person who created the trust is called the "settlor," "grantor," or "trustor."
(*Inter vivos* is a Latin phrase meaning "during lifetime." To avoid using
Latin words, I will refer to an *"inter vivos* trust" as a "living trust").

Testamentary Trust. If a will provides for anything other than an immediate, outright distribution of all assets at death, its terms will create
a trust that will specify what events, dates, or conditions will trigger
distributions from the trust and the designated trustee who will manage
the assets until they are distributed. A testamentary trust is not a separate document, but it is a part of the will.

Avoiding probate. Because testamentary transfers usually require an
expensive probate proceeding, many people use nonprobate transfers to avoid probate. For example, living trusts are frequently used to
accomplish estate-planning objectives without requiring a probate proceeding. Living trusts are discussed in more detail in the next section
of this chapter. In addition, all states recognize at least one form of
joint ownership with a "right of survivorship," which is a right that
allows joint owners to specify that the interest of the owner who dies
first transfers automatically to the surviving owner(s). For centuries, the
most common form of joint ownership with a right of survivorship
has been "joint tenancy," but some jurisdictions recognize additional
forms of ownership that include a right of survivorship. In addition,

all jurisdictions recognize beneficiary designations under contracts, and some jurisdictions have laws that specifically permit transfer-on-death designations for bank accounts, investment accounts, and even real property.

Living trusts. As indicated, a trust is an ownership arrangement by which a "trustee" owns and controls one or more assets for the benefit of specified persons called "beneficiaries." A living trust is a combination of law and contract and can be revocable or irrevocable. In simple terms, a "revocable" trust can be amended or revoked, while an "irrevocable" trust cannot.

Creation. A living trust is created by: (1) signing a declaration of trust or trust agreement that declares the intent to create a trust, designates the trustee and the beneficiaries, and specifies the terms on which the distributions are to be made; and (2) transferring the title to, or ownership of, assets to the trust or its trustee. Once created, a trust can be also designated as the beneficiary of life insurance, retirement plans, and other contractual interests. The most typical trust used for probate and guardianship avoidance is revocable, and the settlor (or creator) of the trust is usually also the initial trustee and initial beneficiary. Married couples can establish a joint trust or separate trusts, which primarily depends on whether or not they have the same beneficiaries. Where spouses have children from prior marriages, separate trusts are usually advisable.

Advantages. Revocable trusts are primarily used for avoiding court-supervised administration of trust assets, which include guardianship proceedings for incompetent adults or minors and probate proceedings at death. Irrevocable trusts also avoid guardianship and probate proceedings, but they can also provide additional tax planning and asset-protection planning, both of which are beyond the scope of this chapter.[12] Unlike Wills, trusts are usually not made public, allowing the family to take care of family affairs privately. One significant benefit of trusts is the ability to encourage or discourage certain behavior.

Distributions can be triggered by favored behavior and reduced, deferred, or eliminated by unwanted behavior. This is discussed more fully in the next section of this chapter.

Disadvantages and pitfalls. A living trust sometimes costs more than a will, but that is not always the case. A living trust does not have any impact on assets not owned by the trust or its trustee, and so formal title changes or beneficiary changes are required to make the trust effective. Over the years, care must be taken to make sure that newly acquired assets are owned in a way that makes them subject to the trust. To be cautious, a trust should be accompanied by a will that designates the trust as the beneficiary of any assets requiring probate.

Power of attorney documents. A "power of attorney" is a document that you sign as "principal" to appoint another person as your "agent" or "attorney-in-fact" to act for you. For estate-planning purposes, there is a financial power of attorney and a healthcare power of attorney.

Financial power of attorney. Under a financial power of attorney, you can authorize your agent to act on your behalf in financial matters. The power can be effective immediately, or it can be triggered at the time you become incapacitated. Most jurisdictions permit a power of attorney to be effective while you are legally incompetent or otherwise incapacitated, but usually specific language to accomplish that is required. The effectiveness of a power of attorney varies from jurisdiction to jurisdiction, and there are some financial institutions that decline to honor them unless required by law.

Your power of attorney will normally expire when you die, making it ineffective to deal with financial affairs after your death. Some people give post-death access to financial accounts by having joint tenancy bank accounts, or by providing for life insurance policies to be paid to designated beneficiaries, but if those arrangements are not coordinated with your will or trust, the family members designated as joint tenants on bank accounts or as beneficiaries on insurance policies can receive the funds without any obligation to use them for any particular purpose. A financial power of attorney is a supplemental estate-planning tool at best. It is inappropriate to rely on a power of attorney to accomplish major estate-planning objectives, and care must be taken to make sure that any agent appointed cannot use the power to provide unfair benefits to himself or herself.

Healthcare power of attorney and living will. A power of attorney for healthcare—also known as an "advanced directive for healthcare"—is a document in which you, as "principal" authorize your "health-care agent" to make decisions relating to your healthcare when you are unable to make those decisions for yourself. Potentially, a healthcare power of attorney can deal with traditional medical care, emergency medical care, care in a nursing home or assisted-living facility, as well as issues relating to the administration of life-sustaining and life-extending procedures, sometimes referred to as "artificial life support." In most jurisdictions, the term "living will" is a limited healthcare directive related to the resuscitation of a dying person and/or artificial life support. A "living will" sometimes takes the form of a declaration of desires, but in some jurisdictions it is more like a healthcare power of attorney because it designates someone who has authority to instruct healthcare personnel to carry out those desires.

In almost all jurisdictions, the healthcare power of attorney is more comprehensive than a living will, and in some jurisdictions you need both. It is important to make sure that you put your desires into a healthcare power of attorney and/or a living will, because it is a lot less stressful for families to make difficult decisions when they know that they are consistent with your wishes. You do not want your family members to have to guess as to what you want, especially as to important decisions that are being made when emotions are running high. Ideally, the issue of how much life-sustaining care we may wish in a terminal-illness situation should be discussed with family members and appropriate provision made in the living will and/or healthcare power of attorney.

Organ donation. If you wish to donate your organs upon your death, be sure to comply with the law of the jurisdiction in which you live. Sometimes making an organ donation can be done in your living will, your healthcare power of attorney, or even by a notation on your driver's license. While we all intend to die at a ripe old age, our passing may come unexpectedly from a fatal illness or an accident, and some of our organs will be in sufficiently good condition to extend the life of another of Heavenly Father's children for a significant period of time. There is no Church policy against organ donation. Even if you are permitted to make an organ donation by a simple notation on your driver license, I recommend that you make a written declaration of your intent, especially if you want your organs to be used only for the treatment of living human beings and not for scientific or medical research. If you do not want to be an organ donor, that is also good to put into writing.

Burial and funeral instructions. A written declaration of your desires regarding the disposition of your mortal remains and regarding any desired memorial service is recommended. Some jurisdictions require a written declaration to authorize someone to make arrangements for burial. Funeral and burial arrangements are discussed more fully in chapter 17.

Asset ownership and beneficiary designations. Proper asset ownership and beneficiary designations are an essential element of effective estate planning. Far too often, a person's ownership and beneficiary-designation documents are inconsistent with his or her will or trust and with his or her true objectives. Here are some illustrations:

If you have a trust that provides for your children to receive assets when they graduate from college, but only if they are not using illegal drugs, but you designate your children (and not the trust) as the beneficiary of life insurance, the children (or a court-appointed guardian for each minor child) will get the insurance proceeds at your death, and the trust—including its provisions to encourage a college education and to discourage drug abuse—will be ignored.

If you have a will that leaves your home to a child, but you own your home in joint tenancy with your spouse, the home will become your spouse's by right of survivorship. The will is disregarded because it does not apply to nonprobate transfers.

If you designate a sister as a beneficiary under a life-insurance policy, the proceeds will belong to that sister, and you cannot expect her to share with your children or to use the insurance proceeds to pay off debts or pay funeral expenses unless your sister is contractually required to do so. Even worse, if your sister has unpaid debts, her creditors will have first claim on the insurance money.

Designing Your Estate Plan to Make a Difference

Most estate planning is behavior neutral, which means that the distributions are made regardless of the conduct of the beneficiary. Sometimes distributions to a beneficiary are deferred until he or she reaches a particular age, but that does not necessarily mean that the beneficiary is more mature or more capable of dealing with the assets that are distributed. Incentive-based estate planning provides a method to encourage or discourage certain behavior. This will almost always require a trust, but it can be a testamentary trust (created under a will) or a living trust.

No-contest clause. A very common provision that is sometimes included in a will or trust is a "no-contest clause" (or "*in terrorem* clause") that declares that a beneficiary's share is reduced or eliminated if the beneficiary contests the will or trust, objects to the appointment of the executor or trustee, or otherwise interferes with the implementation of the will or trust. These clauses are not allowed in every jurisdiction,[13] and where they are allowed, they are "strictly construed," which means that the court will only apply the clause to situations specifically mentioned in it. If you are concerned about litigation, harassment, disruption, and interference with the administration of your estate or trust, consider including a no-contest clause, and if your document already has one, consider customizing it to more specifically apply to your beneficiaries.

Delay of distribution. There are situations in which it is better for a trustee to delay distributions to beneficiaries.

Age. The most common criterion for distribution is age. Most people do not want a child, grandchild, or other beneficiary to receive a distribution before the beneficiary is at least 25 years old. Some pick age 21, others use age 30, and others even specify age 65. Many people provide for lump-sum distributions, but it is also very common to stagger a large distribution over three distributions at various ages, such as 25, 30, and 35.

Installments. You may wish to have a beneficiary's share distributed in periodic installments unrelated to age, for example, one third upon your death, one third five years later, and the final third five years after that, or, for another example, 10% a year for 10 years.

Goals. Some provide for distributions upon graduation from college or vocational training or after three years' employment in the beneficiary's career field. To encourage a college education, a trust might provide for a bonus for college graduation before a specified age or for obtaining an advanced degree or specific credentials (such as graduation from medical school or becoming a certified public accountant). To encourage a beneficiary's gainful employment, a trust might direct a distribution of an annual amount equal to fifty cents (50¢) for each dollar of "earned income" that is shown on the beneficiary's income tax return (IRS Form 1040) for the prior year. To encourage a full-time mission or other public service, a trust might provide for a "bonus" for such service. Some people have set aside a college education fund for grandchildren to give them an incentive to go to college, and to encourage them to help themselves; distributions from a college fund might be made only to match funds provided by the beneficiary from personal earnings or from scholarships.

Negative behavior. You may wish to discourage certain behavior. This is frequently done by giving the trustee discretion to delay a distribution that is otherwise required under the terms of the trust. For example, if a beneficiary receives a distribution while he or she has a gambling habit, or has a substance-abuse problem, that distribution may make a bad situation worse. This can be coupled with a provision that allows the trustee to require drug testing, to pay for rehabilitation programs, and to pay *for* the beneficiary's needs rather than making a direct distribution *to* the beneficiary.

Beneficiary protection. You may wish to protect a beneficiary from bad circumstances, whether or not such circumstances are the beneficiary's fault. If a beneficiary is imprisoned, is heavily indebted, is involved in a divorce, or is involved in a lawsuit, making a distribution might benefit the beneficiary's creditors or ex-spouse more than the beneficiary. In such circumstances, the beneficiary's best interests can be protected by including a trust provision that gives the trustee the authority to delay distributions to the beneficiary until the circumstances change.

Generally, if distributions or the timing of distributions are based on conditions, the terms and conditions must be clear, a time limit for meeting each condition must be given, and an alternate provision must be included in the event any condition is not met. To avoid legal challenges, the trust provisions must be unambiguous. Some discretion can be given to the trustee, but be careful not to make the job too burdensome.

DESIGNING YOUR ESTATE PLAN TO FIT YOUR BENEFICIARIES

Creditor protection. An ongoing trust managed by a well-qualified trustee is ideal for a beneficiary who does not manage money well. Similarly, it is ideal for a beneficiary who has problems with creditors. Most jurisdictions allow a trust to be designed as a discretionary "spendthrift trust," the assets of which cannot be reached by a beneficiary's creditors. If you wish, the beneficiary can be given the right to designate the successor beneficiaries for his or her share of the trust.

Special needs. If you have a dependent parent or child, it is usually best not to direct the trustee to give such a beneficiary an outright distribution. Any benefits should be discretionary so that the trust qualifies as a spendthrift trust that is not subject to assessment by public agencies or attachment by creditors. In most jurisdictions, a trust can be written so that a beneficiary's share is not considered as a resource that would make the beneficiary ineligible for public-assistance programs such as Supplemental Security Income (SSI) and Medicaid.

Disparity. Most clients want to treat their children equally, and this is perceived as being the fair thing to do. On the other hand, if there is a significant disparity in your various children's needs, do not be afraid to treat them unequally. Most parents, while they are alive, provide for their children according to their relative needs. Why should this stop at death? One beneficiary's needs might be appropriately met with an outright distribution without conditions, while another beneficiary's needs might require that he or she receive distributions only in the discretion of a cautious trustee. Perhaps one beneficiary needs a larger share due to personal limitations and handicaps, and another beneficiary should have his or her share reduced because they have already been assisted generously. There are situations when a complete disinheritance may be the right thing to do.

Omitted heirs. If you choose to omit an heir, say, "I leave my son John absolutely nothing." It is best not to explain your reasons.

Improper gifts. Some provisions encourage litigation or create other problems. For example, you should *never:* (a) give a beneficiary $1 or any other token gift; (b) make a gift contingent upon any unlawful act; (c) ridicule or defame any person; or (d) give a substantial gift to a minor without designating a trustee or custodian.

Alternate beneficiaries. The will or trust should make it clear what happens to the property that is allocated to a beneficiary who fails to survive you for a specified number of days or who fails to meet a condition that is required. The alternate beneficiaries might be the children or siblings of the original beneficiary, but if all close members of your family are gone, you may wish to name collateral relatives, friends, and/or one or more charities as alternate beneficiaries.

SELECTING FIDUCIARIES

In general, a "fiduciary" is a person selected or appointed to act on another's behalf. A fiduciary can have broad or limited powers that relate to assets and financial affairs or that relate to personal care and medical decisions. Fiduciaries include the executor of a will, the trustee of a trust, an agent under a power of attorney (whether for asset management or for health-care decisions), a conservator (who manages assets for a minor or incompetent adult), and a guardian (who makes decisions related to the care of someone incapable of caring for himself or herself). A fiduciary must be (1) honest, (2) capable, (3) available, and (4) compatible. The lack of any one of these qualities can potentially lead to disaster. For example, if a guardian for minor children is incompatible with those children, the other qualities will not matter much. If a trustee cannot be trusted, the other qualities will not save the trust from embezzlement. Co-fiduciaries can be appropriate, but they, too, must be able to work together. Designating alternate fiduciaries is very important. Sometimes a bank or trust company or a nonfamily advisor may be a better choice than a family member. This is particularly true if the appointment of a family member as a fiduciary might trigger tension or discord between family members.

Other issues. There are a number of issues that are beyond the scope of these materials, including tax planning, asset-protection, and charitable giving. Even though not discussed here, they may be important to you, and you should consult qualified professionals to find out what laws and planning opportunities may be appropriate for you.

CONCLUSION

Planning. The operative word in estate planning is "planning." The best estate plans are crafted after careful and prayerful consideration of one's beneficiaries and their individual strengths, weaknesses, and needs. If you think of your estate as part of your temporal stewardship for which you must account, your estate plan should be crafted so as to optimize the temporal and spiritual legacy you are going to leave behind.

Prudence. Proper planning requires prudence. I strongly caution all folks against a do-it-yourself approach to estate planning if you can afford to involve a qualified estate-planning attorney. Poorly written documents almost always trigger higher costs than the legal fees charged to set it up correctly in the first place. Even worse, the unintended consequences of poor estate planning can result in wounded feelings and family discord that can create years of disharmony. Whatever your estate consists of, it is the result of your life-long investment of time, effort, and sacrifice. To protect that investment, it is prudent to make the additional investment of paying qualified professionals to help design and implement a well-crafted estate plan.

Your legacy. Prudence and charity both require action. If you wish to leave a legacy, do something about it. If you already have, be sure to keep it current as time goes by.

Notes

1. 1 Corinthians 12–13.
2. 1 Corinthians 13:13.
3. Dennis E. Simmons, "But if Not . . .," *Ensign*, May 2004, 73–75.
4. In the scriptures, "hope" is equivalent to "expectation." President Dieter F. Uchtdorf has taught us that hope "is believing and expecting that our prayers will be answered. It is manifest in confidence, optimism, enthusiasm, and patient perseverance." (Dieter F. Uchtdorf, "The Infinite Power of Hope," *Ensign*, Nov. 2008, 22.)
5. Moroni 7:47.
6. D&C 64:34–35.

7. 1 Timothy 5:8; see also Keith B. McMullin, "Lay Up in Store," *Ensign*, May 2007, 51–53.
8. Mosiah 4:16; D&C 81:5.
9. The Apostle Paul said that "the love of money is the root of all evil" (1 Timothy 6:10), but even the love of money is rooted in selfishness.
11. "Estate," "assets," and "property" are used interchangeably to refer to everything a person owns. Of course, the term "estate" can be modified to refer to only part of one's entire estate. For example, "probate estate" refers to the property subject to administration in probate proceedings, and a "trust estate" refers to the property that is subject to the terms of a trust.
12. Some very general estate-planning information can be found on the author's educational web site at http://rushforth.net. Because the author practices law in Nevada, the emphasis is on Nevada law, but the general principles discussed apply in most states.
13. For example, no-contest clauses are not enforceable under Florida law [Fla. Stat. 733.517 (2009)], and effective January 1, 2010, California has strictly limited the application of such clauses [Calif. Prob.C. §§ 21310–21315]. In contrast, Nevada law specifically directs the court to enforce no-contest clauses [NRS 137.005 as to wills and NRS 163.00195 as to trusts]. These statutes recognize that a beneficiary may seek enforcement of the will or trust or seek a judicial ruling as to the meaning of the will or trust. The statutes also recognize an exception where legal action challenging the validity of the document is "instituted in good faith and based on probable cause that would have led a reasonable person, properly informed and advised, to conclude that there was a substantial likelihood that the trust or other trust-related instrument was invalid."

19

CRITICAL CONVERSATIONS: TALKING ABOUT DEATH, DYING, AND LIFE SUPPORT

Dr. Daren K. Heyland

INTRODUCTION

We live during an unprecedented period in human history. For the first time ever, the number of persons older than 65 worldwide will soon outnumber children under the age of five. The aging of our western society will accelerate in 2011 when the first baby-boom cohort (born in 1946) reaches the age of 65. In Canada, this rapid growth in the aged population is projected to last until 2031, when it is anticipated that seniors over 65 will account for between 23%–25% of the total population, almost double their current proportion of 13%.[1] The age group growing most rapidly is people over age 85, sometimes referred to as the "*old* old" or "very elderly." Coupled with the decline in birth rates worldwide, the changing demographic will have important

Daren K. Heyland, MD, FRCPC, M.Sc., is a professor of medicine and epidemiology at Queen's University, Kingston, Ontario, Canada. For several years, Dr. Heyland has chaired the multidisciplinary Canadian Researchers at the End of Life Network (CARENET), which explores issues related to communication, decision-making, and quality of care provided at the end of life.

social, ethical, and economic implications, not the least of which may be how healthcare systems adapt.

A century ago, when any person contracted a terminal disease or suffered a serious injury, regardless of age, little could be done to reverse the underlying disease, and death frequently ensued. As Plato stated, "For that [death] which takes place according to nature is pleasant, but that which is contrary to nature is painful. And thus death, if caused by disease or produced by wounds, is painful and violent; but that sort of death which comes with old age and fulfills the debt of nature is the easiest of deaths, and is accompanied with pleasure rather than with pain."[2] Most of us would agree with Plato that death at an old age could be a natural event, whereas death of a young person, by "disease or wounds," may be more tragic and filled with a sense of injustice.

Over the last few decades, intensive care units (ICUs) and life-sustaining technologies—such as mechanical ventilators or dialysis machines—have been developed. Some were initially intended to prevent the premature death in young polio or trauma victims. However, in the last 10–20 years, these technologies are increasingly applied to the very elderly with the result that death due to illnesses common in aging has shifted from being a natural life event observed by family and friends to an institutionalized, technologically supported, potentially isolating experience.

Currently, in many parts of the Western world, the majority of deaths occur in a hospital, with a significant proportion of them in an ICU, where life-sustaining technologies are applied to forestall death and prolong life. In the 1990s, only about 10% of ICU admissions were people 80 years of age or older. Moreover, it was rare to have an octogenarian undergo open-heart surgery. Today, almost 20% of ICU admissions are for patients 80 or older, and open-heart surgery has become commonplace in this age group. What is even more striking is that the occurrence of co-morbid illnesses (associated medical problems like cancer, heart disease, and high blood pressure) for these very elderly patients has tripled over the last decade, suggesting that elderly patients with significant, chronic, advanced medical problems are being admitted with increasing frequency to ICUs when they contract a life-threatening illness.

It appears that rather than seeing aging and death as natural processes, we now perceive them as if they were diseases from which a person can recover. The more technology is applied, the greater the chance of treating the aging and forestalling death. From a family's perspective, providing good care to your loved one is often equated with doing everything possible to sustain life. With the advent of more invasive and sophisticated technology, this "doing everything" knows no bounds. In 10–20 years, as society continues to age, the demand for life-preserving medical technologies is expected to explode and will far exceed our ability to supply such services.

Intensification of Care at the End of Life

At times it may be appropriate to provide life-sustaining technologies to very elderly, sick patients. However, I would like to make the point that such technologically supported deaths may not be in patients' or families' best interests. Despite our best efforts as healthcare professionals, many elderly, critically ill patients die from their underlying illness or injury. Recent literature supports the assertion that the intensification of care at the end of life (admission to ICU, use of mechanical ventilators or respirators, dialysis machines, aggressive chemotherapy or tube feeds) is often associated with worse health outcomes for both the patient and the family. To illustrate intensification of care, below are three clinical examples:

An 82-year-old man with severe heart disease and limited ability to care for himself and get around had an unwitnessed cardiac arrest at home. His distraught wife called the ambulance. Resuscitative procedures were initiated, and he was transferred to the local hospital, where his heart was stabilized. A tube was put into his windpipe, and he was hooked up to a breathing machine. Another tube was inserted into the veins in his neck to provide powerful medications to keep the heart pumping steadily. A third tube was placed through his nose into his stomach to feed him. Finally, a tube was inserted into his bladder to drain urine. The elderly gentleman was deeply comatose and had likely sustained a severe brain injury because of a lack of oxygen when he collapsed. Doctors initiated procedures to reduce his body temperature in hopes of minimizing the brain injury. He was kept "on ice" for 24 hours then monitored in the ICU for several days to see if he had any brain function. After one week in the ICU, the doctors informed the family that he was not likely to wake up and regain any normal function. The decision was made to withdraw the life supports, and the patient expired. Months later, family members were still troubled by their memories and images of their loved one "on ice" and with tubes all over his body.

A 76-year-old woman was diagnosed with ovarian cancer that had spread throughout her abdomen. She was offered chemotherapy in an attempt to shrink the tumors and retard their growth. The first round of drugs made her sick to her stomach, her hair fell out, and she lost all her energy. Her symptoms from chemotherapy lasted a month or so. Unfortunately, the treatments were unsuccessful. Her cancer continued to spread, causing her abdomen to swell and making her constantly short of breath. She was hospitalized and underwent another round of chemotherapy. The same symptoms reoccurred, only worse; she was nauseated, short of breath and in considerable pain and discomfort. She rapidly became immobilized. Within seven days of her admission to the hospital, she was bedridden, slipped into a coma, and died. Her loved ones were left questioning why therapies were offered that only made her remaining time on earth miserable for her.

A 72-year-old woman with established dementia from Alzheimer's disease became too much for her family to handle at home and was admitted to a local nursing-home facility. She did not recognize nor interact with her family. The woman was unable to eat on her own and was dependent on family members and attendants to feed her. After one month, the patient lost weight and became malnourished. A feeding tube was inserted through the abdominal wall and into the intestines, and a liquid feeding solution was provided. Because of the tube in her belly, she was restricted in movement and remained in bed or a chair for most of the day. She became progressively weaker to the point where she could no longer get into a chair without considerable assistance. She was unable to look after herself and required assistance with all personal care. After several months in the nursing home, one night she aspirated her oral secretions, started coughing, and became quite distressed. An ambulance was summoned to come to transfer her to the acute-care hospital. Her breathing condition was so severe that the doctors immediately placed a breathing tube into her windpipe, hooked her up to the breathing machine (life support), and provided high-dose oxygen. Despite their best attempts, they could not provide adequate oxygen, and she died in the ICU the next day.

What do these three scenarios have in common? What is your reaction to them? Are you left wondering why such things are done to elderly patients with serious and minimally reversible illnesses? Perhaps you are thinking, "I would never want that to happen to me!" You are not alone. Most elderly people would prefer to be cared for and die at home.[3] Most elderly patients, when provided with a choice, would prefer a less-aggressive treatment plan than a technologically supported, institutionalized death.[4]

There are alternatives. The patient and family always have an option to choose to limit treatments to a certain point and to decline aggressive interventions such as ICU admission or use of a ventilator. They can request a focus only on management of symptoms ("comfort measures") whereby practitioners offer only treatments aimed at alleviating the physical, emotional, and existential distress associated with dying. If these wishes are not made known and advocated for, the system will take over, and aggressive life supports may be provided during the final months of life, even when the patient or family prefers comfort care.[5]

In a study of hospitalized elderly patients in the United States, 70 percent reported that their baseline quality of life was fair or poor and most wanted symptom management as opposed to life-prolonging treatments.[6] Nevertheless, 54 percent of these patients were admitted to ICUs. In another study done in the United States, at least half of seriously ill patients reported pain, and many died after unwanted prolongation of their dying process in an ICU.[7]

These patients, and others like them, report worse quality of life in the period before death compared to dying patients receiving hospice care. Such suffering can cause significant distress to family members during the terminal phase and in the months following death, compared to less-aggressive care that focuses on treating symptoms only.

For those readers who have lost loved ones, the notion may resonate with you that the memories of those final days are often poignant and reside with you for months or years after the event. When that memory is negative—because of the physical, psychological or existential suffering of the loved one—the probability of psychiatric illness experienced by surviving family members (including depression, anxiety, exaggerated grief and even Post-traumatic Stress Disorder) increases.

After death and upon reflection, many family members feel guilty for what they put their loved one through. Unfortunately, despite the best of intentions, applying such technologies at the end of life is often viewed after the fact as intrusive, undignified, and as having a significant negative impact on the quality of the death experience for both the patient and the family. As will be discussed below, this risk can be decreased by ensuring that individuals talk about their thoughts and preferences with all family members who may be asked to make decisions for them in the event of illness.

In a recent landmark study conducted by our group, CARENET, we demonstrated that many elderly, hospitalized, and seriously ill patients value quality of life, not lengthening the dying process.[8] Avoiding unnecessary prolongation of life through technology, and not being a burden to family, are among the most important aspects of end-of-life care for the elderly.[9] They also value having trust and confidence in the physicians looking after them; they want their physicians to be available to them and give them honest information, and to help them make difficult decisions about care near or at the end of life.[10] Unfortunately, this same population of elderly, hospitalized patients is poorly informed about end-of-life treatment options.[11]

ADVANCE-CARE PLANNING

Research has shown that a poorly planned death often equals a poor-quality death, where the experience may be very different than envisioned or desired. Whereas many elderly patients will acknowledge death and have chosen funeral plots and planned their funeral services, few have planned for how they and their families will respond to a serious illness to ensure that their passing is as they hoped. At a church meeting once, I heard an elderly gentleman stand and declare that he was not afraid of death, of what lay behind the veil in the next life, that his understanding of the eternities provided him great comfort that he would be with loved ones again. I wanted to stand up and interrupt him and declare that it was not *death* he should be afraid of, but rather, the *dying process* (what lies between the now and the point of death), and I asked him whether he had carefully planned for *that*. Some religious people, including some Latter-day Saints, tend to have a faith-based approach to planning for the end, meaning they don't plan at all. They don't feel the need to talk about it—they inherently have faith that God will look after them, that their family will know what to do, and that the doctors and nurses will do the best they can. Unfortunately, despite best intentions, reality is often different than this expectation.

For many patients with terminal illness, the absence of end-of-life discussions and planning is associated with worse patient ratings of quality of life in the terminal phase of the illness, worse ratings of satisfaction by the family during the terminal illness, and increased family ratings of anxiety and depression, compared to those who have had had these talks and made plans. Such discussions generally consist of a frank and straightforward disclosure of a prognosis (the chance of surviving the condition and the resultant state of health), a discussion of various treatment options, including comfort care only, a consideration of the patient's values and preferences, and ultimately, a decision about the level or amount of technology that should be applied should the patient require it.

This process, when done in advance of the terminal event, is referred to as "advance-care planning" (ACP). Overall, patients who have this end-of-life communication are much more satisfied with end-of-life care and have higher ratings of quality of life in the final stages of life.[12] ACP should best be viewed as a process or an ongoing dialogue rather than a single event, because perspectives, values, and preferences change over time.

A participant in a research study on improving end-of-life care shared the following after her husband died: "I didn't expect him to die so soon. I got the feeling the doctors weren't entirely honest with us about his condition. The doctors gave us false hope by focusing on his lowered PSA level. My husband was such a private man. He resisted talking about dying, and after 40 years of marriage, I feel he let me down by not opening up, and I guess I let him down for not knowing how to talk about some of the things that I needed to discuss. It would have been nice closure if things had been different in the end. I can never get that time back."

Unfortunately, the quality and quantity of these discussions with elderly patients and their families is insufficient. Healthcare professionals frequently fail to engage patients and families in these difficult conversations, and sometimes if they are attempted they are often of poor quality. As illustrated in the preceding anecdote, patients and families often do not know how to start these conversations and need assistance. Our survey done with hundreds of elderly hospitalized patients demonstrated that the greatest unmet needs at the end of life—the priority areas for improvement of their care—related to helping patients feel at peace, better assessing and treating their emotional problems, improving physician availability, and increasing their satisfaction that the physician took a personal interest in them—that the doctors communicated clearly and consistently to them and listened to them.

Similar priorities were identified from family members' perspectives, but in addition, they wanted more timely information about the patient's condition and better discussions with the doctor regarding the final location of care and use of technology at the end of life. This analysis concluded that better advance-care planning and improved relationships with physicians—including better communication and decision-making—can have the greatest impact on improving the quality of death and dying.[13]

HOW DO WE GET THIS DIALOGUE GOING?

The first place to start is with yourself. Have you considered what kinds of treatments you would want if you were very sick and could die? Have you considered what kinds of conditions would be unacceptable to you, that you would consider to be worse than death? Have you considered who you might trust to make decisions for you if you were too sick to participate in decision-making?

If you are an elderly person, answer the questions in Table 1 and discuss them with a trusted person and other close family members or friends who you would like to include in decision-making should you be unable. Clarify with these loved ones the answers to these questions and appoint one of them to represent you if, due to injury or illness, you are unable to speak and advocate for yourself.

On the other hand, if you have an elderly person in your family, ask them the questions and discuss the answers with other close family members. Have your elderly loved one appoint one of you to be the spokesperson/decision maker if needed.

By going thru the questions on Table 1, you or your family member will be ready to make the best decision in the moment, when such decisions are needed.

The first two questions in Table 1 are meant to create a dialogue about quality of life and what decrease or reduction in quality of life would be acceptable or unacceptable. The remaining three questions tap into one's readiness for death. For example, if there is no unfinished business, the person places an X close to the far right anchor of question #4 (Death), and places an X near far right anchor of question #5 (symptom relief only). The person who answers this way is ready for death, and when a life-threatening illness presents itself, all parties (patient, family, and doctors) will understand that the correct course of action is to provide comfort measures only. On the other hand, if the person has lots of unfinished business and places the Xs closer to the left side of the lines in both questions four and five, this person is not ready to die and may want aggressive, life-sustaining technologies applied when a life-threatening illness develops.

For others, those who place the Xs somewhere in the middle of the scale, the implications will be less clear, and the best answers will only emerge after discussion with a doctor about the specific disease process and therapeutic options available to the patient. Knowledge of the likelihood of benefit from aggressive interventions is crucial as part of this type of discussion. For example, in older people with significant health problems, the chance of successful cardiac resuscitation is less than 10%. The decision to be resuscitated or not is the most common end-of-life decision that elderly hospitalized patient will make when in hospital.

We have created a decision aid to walk patients and their families through this process about deciding about cardiac resuscitation (see www.thecarenet.ca for more details).

A complementary or even alternative approach to beginning this dialogue is the completion of an advance directive or *living will*. Although the terminology may change across various countries or health jurisdictions, basically, an *advance directive* or *living will* is a statement by a person of the kinds of treatments they would like to receive if they became unable to make decisions for themselves. Often, as a part of this documentation, the person specifies who should make decisions pertaining to their health should they become unable to advocate for themselves.

Various planning documents exist, such as My Voice and Respecting My Choices, but the legality and utility of the documents vary depending on local legislation. For examples of such documents in use in Canada, see www.thecarenet.ca. For more information on such documents in the United States, see www.nationalhealthdecisionday.org.

Armed with the answers to such questions, or the completed documents, patients and/or families are ready to engage healthcare professionals in discussions about the kinds of treatments they would like to receive if they experience a life-threatening illness. Don't wait until it's too late to have these discussions. More often than not, when the elderly patient develops a serious illness or injury, they are incapable of having a discussion with the doctor about their wishes. The doctors are left talking to the patient's family. Such families experience considerable distress and anxiety in making life and death decisions on behalf of their loved ones. Opinions in the family may vary considerably, resulting in discord and contention, and long-lasting ill will. Stress, anxiety, and discord are considerably reduced if discussions have already happened, preferences are understood by all, and plans are already in place. Families then know that they are not making a difficult decision, but that they are reflecting the wishes of their loved one.

SAY WHAT YOU NEED TO SAY—NOW!

When I was early in my training as a critical-care physician, I had a significant, poignant experience that touched my life forever. One night while on duty at the local hospital, I was responsible for admitting a middle-aged man to our ICU. Tragically, while at work earlier in the day, this man had collapsed from an intracranial aneurysm. Due to significant bleeding and swelling in the brain, he had suffered a severe brain injury, and his organs where shutting down. It was unclear whether he would survive the night. Even if he did survive the short-term, in the long-term, he would be left with significant disabilities—he would be paralyzed on one side of his body and unable to speak. It was my duty to meet with his wife, tell her what had happened, and explain his expected prognosis.

As I broke the bad news to her, her grief was unbearable. Between her sobs, she shared that earlier that day, before her husband left for work, they'd had a fight, and she'd said some unkind words to him as he went out the door. Now, in his current state, she would never be able to apologize and tell him her true feelings about him. She sobbed at his bedside, wishing she could have the chance to tell him that she truly loved him and was sorry for her harsh words.

From this impactful event, I realized that, but for the grace of God, it could be me or a loved one in the ICU bed, and that each day, I need to have my relationships in order in case I never get the chance to express my love or true feelings again. Repeatedly, I have witnessed illness or injuries rob people of those unspoken conversations. Now is the time to have them.

As John Mayer sings in his hit song, "Say": *say what you need to say . . . it is better to say too much than to never say what you need to say.*

Unhappy with Your Current Care
Near or at the End of Life?

During an interview, the son of deceased woman was asked, "How did things go for you and your mom in the last days of her life?"

He responded, "She got so weak, she wouldn't eat in the last week, and she had trouble swallowing anything, including water. This made it difficult for her to swallow her pain medicine, so she was suffering from a lot of pain. She had a patch, but it didn't cover the pain. There wasn't enough nursing care for her at home, and we didn't know what we were doing with her. The last week was really bad. She kept saying 'Help me,' but I didn't know what to do to help her. I felt so useless. I don't think anyone really knew what was going on with her, and my wife and I sure as heck didn't know what to do for her. I think the whole experience was badly managed, and Mom suffered from it. It is really hard for me—I can't forget how she suffered. I wasn't able to do enough for her."

If you are a patient near the end of your life, or if you have a family member close to the end and are unhappy with or unsure about the current care being received, there are tools that can enable you to begin a dialogue with the healthcare professionals looking after you or your loved one. Our CANHELP questionnaire was developed to help you rate the level of importance of various aspects of healthcare (as either a patient or caregiver) and then rate your current level of satisfaction with each of those aspects. CANHELP has 37 questions and takes about 20 minutes to complete. Once you've completed the questionnaire, you will be provided with a report that can help you to identify the things that are most important to you—and the things you're least satisfied with—and then discuss those things with your healthcare team, family and friends. The questionnaire can be filled out by patients or by family members/friends helping to care for patients. Some patients prefer to bring the report to a social worker or nurse to help them begin the conversation with the healthcare team. For more information, visit: www.thecarenet.ca.

LET'S GET THIS DIALOGUE GOING!

While many older people acknowledge the imminence of death, they neglect planning their dying process. The failure to discuss and plan the nature of treatments provided at the end of life is associated with worse patient and family outcomes. The solution is to engage in a dialogue with family, close friends, and healthcare professionals about the kinds of treatments you want at the end of your life. Those desirable treatments will be a function of your values and preferences, the prognosis of your medical conditions, and the possible treatments available to you.

You always have the option of choosing comfort measures only, whereby practitioners offer only treatments aimed at alleviating the physical, emotional, and existential distress associated with dying. Have these conversations today—and document them in the form of an advance directive—lest you lose the opportunity to say what really needs to be said. Your family will thank you for it—in some cases, posthumously—as you will have alleviated a lot of stress for them in guessing what the right decision was for you.

Table 1. Getting the Dialogue Started

1) In general, how would you rate your *overall health*? Please indicate one answer.

   ☐ Excellent   ☐ Very Good   ☐ Good   ☐ Fair   ☐ Poor

   Please explain what's good and bad about your current situation:

   _____

   _____

   _____

   _____

2) Is there any condition or quality of life that you would consider unacceptable? For example, many people say, "I would rather die than live in a nursing home, where I am totally dependent on others." Think about what health states or conditions would be unacceptable to you and write them in the space provided.

   _____

   _____

   _____

   _____

3) Do you have unfinished business that you really want to get done before you die (assuming you are well enough)? Please describe.

   _____

   _____

   _____

   _____

4) If life were represented by a straight line, where birth is represented on the far left of the line, and death is represented on the far right of the line, place an X on the line where you see yourself on this life line.

   Birth -- Death

5) It is very important for the healthcare team to understand how individual patients who are seriously ill would view the goals of their care. At one end of the spectrum, treatments offered are intended to reduce symptoms such as pain and shortness of breath. Symptom management is not targeted to extend life and may actually shorten it. At the other end of the spectrum, treatments such as breathing machines and dialysis are offered with the primary goal of extending life. These treatments can cause additional pain and discomfort. Please indicate on the line below where you feel would best represent your wishes regarding treatments that *either* extend life as much as possible *or* reduce symptoms (at the far left, the patient values treatments that extend life as long as possible; at the far right, the patient values treatments that relieve distressing symptoms, even if they hasten death).

patient would value←   patient would value
   Extending **L**ife   →**S**ymptom **R**elief
EL_____**SR**

Notes

1. See Statistics Canada, http://cansim2.statcan.ca (consulted Nov. 21, 2007).
2. Timaeus Plato, *The Loeb Classical Library*, 234 (Cambridge, MA: Harvard University Press, 1989), 219.
3. See Department of General Practice, Medical School, University of Otago, Dunnedin, New Zealand, "Attitudes Towards Care of the Dying: A Questionnaire Survey of General Practice Attenders." *FamPract*, 1991; 8 (4), 356–59;Townsend, J, A.O. Frank, D. Fermont, S. Dyer, O. Karran, A. Walgroveet et al, "Terminal Cancer Care and Patients' Preference for Place of Death: A Prospective Study." *BMJ*, 1990; 301 (6749), 415–17; K.I. Stajduhar, D.E. Allan, S.R. Cohen, D.K. Heyland, "Preferences for Location of Death of Seriously Ill Hospitalized Patients: Perspectives from Canadian Patients and Their Family Caregivers." *Palliat Med*, 2008, 22:85–88.
4. See J. Lynn, J. M. Teno, R. S. Phillips, A. W. Wu, N. Desbiens, J. Harrold, et al. "Perceptions by Family Members of the Dying Experiences of Older and

Seriously Ill Patients." SUPPORT Investigators, *Annals of Internal Medicine* (1993), 118:639.

5. Ibid.
6. See E. Somogyi-Zalud, Z. Zhong, M.B. Hamel, J. Lynn, "The Use of Life-Sustaining Treatments in Hospitalized Persons Aged 80 and Older." *J Am Geratric Soc* (2002), 50:930–34.
7. See The SUPPORT Investigators, "A Controlled Trial to Improve Care for Seriously Ill Hospitalized Patients," *JAMA* (1995), 274:1591–98.
8. See Heyland, D. K., P. Dodek, G. Rocker, D. Groll, A. Gafni, D. Pichora, et al., for the Canadian Researchers at the End of Life Network (CARENET). "What Matters Most in End-of-Life Care: Perceptions of Seriously Ill Patients and Their Family Members," *CMAJ* (2006), 174 (5):627–33.
9. Ibid.
10. Ibid.
11. See D. K. Heyland, C. Frank, D. Groll, D. Pichora, P. Dodek, G. Rocker, et al. for the Canadian Researchers at the End of Life Network (CARENET). "Understanding Cardiopulmonary Resuscitation Decision Making: Perspectives of Seriously Ill Hospitalized Patients and Family Members," (*Chest*, Aug. 2006), 130 (2):419–28.
12. See Heyland D. K., D.E. Allan, G. Rocker, P. Dodek, D. Pichora, A. Gafni. "Discussing Prognosis with Patients and Their Families near the End of Life: Impact on Satisfaction with End-of-Life Care," *Open Medicine* (2009), 3 (2):71–80.
13. See D. K. Heyland, D. Cook, G. Rocker, et al. "Defining Priorities to Improve End-of-Life Care in Canada," *Canada Medical Assoc Journal* (2010), in press.

20

FINDING FULFILLMENT
IN LATER LIFE

Lloyd D. Newell

My mother is in her early 80s. She is and always has been a beacon of strength, hope, and faith to me and so many others. She is a positive influence and bright light of optimism and encouragement to all around her. But hers is not a story of a woman without sorrow or pain, and her life didn't unfold the way she expected. No one's life ever does.

She grew up on a farm in southeastern Idaho, the youngest of nine siblings. When she was six, she was kicked in the head by a horse and almost died. At 12 she had an emergency appendectomy that could have taken her life. At 19 she became her parents' caregiver, leaving Brigham Young University to care for them after an accident that could have taken their lives.

Then at 20 she met and married the man of her dreams, my father, and they built a beautiful marriage and family. She served as president of the Relief Society, Primary, Young Women, and the Parent Teacher Association; she reared seven children through adolescent ups and downs, good times and challenging times.

Lloyd D. Newell, Ph.D., is a professor at BYU and author or co-author of more than a dozen books. He has worked as a television news anchor, professional speaker and consultant. Since 1990 he has been the announcer and writer of the Mormon Tabernacle Choir broadcast Music and the Spoken Word. He and his wife, Karmel, are the parents of four children.

At 55, just before my father was to take early retirement from the steel plant where he worked so they could serve missions and enjoy more time together, my father was killed in a tragic industrial accident. Suddenly she was alone, wondering what would become of her. She worked part-time in a retail store, traveled a bit, and spent time with grandkids. Then the next challenge came: at 57 she had brain surgery that left her physically limited and unable to walk, drive a car, or live alone. She could have chosen to wallow in self-pity; she could have given up on life or given in to despair and hopelessness. She could have become bitter and angry that life did not turn out as she had expected. But she had "[laid] aside the things of this world and [sought] for the things of a better"[1] and moved forward with courage, faith and love.

When I am with her and pushing her wheelchair, I sometimes feel like saying to people, "Do you have any idea what an incredible woman this is? Do you know about her strength and courage, her faith and compassion, her wisdom and goodness? She is an amazing woman! Look at her, talk to her, acknowledge her . . . and don't park in the handicapped zone unless you have a permit!" She has a steady stream of people who come to visit her in the assisted-living facility where she lives because of her kind and listening ear, her gentle wisdom and goodness, her ready smile and her interest in others. She has found a measure of fulfillment and joy, even with her difficulties and sorrows. She has come to know that God has not abandoned her.

My mother's life is proof that although life can be difficult, it can also be good—very good. Despite the hardships and heartaches of life, despite our setbacks and shortcomings, despite our aches and pains, we can strive to find joy and purpose in everyday living. As I've watched my mother—and many others like her—I've noticed a few common traits among those who are able to find fulfillment in later life: (1) they've learned how to enjoy living life, (2) they take things one step at a time, (3) they forget themselves and reach out to others, (4) they have a spirit of gratitude, and (5) they are never truly alone, because they walk with God. All of this allows them to find the sweet peace and happiness the gospel brings, regardless of their station in life.

Enjoy Living Life

Several years ago we were driving down the road as a family, busily chatting and laughing along the way. I asked our unusually quiet seven-year-old son, "Jacob, what are you doing back there?"

He enthusiastically responded from the back seat, "I'm just living life!"

Living life: it's not always easy, especially when we know keenly that the years ahead of us are fewer than those behind us. How can we find happiness and fulfillment when our bodies are slowing down, when life hasn't turned out exactly the way we had planned, when disappointment and sorrow have been our companion along life's twists and turns?

We *can* find joy and goodness if we'll look for it. Life is full of everyday moments that bring a smile or warm the heart: the glorious dawn of a new day, the flight of a bird, the melting of an icicle, the smell of bread in the toaster, the toothless smile of a child, the hug of a loved one, the laughter of family and friends, the kindness of strangers. Moments like these bring peaceful assurance that God, the Father of our souls, is in His heaven, watching over His children. With this assurance, we can face any fear, deal with any difficulty, and do more than we may have thought possible.

The longer we live, the more we become aware of the sorrows and sufferings of life—and, ironically, the more we can become aware of life's beauties and blessings. Sometimes it takes courage to believe that life is good, that God will walk with us. We can begin with something as easy as knowing that the sun *will* rise and that winter *will* turn to spring. From there we can trust that good will triumph over evil, that kind and decent people far outnumber those who are not, that losses truly can give way to gains, that the plan of salvation is real and the restored gospel of Jesus Christ is true. We can hope and pray for the sweet assurance, the quiet confidence that comes to those who trust in God and do their best each day. We can choose to believe that life, no matter what its difficulties, really is good. The great writer Victor Hugo advised: "Have courage for the great sorrows of life and patience for the small ones; and when you have laboriously accomplished your daily task, go to sleep in peace. God is awake."[2]

ONE STEP AT A TIME

In 1833, John Henry Newman was traveling from Europe back to his beloved home in England. He was already ill and homesick when he was seized by an attack of malaria. To make matters worse, fog rolled in, and his ship was becalmed at sea. He longed for England—for home—and was discouraged by the delay. Humbled by his infirmity, his heart turned heavenward. Despite the fog that enshrouded his ship, heavenly light penetrated the fog that had enshrouded his soul, and he wrote the words for which he would long be remembered:

> Lead, kindly Light, amid th' encircling gloom;
> Lead thou me on!
> The night is dark, and I am far from home;
> Lead thou me on!
> Keep thou my feet; I do not ask to see
> The distant scene—one step enough for me.[3]

When fog seems to obscure our view of the days ahead, often one step *is* enough. We may be paralyzed by fear, pride or discouragement, unwilling to take another step unless we know exactly where it leads. We may feel that the best has passed us by, that life is to be waited out, not *lived*. As John Henry Newman learned, patience and peaceful resignation are sometimes needed. Sometimes we just have to wait, to stay awhile in life's present moments. During those seasons of life, inspiration and humility can be born; faith in everlasting things can be rekindled; hope in the Lord and His gospel can be strengthened. We can take comfort in the words of the Psalmist: "Wait on the Lord: be of good courage, and he shall strengthen thine heart."[4]

In his brokenness and despair, John Henry Newman found the Lord's strengthening and healing balm. President Thomas S. Monson has encouraged us in our day to "look to the lighthouse of the Lord. There is no fog so dense, no night so dark, no gale so strong, no mariner so lost but what its beacon light can rescue. It beckons through the storms of life. The lighthouse of the Lord sends forth signals readily recognized and never failing. . . . The Lord loves us, my brothers and sisters, and will bless us as we call upon Him."[5]

Life is lived one step at a time. If we're patient, we can learn a lot from taking one step of faith—and then another and another. Especially later in life, when our passions and exuberance may be dimmed with aches and pains, with disappointments and worries, we may feel too weary to carry on. But carry on we must. President Dieter F. Uchtdorf taught: "Patience is not passive resignation, nor is it failing to act because of our fears. Patience means active waiting and enduring. It means staying with something and doing all that we can— working, hoping, and exercising faith; bearing hardship with fortitude, even when the desires of our hearts are delayed. Patience is not simply enduring; it is enduring well!"[6]

It has been said that "the best thing about the future is that it only comes one day at a time." Acknowledging that fact may not always diminish our current sorrow or suffering, but it can help us endure it well. We need only thank the Lord for another day of life and trust Him to light our way. As we do, joy will fill our hearts, and purpose will come to our days—one step at a time.

Reach Out to Others

You and I know stories of people who at age 70 go to law school, who at 75 start a business, who at 80 take up skydiving and motorcycle riding—remarkable stories affirming that a zest for life does not have to die within us. But sometimes these stories may discourage more than they inspire.

I'm inspired by a neighbor, now 73, who "adopted" us as her family and has become a beloved "grandmother" to our children. I'm inspired by a couple, now in their late 70s, who continue to serve others although their physical health makes it impossible for them to go on a mission together. I'm inspired by our prophets, seers, and revelators, past and present, who, despite advanced years, continue to bless and minister and serve passionately and faithfully.

President Gordon B. Hinckley taught, "He who lives only unto himself withers and dies, while he who forgets himself in the service of others grows and blossoms in this life and in eternity."[7]

We are to be anxiously engaged in good causes,[8] as much as we are able, over the course of our lives. President Uchtdorf said to the "seasoned" brethren of the priesthood: "Retirement is not part of the Lord's plan of happiness. There is no sabbatical or retirement program from priesthood responsibilities—regardless of age or physical capacity."[9]

We can all do something. Expectations may need to be adjusted, tasks may need a little more time, and we may not move as fast as we once did, but we can all serve in some way. It doesn't have to be something big; it just has to come from a willing heart.

I know so many who have served so faithfully for so long, but now is a different season for them. We have a sweet friend who is approaching 90. She, too, has made us a part of her family. We have family home evening together from time to time. We are strengthened by her faith and courage, and we are inspired by her testimony. She may not have an official church calling, but she blesses the lives of countless individuals and families. She finds joy and the antidote to loneliness by reaching out to others.

I think of another friend, now in his early 70s and a widower of eight years, who once or twice a month visits an assisted-living center to sing show tunes from the past and share his life and talent with others. He told me, "I could sit home and feel sorry for myself. I could spend my day watching TV and waiting for the phone to ring. Instead, I decided a few years ago to get out and try to brighten someone else's day. My singing may not be the best, but the groups I sing for seem to enjoy it. I sure enjoy it . . . and it keeps me young!"

We all need to reach out to others, and we all need to be reached out to. When someone close to you has suffered a loss—whether a death, a divorce, the loss of a job, or the loss of a dream—take the time to find out what would help him or her most. When someone you know is discouraged, disheartened, and struggling, reach out in love and kindness. Extend a friendly, caring hand. Lend a listening, compassionate ear. More often than not, what we offer won't be something that costs money, but rather a gift of time, a gift of self. Life is not over as long as we think of others, as long as we can reach out in love and kindness.

DAILY GRATITUDE AND THANKSGIVING

A few years ago, researchers conducted what they called the Research Project on Gratitude and Thankfulness. They found scientifically what most of us know intuitively: gratitude makes people happy.[10]

For the study, several hundred people were divided into three groups and asked to keep diaries. The first group listed the day's events in their diaries, the second group recorded any unpleasant experiences they had during the day, and the last group made a daily list of things they were grateful for.

The researchers found that the simple act of taking time each day to count your blessings makes a person more enthusiastic, determined, optimistic, and energetic. Those who expressed gratitude experienced less depression and stress, exercised more regularly, and made more progress toward personal goals. Researchers even noted a relationship between feeling grateful and feeling loved, and they observed how gratitude inspires acts of kindness and compassion.

Remarkable, isn't it? All this from daily gratitude and thanksgiving.

When we daily count our blessings, we feel better about life, even in the midst of adversity; we garner strength of character and largeness of soul that will help us through hard times; and we see life as basically good, despite its challenges and heartaches. That's why the scriptures exhort us to "live in thanksgiving daily, for the many mercies and blessings which [God] doth bestow upon [us]."[11] If we open our hearts and look, we'll find reasons for gratitude and thanksgiving each day, all around us.

President Thomas S. Monson said:

> Our realization of what is most important in life goes hand in hand with gratitude for our blessings. Said one well-known author: "Both abundance and lack [of abundance] exist simultaneously in our lives, as parallel realities. It is always our conscious choice which secret garden we will tend . . . when we choose not to focus on what is missing from our lives but are grateful for the abundance that's present—love, health, family, friends, work, the joys of nature, and personal pursuits that bring us [happiness]—the wasteland of illusion falls away and we experience heaven on earth.". . . Despite the challenges which come into our lives and with gratitude in our hearts, may we fill our days—as much as we can—with those things which matter most. May we cherish those we hold dear and express our love to them in word and in deed.[12]

So often we fail to be grateful for the present moments of life. We may consume the joys of the here and now with a longing for something else. When we're working, we may think of retirement; when we're in retirement, we may long for a busy career. Or, when the children are young and energetic, we may wish for a quiet and clean house; and when they're gone, how we yearn for the joyful noise of children to fill our empty home. Life teaches us that the longer we live, the more we learn to value present moments.

God's creations are an abundant source of such moments. As Elder M. Russell Ballard has said: "Take time to observe the marvels of nature. . . . Share with your family the miracle of buds changing to fragrant blossoms. Take time to sit on a hillside and feel the tranquility of the evening, when the sun casts its last golden glow over the horizon. Take time to smell the roses."[13] Taking time to feel grateful will fill your heart with peace and joy.

Grateful people know that life has its challenges and heartaches, its satisfactions and joys. To be grateful doesn't mean to deny the difficulties of life. It means to recognize that the blessings outweigh the trials and that more often than not, things tend to work out. It means to see beauty even when it's surrounded by ugliness, to see peace amid the storms of life. In fact, the ugliness and the storms seem to make the beauty and peace more noticeable. Our sorrows and trials may become the very things that help gratitude grow in our hearts.

A truly grateful heart is an abundant heart that builds bridges of understanding and opens doors of friendship. At times it may seem easier to turn inward, to keep others at a distance, to withhold our time, our means, and our hearts from others. But that can lead to unhappiness and smallness of heart.

When we feel grateful, our hearts overflow with good feelings for others. Rabbi Harold S. Kushner writes of a man whose small plane crash-landed but who was fortunate enough to escape before it burst into flames. A reporter asked him what was going through his mind as the plane neared the ground. His answer revealed the abundance of his heart: "I realized I hadn't thanked enough people in my life."[14] Before another opportunity passes, let's open our hearts to others, count our blessings, and give thanks. In doing so, we find joy and fulfillment.

WALK WITH GOD

Many of us are familiar with the show tune "You'll Never Walk Alone," from the 1945 Rodgers and Hammerstein musical *Carousel:*

> Walk on, walk on, with hope in your heart
> And you'll never walk alone.

Who among us has not felt lonely, even afraid at times? A loved one dies, friends and family move away, visits come to an end, and silence is all we hear. The quiet of loneliness can be deafening. At other times we may feel alone even when surrounded by people. Perhaps our loneliness stems from the nagging feeling that we're not valued or appreciated. It may be that we're discouraged. Or maybe resentment and heartache has led us to detach ourselves from others. Whatever the reason, feelings of loneliness can range from momentary sadness to the crushing weight of despair.

There is a way to the other side of loneliness. The Lord taught that the peacemakers, the pure in heart, the meek and merciful would be blessed here and hereafter with comfort and joy.[15] Purposeful activity, worthwhile endeavors, service to others, family, and friendship and fellowship with good people will help us feel less lonely.

Loneliness is never permanent when we walk on with hope and faith in our hearts. You've had such faith during your life, and you can be inspired now by the examples of people you know. I have a friend in her mid-60s who has suffered great loss and could brood about her loneliness and heartache. Instead, over time and with great willpower, she has chosen to lift and bless others. She knows that while she hasn't changed the world, she has made a difference. She has been a friend. She has listened and been kind. You know people like her—people who reach out to God and to others while in the midst of loneliness. The Lord blesses them and each of us—for if we walk with Him, we'll never walk alone.

WHENCE HAPPINESS?

And so we ask the question: "How do we find happiness?" Obtaining happiness can be like catching a butterfly—it seems so elusive, always out of reach. Yet happiness is what we long for more than anything else in the world. The Prophet Joseph Smith said, "Happiness is the object and design of our existence; and will be the end thereof, if we pursue the path that leads to it; and this path is virtue, uprightness, faithfulness, holiness, and keeping all the commandments of God"[16]

President James E. Faust said, "Happiness is not given to us in a package that we can just open up and consume. Nobody is ever happy 24 hours a day, seven days a week. Rather than thinking in terms of a day, we perhaps need to snatch happiness in little pieces, learning to recognize the elements of happiness and then treasuring them while they last."[17]

Elder Richard G. Scott suggested that happiness can come from something as simple as learning a new skill:

> After their noble husbands were called home, Sisters Camilla Kimball, Amelia McConkie, and Helen Richards learned to paint. They not only leave legacies of art, but they will never see a sunset, a face, or a tree the same again. They now perceive subtle nuances of color and form and rejoice in the abounding beauty around them. Select something like music, dance, sculpture, or poetry. Being creative will help you enjoy life. It engenders a spirit of gratitude. It develops latent talent, sharpens your capacity to reason, to act, and to find purpose in life. It dispels loneliness and heartache. It gives a renewal, a spark of enthusiasm, and zest for life.[18]

President Hinckley's personal motto is one to remember as we seek joy and fulfillment in later life: "Things will work out. If you keep trying and praying and working, things will work out. They always do. If you want to die at an early age, dwell on the negative. Accentuate the positive, and you'll be around for a while."[19]

Those of us who *have* been around for a while have had many opportunities to see the truth of President Hinckley's words. Life really is good, and in many ways it gets better as it goes along—particularly for those who have learned to enjoy living life, to take things one step at a time, to reach out to others, to live in thanksgiving daily, and to overcome loneliness by walking with God. They look for happiness in little pieces: a beautiful vista, a child's laughter, a worthwhile accomplishment, a simple act of service. Because these things seem small, we're inclined to miss them in our pursuit of happiness and fulfillment. Maybe fulfillment and happiness are simpler than we sometimes think. Maybe instead of trying to catch the butterfly, we can just enjoy her visit for a while.

Sweet Is the Peace the Gospel Brings

The Mormon Tabernacle Choir's 2009 CD release, *Come, Thou Fount of Every Blessing*, contains one of my favorite Mack Wilberg arrangements, "My Song in the Night." The words are partly an adaptation from Joseph Swain's poem "Redemption" (published in London in 1789):

> O Jesus, my Savior, my song in the night,
> Come to us with Thy tender love, my soul's delight.
> Unto Thee, O Lord, in affliction I call,
> My comfort by day and my song in the night.

In these troubled times, it's reassuring to know that God is watching over His children. This promise is perhaps best expressed in the

Psalm: "He that keepeth thee . . . shall neither slumber nor sleep. The Lord *is* thy keeper."[20] The Good Shepherd is vigilant by day and by night. When the shadows get darker and the threats seem more real, He stands ready to help. When disquieting sounds and hidden dangers intensify our fears and shake our peace, He offers comfort as He did to the Psalmist, who testified, "In the night his song *shall be* with me."[21] That song is a song of peace amid the storms of life, of comfort despite heartache and pain, and above all, it is a song of love and tender watchcare.

Recently, I asked a dear elderly widow if she ever felt afraid, living alone as she does. She replied with the kind of faith and conviction that had seen her through many years and many difficult circumstances. She explained that she does not feel afraid because, with all her heart, she knows that God loves her and is watching over her.

No matter how dark the night, we can feel heaven's light. That doesn't mean bad things won't happen. Good people will suffer, hearts will be broken, and anguish in one form or another comes to us all. But we can trust in the Lord's promises: "For after much tribulation come the blessings. Wherefore the day cometh that ye shall be crowned with much glory; the hour is not yet, but is nigh at hand."[22] It may even be that after opposition and hardship, we may yet have greater joy and rejoicing in the fulfillment of our lives. In our quiet moments, we listen to Him whose song in the night whispers peace, comfort, and joy to the soul. In our suffering, we remember and take strength from the Savior's promise: "My peace, I give unto you: not as the world giveth, give I unto you."[23]

Advancing years give us time to come to some measure of resolution or peace concerning many troubling issues and worries; they give us opportunity to feel the serenity and fulfillment that may come with a life well-lived, and a fuller understanding of its meaning and purpose. True joy and abiding peace distills upon our souls as the dews of heaven as we reap the benefits of long association with the Spirit of the Lord.

Over the years we become, as it were, better friends with the Lord and
with the Spirit. President Ezra Taft Benson said, "Spirituality—being in
tune with the Spirit of the Lord—is the greatest need we all have. We
should strive for the constant companionship of the Holy Ghost all the
days of our lives."[24] As the apostle Paul wrote, "The fruit of the Spirit
is love, joy, peace, longsuffering, gentleness, goodness, faith, meekness,
temperance."[25] In the meekness and humility of our lives—perhaps
reflected in the mellowing that frequently accompanies aging—the
Spirit may teach us that ultimate of human virtues: perfect love.[26] Our
joy will be deeper, and our preparation to meet the Savior will be enhanced, as we acquire these godly attributes.[27] We come, in the end, to
the sweet peace the gospel brings and a comforting assurance of the
Lord's promise: "But learn that he who doeth the works of righteousness shall receive his reward, even peace in this world, and eternal life
in the world to come."[28]

Now is the time to prepare and look forward to the next stage of
our eternal journey. Now is the time to rejoice in the blessings of life,
the wisdom gained and lessons learned, to recognize the Lord's out-
stretched and compassionate hand, to acknowledge worthy and ongoing efforts to change and repent and forgive, to exult in the joy that
comes as our children walk in truth[29] and to be patient and understanding with both ourselves and with others who struggle. No matter our
age or stage of life, we're all in this together.[30]

Notes

1. D&C 25:10.
2. Richard L. Evans, *Richard Evans' Quote Book* (Salt Lake City: Publisher's Press, 1971), 139.
3. "Lead, Kindly Light," *Hymns of The Church of Jesus Christ of Latter-day Saints* (Salt Lake City: The Church of Jesus Christ of Latter-day Saints, 1985), no. 97.
4. Psalm 27:14.
5. "A Word at Closing," *Ensign*, May 2010, 113.
6. "Continue in Patience," *Ensign*, May 2010, 57.

7. *Teachings of Gordon B. Hinckley* (Salt Lake City: Deseret Book Co., 1997), 588.
8. See D&C 58:27.
9. "Two Principles for Any Economy," *Ensign*, Nov. 2009, 57.
10. See Robert A. Emmons and Michael E. McCullough, "Highlights from the Research Project on Gratitude and Thankfulness," http://psychology.ucdavis.edu/labs/emmons; see also "Gratitude Theory," http://www.acfnewsource.org/religion/gratitude_theory.html.
11. Alma 34:38.
12. "Finding Joy in the Journey," *Ensign*, Nov. 2008, 86–87.
13. "The Handiwork of God," *New Era*, Mar. 2006, 7.
14. *The Lord Is My Shepherd: Healing Wisdom of the Twenty-third Psalm* (New York: Alfred A. Knopf, 2003), 154–55.
15. See Matthew 5:3–10.
16. Joseph Smith, *History of the Church* (Salt Lake City: Deseret Book, Co., 1991), 5:134–35.
17. "Our Search for Happiness," *Ensign*, Oct. 2000, 2.
18. "Finding Joy in Life," *Ensign*, May 1996, 26.
19. Sheri Dew, *Go Forward with Faith: The Biography of Gordon B. Hinckley* (Salt Lake City: Deseret Book Co., 1996), 423.
20. Psalm 121:3–5.
21. Psalm 42:8; emphasis added.
22. D&C 58:4; see also 122:7.
23. John 14:27.
24. "Seek the Spirit of the Lord," *Ensign*, April 1988, 5.
25. Galatians 5:22–23.
26. See Moroni 8:26, 7:44–48.
27. See 2 Peter 1:2–8.
28. D&C 59:23.
29. 3 John 1:4.
30. I wish to acknowledge that some of the ideas and expressions in this chapter were presented earlier in Spoken Word messages I wrote for the Mormon Tabernacle Choir broadcast, Music and the Spoken Word. Revised portions of the following are included: "In Times of Loneliness," Sept. 12, 2004; "Life Is Good," Feb. 4, 2007; "The Elements of Happiness," Nov. 4, 2007; "A Song in the Night," Oct. 3, 2010.

21

BEYOND MORTALITY:
PATHWAY TO ETERNAL LIFE
Joseph Fielding McConkie

As we approach our later years, the question of life after death has much greater poignancy as "all must die." The great question that Job posed was, "If a man die, shall he live *again?*"[1] Conceived before the foundation of the world, Heavenly Father's plan for the salvation of His children provided that after a mortal probation on earth, man would pass through the portals of death as part of his eternal journey. Seen in the eternal perspective, the passage into the realm of spirits to await the resurrection is part of the pathway leading to eternal life as provided for in the plan of salvation.

A knowledge of the plan of salvation, or the path to eternal life, is—and always has been—the exclusive province of those who believe in the principle of revelation. It is not historical revelation of which I speak—revelation given to another people in another time—but rather revelation that is immediate and personal to those involved. Living revelation is the key by which all that has been revealed in the past is unlocked and the continued light of heaven is received and understood.

Joseph Fielding McConkie served as a seminary teacher, LDS chaplain (including a year in Vietnam), Institute director at the University of Washington, mission president in Scotland, and professor of scripture at BYU for 30 years, where he also received his doctorate. He is the author or co-author of 28 books on gospel subjects.

THESE SIGNS WILL FOLLOW

Three signs always identify those to whom the plan of salvation has been revealed: prophets, priesthood, and the ordinances of salvation. Without these, the keys of the mysteries of the kingdom cannot be had. These keys, which unlock the gates of heaven and identify the path we must follow, are entrusted only to prophets.

The word *keys* is used in the revelations of the Restoration with two distinct meanings. The first describes the power to unlock or open the heavens so that God either stands revealed or remains unknown. All true religion is revealed religion. Anything that stands this side of revelation, relative to the plan of salvation, is simply speculation.

The second usage of *keys* is an extension of the first and centers on the authority by which the priesthood is governed or disciplined.

With regard to the first meaning, often when you read the word *keys*, it will be associated with the word *mysteries*. In the scriptural sense, *mystery* refers to that which can be had and understood only by revelation.

The concept of a *mystery* is inseparably associated with sacred ordinances. The phrase *mystery religions* in ancient times was used to describe those religions which had preserved, to one degree or another, the temple ceremony as it was had from the days of Adam. The term *mystery* is used thirteen times in the New Testament, where it is the translation of a Greek word meaning *initiatory*. Its primary reference was to sacred ordinances by which the veil was lifted so that people could receive knowledge of their destiny. Often this involved communication with the temple oracle.

The usage of the phrase *keys of the kingdom* has reference to *the right of presidency*.[2] The keys of presidency govern and discipline the use of priesthood authority. For instance, though a man may hold the authority to baptize, he can baptize only under the bishop's direction and with his permission. A baptism not performed under the direction of keys is void and meaningless.[3] So it is with the administration of the sacrament or any other gospel ordinance—to be valid, all ordinances must be performed under the direction of the presiding officer who holds the appropriate keys, which come only by the laying on of hands.

Those ordinances, in turn, constitute *key words*, meaning that they bring with them knowledge and understanding that can be had in no other way.

Of necessity, this means that the Lord's people have always been a temple-building people. The temple is the sacred space in which all the ordinances of salvation are performed. Participation in these ordinances brings with them the knowledge of the path to be followed in obtaining eternal life. Such principles cannot be found in a book. It is one thing to read about Christ's baptism and quite another to be baptized. It is one thing to read about the power of the priesthood and quite another to hold that power. Thus, in the full and complete sense, only those who have participated in these ordinances can have a complete and meaningful understanding of the plan of salvation.

Many in our day profess their religion to be Bible religion. Salvation, they declare, comes from their faith in the Bible and in their profession of Christ. The declaration itself is unbiblical. Remember that those of whom we read in the Bible never had a Bible; and that the revelation of Christ bringing with it the power of salvation requires participation in the same ordinances that Christ and His disciples participated in. While Christ died that we might live, we must live in a manner that justifies His death if we are to obtain eternal life. If we are to receive the same blessings granted to the saints in ancient days, we must receive the same ordinances in the same manner that they received them. To follow a different path is to end up in a different place.

KNOWLEDGE RESTORED

It follows as the night the day that, in the meridian of time, when the principle of revelation was lost and the canon of scripture declared complete or closed, that the power and authority of the priesthood had been lost. You cannot speak for God if God does not speak to you. If

He speaks to you, the canon of scripture cannot be closed. With the loss of the priesthood comes the loss of the ordinances of salvation. As a result, we immediately find what could be called *ordinance drift*, meaning that ordinances will be changed—either added to or taken from—but most importantly, they are without the power of revelation and are no longer *key words* bringing with them an understanding of the mysteries of heaven.

Thus the Restoration centers in the opening of the heavens, meaning the restoring of the principle of revelation; the restoration of the priesthood, which always follows immediately upon the heels of the heavens being opened; and the covenants of salvation being restored with the knowledge and understanding that comes only through them.

Because of this sequence of events, we as Latter-day Saints know a number of important things.

We know that God is a personal being—having body, parts, and passions. We know that He is an exalted, glorified man.

We know that we were first born as spirits to heavenly parents—that we are literally children of God and His eternal companion, our Heavenly Mother.

We know that our spirits are in the image and likeness of our physical tabernacle and that we came to earth to gain a physical body, which will house our spirits throughout the endless expanses of eternity.

We know that birth into this mortal sphere is the process whereby our spirit is enabled to obtain a physical body. The union of body and spirit constitutes life here in our second estate, while the separation of body and spirit constitutes death.

We know that in and through the Atonement of Christ all things that have life, and thus became subject to death through Adam's Fall, will be resurrected. The resurrection is the inseparable union of body and spirit.[4]

We know that the nature of our resurrected body will be determined by the law we choose to obey in our mortal probation. Those who have been responsive to things of a celestial order will come forth from the grave with a celestial body. Those who have been responsive to a terrestrial order will obtain bodies that are terrestrial, and those who have assumed a telestial nature will receive a body that is telestial.[5]

We know that at the time of our birth as spirits, we were granted the gift of agency. Agency, the power to act, enables us to determine our own destiny. This gift was given to us anew at the time of our birth into mortality. As this gift was given to all of God's children, so all of His children have the power and capacity to become as He is. Doing so constitutes our salvation, or what we commonly refer to as exaltation in the celestial kingdom.

THE SPIRIT WORLD

This knowledge places us in a position to ask and answer questions that others cannot. For instance, at death (the separation of the body and spirit), what becomes of the spirit while we wait for the time of our resurrection? Having asked this question of an angel, Alma was told that those who chose wickedness over righteousness will, at death, be cast out into "outer darkness."[6] This is not the hell reserved for those sons of perdition who have denied the Holy Ghost, but a place for the mending of their ways.[7]

Those who chose to live righteously—meaning those who comply with the laws and ordinances of the gospel—will go to a place in the spirit world which the angel called *paradise*, where they will enjoy a "state of happiness."[8] There, he said, they would rest, being freed from the burdens of this mortal state, such as hunger, pain, fatigue, and all other forms of physical corruption.

From Joseph F. Smith's vision of the redemption of the dead, we learn that men will join their various priesthood quorums and continue the work and labor of teaching the gospel both to those who were faithful to what they knew, and to those who did not have the opportunity to hear it in this life. That women will be involved in the same labor is axiomatic; indeed, for the most part they will labor with their husbands in the teaching of the gospel to their own progenitors. Often women will be found teaching women, while the men will instruct their counterparts, just as in this life. In the family setting, men and women will teach together as is the eternal order.

We will take the knowledge of the gospel that we have obtained in this life with us into the world of the spirits. Given that you cannot teach what you do not know, those who are not prepared to teach will have to labor to prepare themselves to do so, just as those called on missions in this life must learn.

Not birth, death, or the resurrection will alter any gospel principle. Gospel principles are absolute and eternal, meaning that they are endlessly the same. Those who leave this life filled with light and truth will be filled with light and truth in the world to come. Those who are ignorant of such truths do not become equal to them simply through death. Death does not bring with it a restoration of our pre-earth memory (a matter to which we will come); thus their minds will be as dark or light then as they are now.[9] This concept is particularly important for Latter-day Saints, who may be scripturally and doctrinally lazy and who have done little else than find some authority to quote when called on to speak or teach. Just as revelations given to others do not empower us to act, our salvation cannot rest on what others know and do.

As the gospel centers in faith, repentance, baptism and the receipt of the Holy Ghost, in the spirit world it will also center in those same principles. The gospel remains unchanged. Faith must be exhibited in the same proportion there to obtain salvation as was the case in this life. Nothing will change relative to the process of repentance. That which we failed to overcome here must be addressed on the same conditions there. Revelation states: "The dead who repent will be redeemed, through obedience to the ordinances of the house of God. And after they have paid the penalty of their transgressions, and are washed clean, shall receive a reward according to their works, for they are heirs of salvation."[10]

COMMON MISCONCEPTIONS

While it is appropriate to offer words of consolation on behalf of the mourners and to celebrate the life of the deceased, often the emotions that surround funeral sermons cloud a clear understanding of the plan of salvation as declared in the scriptures. If funerals are our standard, it would appear that only the righteous die. In like manner, Sunday School and other auxiliary classes often pass notions from generation to generation that could be greatly improved upon by a careful reading of scripture and thoughtful attention to those principles taught in our temples.

It is commonly taught that at death, those who do not go to paradise are consigned to spirit prison. This does not accord with scripture. *Spirit prison* and *hell* are the scriptural phrases used to describe the place of departed spirits in the Bible. The Bible Dictionary explains that *hell* is an English word representing the translation of the Hebrew word *Sheol* or the Greek word *Hades*, both of which refer to the abode of departed spirits. We have ascribed to them the idea of a place of torment for the wicked, but this was not their original or primary meaning.[11]

In Moses, we read Enoch's prophecy about the events surrounding the Resurrection of Christ. He said, "the saints arose, and were crowned at the right hand of the Son of Man, with crowns of glory; and as many of the *spirits as were in prison* came forth, and stood on the right hand of God; and the remainder were reserved in chains of darkness until the judgment of the great day."[12]

The true understanding is that death itself is a bondage imposed upon all because of the Fall of Adam. All are prisoners, and at death, all are consigned to spirit prison, which as Alma taught us, is divided into *outer darkness* and *paradise*. Only through Christ and His Atonement and the resurrection can even the most righteous be redeemed or freed from its effects.

This concept receives considerable emphasis in Joseph F. Smith's "vision of the redemption of the dead," where the righteous dead are described as a "vast multitude" awaiting "the hour of their deliverance from the chains of death," to whom the Son of God appeared, "declaring *liberty* to the *captives* who had been faithful. . . . But unto the wicked he did not go, and among the ungodly and the unrepentant who had defiled themselves while in the flesh, his voice was not raised; Neither did the rebellious who rejected the testimonies and the warnings of the ancient prophets behold his presence, nor look upon his face. Where these were, darkness reigned, but among the righteous there was peace; And the saints rejoiced in their redemption, and bowed the knee and acknowledged the Son of God as *their Redeemer and Deliverer from death and the chains of hell.*"[13]

Understanding these principles brings with it a more healthy understanding of the significance of the Atonement of Christ. Adam's Fall brings the bondage of death to both the righteous and the wicked, and both are fully dependent on Jesus Christ for their redemption from its effects. The full blessings of the Atonement come only to those who have chosen to live in such a manner that they come forth in a celestial resurrection.

As noted earlier another common misconception deals with the idea that at death we receive a restoration of our pre-earth memory. In fact there are no bonuses for dying, no immediate restoration of pre-earth knowledge. If this were the case, there would be no test of faith in accepting the gospel in the spirit world. The citizens of that estate could not be "judged according to men in the flesh," as declared by Peter, and Joseph F. Smith in their respective revelations.[14] On this matter Alma taught thus:

"It is given unto many to know the mysteries of God; nevertheless they are laid under a strict command that they shall not impart only according to the portion of his word which he doth grant unto the children of men, according to the heed and diligence which they give unto him. And therefore, he that will harden his heart, the same receiveth the lesser portion of the word; and he that will not harden his heart, to him is given the greater portion of the word, until it is given unto him to know the mysteries of God until he know them in full. And they that will harden their hearts, to them is given the lesser portion of the word until they know nothing concerning his mysteries; and then they are taken captive by the devil, and led by his will down to destruction. Now this is what is meant by the chains of hell."[15]

DEATH

"Death hath passed upon all men, to fulfill the merciful plan of the great Creator."[16] It brings an end to our experience in a corruptible world.

"[Death] is one of the most important and desirable events that can transpire in the eternal existence of the spirit offspring of Him who ordained the great plan of mercy of which it is a part. It is just as important to die as to be born, for the spirit to leave the body as for it to enter that same body. Mortality is a necessary prelude to immortality; it is by passing the test of this life that men obtain eternal life in the world to come. If there had been no creation, there would have been no fall. If there had been no fall, there could have been no birth into mortality. If there were no mortality, there would be no death. And without death there would be no resurrection, and hence no immortality or eternal life. Thus to do away with death would frustrate the whole plan of redemption."[17]

JUDGMENT

Given that resurrection is the inseparable union of body and spirit, and that it comes before we are invited to stand before the bar of God, it is also a judgment. Nephi's brother Jacob explained the doctrine in this manner: "And it shall come to pass that when all men shall have passed from this first death unto life, insomuch as they have become immortal [that is, have been resurrected], they must appear before the judgment seat of the Holy One of Israel; and then cometh the judgment, and then must they be judged according to the holy judgment of God."[18]

But before that great day, there are a number of preliminary judgments. Alma explains that death itself is a judgment. The spirits of the righteous, he said, are "received into a state of happiness, which is called paradise, a state of rest, a state of peace, where they shall rest from all their troubles and from all care, and sorrow." There is no apostasy from paradise.[19] It will be with them as it is with translated beings: Satan simply has no power over them.[20] By contrast, in death the "spirits of the wicked," those who had no "part nor portion of the Spirit of the Lord" but chose "evil works rather than good" will be "cast out into outer darkness," where there will be "weeping, and wailing, and gnashing of teeth, and this because of their own iniquity, being led captive by the will of the devil."[21]

In the resurrection those who are celestial will be called forth first, then will come the resurrection of those who are terrestrial, and these will be followed by those who are telestial. The order of the resurrection is from the most righteous to the most wicked—in that order. As to standing before the judgment bar of God, the degree of glory you have inherited will already be known to you and not subject to change because you have already received your resurrected body. This experience will simply affirm the justice of God.[22]

This means that those in the celestial kingdom cannot fall from their exalted position—no one apostatizes from exaltation. To suppose that this could be the case would be the same as supposing that God could err in judgment, retire, get old and sick, or even just choose not to be God any longer. As this cannot happen, neither can those who are telestial become terrestrial or those who are terrestrial become celestial.

Each will already have a body and spirit that are "inseparably" united together that accords with the law of the kingdom they have merited.

DEGREES OF GLORY

Those resurrected in what we call "the morning of the first resurrection" inherit the highest of the three degrees of the celestial kingdom. Only in this ultimate degree of glory is the power of eternal lives, or eternal increase, enjoyed.[23] Entrance to this kingdom is in and through eternal marriage. Godhood can only be obtained through the union of a man and a woman. This is the greatest of all God's gifts and consists of "a continuation of the seed forever and ever. . . . For strait is the gate, and narrow the way that leadeth unto the exaltation and continuation of the lives, and few there be that find it. . . . Broad is the gate, and wide the way that leadeth to the deaths; and many there are that go in thereat, because they receive me not, neither do they abide in my law."[24]

THE TEMPLE

In the full and proper sense, it is in the temple that we obtain the knowledge of the path that leads to eternal life. Here it is that we are endowed with power from on high. The root meaning of *endow* is "to clothe," which embraces the idea of a garment of protection and the arming of those involved with spiritual knowledge and power. Thus we are prepared for the journey of mortality and entrance into eternal life. In all of this Christ stands, as would be expected, as the perfect example.

Joseph Smith stated the matter thus: "If a man gets a fullness of the priesthood of God, he has to get it in the same way that Jesus Christ obtained it, and that was by keeping all the commandments and obeying all the ordinances of the house of the Lord."[25]

A correct understanding of gospel principles related to man's eternal journey—including death, life in the spirit world, phases of judgment and the resurrection—provides great consolation to those who have received all of the ordinances of the temple and, having lived righteous lives, live in hope of a glorious resurrection and being "raised unto life eternal."[26] Indeed their death "shall be sweet unto them,"[27] for it is but a step forward toward that ultimate goal of exaltation in the presence of God with eternal family—husbands and wives, fathers and mothers, parents and children, united forever. This glorious condition is made possible through the Atonement of Jesus Christ, who has marked the path to eternal life.

Notes

1. Job 14:14.
2. D&C 107:8.
3. See D&C 22.
4. See Alma 11:45; D&C 138:17.
5. See D&C 88:20–31.
6. Alma 40:13–14.
7. See D&C 19:4–12.
8. Alma 40:11–12.
9. See D&C 130:18–19.
10. D&C 138:58–59.
11. See Bible Dictionary, 699.
12. Moses 7:56–57; emphasis added.
13. D&C 138:18–23; emphasis added.
14. 1 Peter 4:6; D&C 138:10.
15. Alma 12:9–11.
16. 2 Nephi 9:6.
17. Bruce R. McConkie, *Mormon Doctrine*, 2nd ed. (Salt Lake City: Bookcraft, 1966) 185; see also 2 Nephi 9:6–16.
18. 2 Nephi 9:15.
19. See Abraham 3:26.
20. See 3 Nephi 28:38–39.
21. Alma 40:13.
22. See 2 Nephi 9:15; D&C 84:20–31.
23. See D&C 132:24, 131:4.
24. D&C 132:19–25.

25. Joseph Smith, *Teachings of the Prophet Joseph Smith*, comp. Joseph Fielding Smith (Salt Lake City: Deseret Book Co., 1976), 308.
26. Moroni 7:41.
27. D&C 42:46.